PHYSICAL FITNESS AND ATHLETIC PERFORMANCE

Second edition

PHYSICAL FITNESS AND ATHLETIC PERFORMANCE
Second edition

A W S WATSON

Chapter 4 revised and updated by L C M Hennessy

LONGMAN
LONDON AND NEW YORK

Longman Group Limited,
Longman House, Burnt Mill,
Harlow, Essex CM20 2JE, England
and Associated Companies throughout the world

*Published in the United States of America
by Longman Publishing, New York*

© A. W. S. Watson 1983, 1995

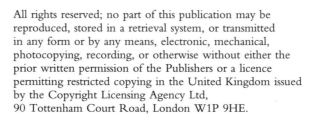
First published 1983
Second edition 1995

ISBN 0 582 091101 PPR

British Library Cataloguing-in-Publication Data
A catalogue record for this book is
available from the British Library

Library of Congress Cataloging-in-Publication Data
Watson, A. W. S.,
    Physical fitness & athletic performance : a guide for students,
athletes & coaches / A.W.S. Watson. – 2nd ed.
        p.   cm.
    Includes bibliographical references and index.
    ISBN 0-582-09110-1 (paper)
    1. Physical education and training.   2. Physical fitness–Testing.
I. Title.   II. Title: Physical fitness and athletic performance.
GV711.5.W37   1995
613.7′1–dc20   94-44802
                                                                    CIP

Set by 6 in 10 on 12pt Bembo
Produced by Longman Singapore Publishers (Pte) Ltd
Printed in Singapore

CONTENTS

PREFACE TO THE SECOND EDITION

The twelve years since the publication of the first edition of this book have seen a considerable increase in participation in sport. 'Sport for All' initiatives have been held in most European countries and active participation in many different forms of physical activity is now very common. The fitness levels of those who are active have also risen considerably. Not long ago running a marathon was considered a tremendous achievement – to be contemplated only by individuals who were of almost super-human constitution: today everyone has a relation, friend, or neighbour who has completed a marathon – even if they have not run quite that far themselves. The health benefits of proper programmes of exercise have also become established over this period and those who aspire to be active are now the rule rather than the exception.

A number of other changes have paralleled the above developments. These include: increasing professionalism in sport and a decline in genuine amateur participation in top level competitition; a considerable increase in the number of sports science and sports studies courses and students engaged in such disciplines; the introduction of structured and certified courses for coaches; the introduction of commercial fitness centres in hotels and other leisure facilities; the much wider availability of fitness testing; a very large increase in the number of sports injuries.

The second edition of this book has been produced in order to bring the original title up-to-date and to address some of the changes that have occurred since the first edition appeared. The most significant modification is the introduction of an additional chapter on sports injuries and their prevention. Many books are available that give their author's opinion on this subject: but this is the first, easily accessible, account of the scientific evidence on the causes and prevention of injuries in sport. I hope that athletes and coaches will find this chapter useful and that it will help to make their activities safer and less prone to disruption through sports injury.

The introduction of systematic training courses for coaches is a very welcome development and I hope that participants will find that the content of this book will assist them in their studies and in their subsequent work with athletes.

I also hope that students of physical education, sports studies and sports science will find the updated version of this book useful. Several new sections have been added. These deal with research completed since the first edition was published and also discuss some limitations of physiological investigations and measurements. This material is intended to assist in the design and execution of projects.

In the last ten years sports training has become more scientific and the assessment of various aspects of physical fitness more common place. Unfortunately, the quality of fitness testing has not always paralleled the rise in quantity and I have addressed this problem in a re-written version of chapter five. I hope that those involved in the field will find that it helps them to improve the accuracy of the measurements that they take and the quality of the advice that they are able to give. I also hope it will put athletes and coaches in a better position to understand scientific information and to demand a high quality service from testing centres.

A large number of people have made a contribution to the revision of this book but I would like to mention four in particular. Dr Richard O'Flaherty has encouraged and assisted in the production of this book since it was first suggested many years ago: for the second edition he has acted as a consultant on the chapter on sports injuries. Professor D J O'Donovan, of the Department of Physiology University College Galway, and Tony Wallace, head of the haematology laboratory of the Regional Hospital Limerick, also deserve special thanks for their contributions as well as their encouragement and support.

Dr Liam Henessy, of the Blackrock Clinic Dublin, has acted as co-author of the second edition of this book. He has re-written the chapter on training from the stand-point of a sports scientist who is also a successful coach. In addition, he has reviewed the whole of the remainder of the manuscript, offering expert advise on many topics. He has also offered considerable encouragement and support throughout the long process of revising this book.

A W S Watson
Wimbotsham, Norfolk   September 1995

PREFACE TO THE FIRST EDITION

This book is concerned with athletic performance: its biological basis, the factors which influence it, and how it can be evaluated, and then improved, through training. It is the product of a number of years of lecturing on such topics and of advising athletes from a wide variety of sports. This experience has suggested the need for a volume which gives an account of some of the recent research into physical performance, fitness and the effects of training, in a form that is useful to the serious athlete and those who advise him. A number of reviews of the research literature are available but these are often extremely specialised and usually very limited in scope. At the opposite end of the spectrum there is no shortage of 'recipe books' of training exercises. Useful as these are to the beginner, they are inadequate for the serious practitioner and are seldom up-to-date. This volume is an attempt to bridge the gap between these two types of publication and to provide some of the information required by the serious coach and those who work with sportsmen in a professional capacity as teachers, organisers, medical advisers, etc.

The information available on the effects of exercise has increased dramatically over the last few years. In particular, much more is now known concerning the specific effects of different types of training and of the important biochemical changes that occur as a result of physical activity. Some of this recent work challenges many of the traditional approaches to exercise and training, and as more detailed research is carried out it is becoming clear that the effects of conditioning programmes are often more subtle and less general than had previously been supposed. This suggests that the modern exercise practitioner must be prepared to develop his own techniques based on the specific needs of the individual athlete and the activity he is undertaking. If the coach or adviser is to do this effectively, he requires a sound understanding of basic biological principles and the ability to establish the training requirements of the individual sportsman.

It is my pleasure to thank the many people who have contributed to the production of this book. Professor G. R. Kelman, Professor Risteard Mulcahy, Dr Dan McCarthy and Dr Richard O'Flaherty have read parts of the manuscript and have provided valuable assistance in particular areas. My thanks are also due to other individuals too numerous to mention by name: friends, students, colleagues, coaches and athletes who have given me the benefit of their specialist knowledge of particular sports and training methods – and I hope I have learned something from them; however, the errors which remain are my responsibility, and the views expressed are my own. Finally, I am most grateful to all those who assisted so skilfully in the production of the illustrations, and to Eileen Healy for her secretarial assistance.

TONY WATSON
Wimbotsham, Norfolk

1 INTRODUCTION

Factors influencing physical performance

At the most general level, physical performance is a function of all the physical and mental characteristics of the individual. Some of these are determined at the moment of conception by the genetic material derived from the father and mother. The most obvious is the individual's gender. Some characteristics may be acquired later through the processes of growth, maturation and learning, while others result from the interaction of the individual's basic genetic make-up with his or her environment. All this may seem rather far removed from the scoring of goals in a football match or the winning of an athletic event, but in fact such achievements are subject to just these constraints. Sporting achievement is a complex mixture of genetic make-up and environmental influences – including training – and in attempting to reach any meaningful conclusions about physical performance it is useful to try to separate these two factors. There have been several studies of genetic effects in athletes and it is becoming clear that they have a most important influence (see pp. 76–7). In the case of a few characteristics the effect is entirely genetic, but in many others there is interaction with environmental factors such as training. Training can 'fine tune' the characteristic, but the limits of achievement are genetically predetermined.

Certain environmental influences occurring after conception have permanent effects and, together with genetic factors, these represent 'invariable' constraints on the athlete's performance. Characteristics that are relevant to physical performance and over which the individual has little or no control include gender, age, somatotype, height, and the distribution of motor unit types. Many of the effects of the first two factors are obvious, but a few of the lesser known points are referred to elsewhere. 'Physique' is briefly considered later in this chapter and 'motor unit distribution' is discussed in Chapter 3.

At a less general level it is possible to demonstrate that physical performance is influenced by specific characteristics, many of which can (at least in theory) be measured or otherwise described. These include such variables as strength, joint mobility (flexibility) and the capacity for various types of physical work (endurance). These are frequently classified as components of *physical fitness*. This, too, is a useful way of analysing physical performance because it highlights variables which can generally be modified or improved through training. As more is known about the biological effects of exercise it has become clear that the changes are all due to definite anatomical, physiological and biochemical adaptations. It seems convenient to group these variable aspects of physical performance under one heading since they are all factors over which the individual has some control. In this book they are considered as components of fitness and their biological basis is discussed in Chapter 2.

Chapters 3 and 4 are concerned with the effects of training. Considerable difficulties are encountered when writing in this area as athletes trained long before physiology became fashionable and much of the available information has been acquired by trial and error rather than by the processes of science. When scientific investigations were started they tended to concentrate on matters occurring *during* exercise, and it is only recently that carefully controlled studies have been made of the merits of different training methods. Some of the most useful information available about training has come from such studies but they are few in number and, due to the nature of scientific investigation, are limited in scope. The investigations are usually of short duration because it is very difficult to ensure that individuals train under controlled conditions for long periods. And they have to be confined to one particular kind of subject – quite often, college students. It must be a matter of speculation as to how far the results of such studies can be applied to other types of subject. In particular, it is difficult to be sure they will relate to the élite athlete who is already highly trained and whose invariable physical characteristics are far from average. Although controlled studies on such an individual are theoretically possible, they are, in practice, extremely difficult to organise.

Another problem is the uneven coverage of different areas. A good deal of work has been carried out on endurance training – some on strength, but very little on many other aspect of fitness.

Because of these difficulties the approach to the sections on training is different from that adopted in Chapter 2. The authors have taken the view that the athlete is not going to wait to begin training until all the research has been completed, and we have tried to make comments on all the major areas. Where possible these have been based on carefully controlled experimental studies, but where such information is not available we have made use of the best information available.

A training programme is most likely to be beneficial if it is specifically designed to meet the individual sportsperson's needs. Thus some kind of evaluation of the fitness levels of the athlete is necessary, and this topic is considered in Chapter 5. As with the work on training methods, the information available is less complete and up-to-date than that which exists on basic physiology. Although a large number of general tests have been described, many were developed before the highly specific effects of training were fully appreciated. There is a need to adapt many of these for use with particular types of athlete. The field is so wide that it is impossible to consider all the tests necessary in different situations. We have therefore described tests with general applications and have tried to include material which may help the readers to develop more specific techniques of their own.

Physique

Physique has an important influence on athletic performance but is only to a very limited extent under the individual's control. A large number of studies have shown that successful sportspeople tend to have particular types of physique and that this is related to athletic success.

Size

Apart from such obvious observations that height is an advantage to rugby forwards, basketball players and throwers, there are also more subtle effects of differences in body size. These occur because the human is three dimensional. If the height of a three-dimensional object is doubled its surface area increases four times and its mass is

	Function	Proportional to	Effect on the function of increasing height by a factor of 1.5	Example or comment
Table 1.1. The influence of body size on some physiological functions and aspects of human performance. Body shape is assumed to remain constant.	Body surface area	Height^2	×2.25	Body surface area increases at a faster rate than height
	Body weight	Height^3	×3.375	Weight increases at a much faster rate than height
	Body surface area per kg body weight	1/height	×0.67	Better heat conservation in large individuals – an advantage in activities where cold is a problem. Better heat dissipation in small individuals. Preserves cardiac output – an advantage in endurance activities
	Blood and lung volumes	Height^3	×3.375	
	Strength	Height^2	×2.25	Strength increases at a faster rate than height
	Work-rate	Height^3	×3.375	Larger individuals have a much higher work rate
	Anaerobic power	Height^2	×2.25	
	Ability to accelerate external object	Height^2	×2.25	Large size an advantage to throwers
	Ability to accelerate own body	1/height	×0.67	Large size is a disadvantage in activities where acceleration is important
	Lifting own body weight	1/height	×0.67	Size is a disadvantage
	Running at constant speed on the level	1	None	Size has no influence
	Running up hill	1/height	×0.67	Size is a disadvantage
	Long jump	1	None	Size has no influence
	High jump	1	See comment	Size has no influence on the trajectory of the jump but extra height raises the centre of gravity which is an advantage

Table 1.1. The influence of body size on some physiological functions and aspects of human performance. Body shape is assumed to remain constant.

multiplied eight-fold. Thus, when individuals of different size are considered, the body surface area and the cross-sectional area of muscle (and therefore strength) tend to vary in proportion to the square of height. Variables such as weight and blood volume increase in line with height cubed. Thus changes in size tend to produce differences in the relationships between such variables as strength, weight, power output, acceleration and work capacity. This means that individuals of various sizes are better equipped for different types of activity. A detailed analysis of the mechanical and physiological consequences of changes in size has been made by Asmussen and Christensen (1967) and some of this work is summarised in Table 1.1.

Table 1.1 illustrates that size on its own has a considerable influence on athletic performance. If body shape remains constant, measures such as body surface area and the cross-sectional area of muscle increase in proportion to the square of the individual's height. This means that a large individual will be considerably stronger than a small person of the same shape. This will be an advantage in such situations as rugby scrums and throwing events. However, measures that are related to body volumes increase in proportion to height cubed. Thus body weight increases at a faster rate than strength and therefore a large person finds it harder to lift his or her body weight and also has poorer acceleration. This explains why small athletes tend to be more agile than larger ones. There are also many other implications of the three-dimensional nature of the human body. Some of these are summarised in Table 1.1.

Somatotypes

Somatotyping is a technique for quantifying body shape. It is based on the assumption that every physique can be expressed in terms of the contribution of three basic components that are genetically determined. These are known as **endomorphy**, **mesomorphy** and **ectomorphy**. Somatotyping has been used successfully in analysis of the physique of athletes and children by a number of investigators. The most significant work is a study of the physique of Olympic athletes carried out by Tanner (1964a).

On the basis of somatotype alone there are considerable differences between the physiques of successful athletes and members of the general population. These differences are illustrated in Figure 1.1, which shows that less than half the somatotypes found among the general population are represented at the Olympic games.

Tanner's classic study of physique also demonstrated that athletes competing in different Olympic events tended to have different somatotypes. There were clear differences between competitors in power and endurance events but overlap occurred in the somatotypes of athletes who competed in similar events. The best discrimination was obtained when other measurements were also included in the analysis, using the technique described below.

Anthropometric measurements

A second approach to the quantification of physique is the analysis of linear and circular measurements taken on the body: **anthropometric measurements**. These normally include the lengths of bones and segments of the body, bone widths, skinfold thicknesses and muscle circumferences. A large number of such measurements are possible: studies on athletes often employ between 20 and 50.

Discriminant analysis

It is difficult to assemble a picture of an individual from such a large number of isolated measurements and various complex statistical techniques are necessary in

Figure 1.1.
Distribution of somatotypes in (*above*) students attending Oxford University and (*below*) track and field athletes at the 1960 Olympics. The diagram shows that only about half the physiques present in the general population were represented at the Olympics. (Redrawn from Tanner 1964a.)

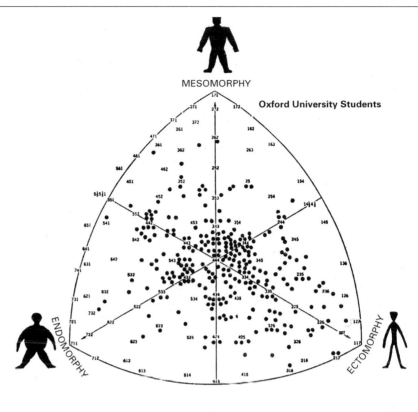

Oxford University Students

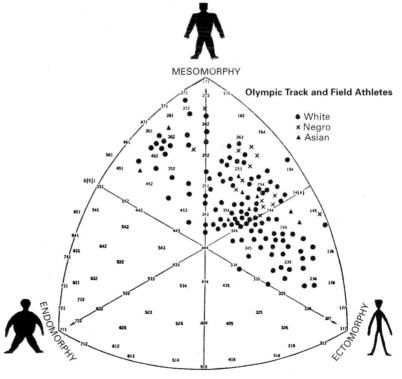

Olympic Track and Field Athletes

● White
× Negro
▲ Asian

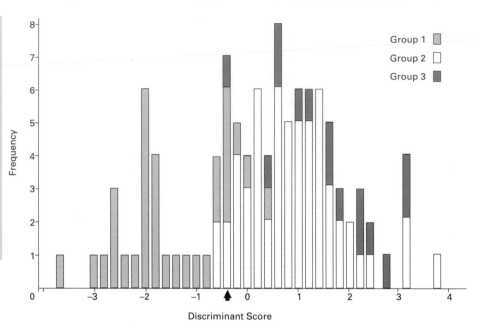

Figure 1.2. Discriminant analysis of the physiques of successful schoolboy rugby players and hurlers compared with those of non-team members. Group 1 = non-team members. Group 2 = members of school rugby and hurling teams. Group 3 = members of a UK school rugby team. See text for explanation. (Data adapted from Watson 1988a.)

order to make sense of such an extensive amount of data. When the individuals can be classified into groups such as 'athletes' and 'non-athletes' or according to the event in which they specialise, **discriminant analysis** is the method most often used. Discriminant analysis selects the measurements that produce the best discrimination between the various groups of subjects. It also provides a mathematical equation that weights these measurements in order to produce a score for each subject. This allows the physique of different individuals to be compared.

Figure 1.2 illustrates the use of discriminant analysis on a range of 31 anthropometric measurements that were taken on a group of senior Irish schoolboys. Thirty-four were successful rugby players, 25 were successful hurlers and 34 were non-team members. The discriminant function produced in the study was correctly able to classify 92 per cent of the boys as 'players' or 'non-players'. When the same function was applied to the members of the rugby team of an English school, 14 out of 15 boys were correctly classified as 'players'. This study demonstrates the use of discriminant analysis and also the strong influence of physique upon team membership in school sport. However, the results do not suggest that all the team members had physiques that were identical. Various combinations of muscle mass, and muscle size in relation to height and bone size, all favoured team membership. Many different physiques were found among the team members, but these were all quite distinct from the physiques of the non-players.

When discriminant analysis was applied to anthropometric measurements taken on Olympic athletes a similar result was obtained. It was possible to identify a small range of characteristics of physique that were different and unique for most of the major types of event.

Physique also has a direct influence upon a number of physiological variables and physical performance tests that are commonly used as measures of physical fitness. A summary of published relationships is summarised in Figure 1.3.

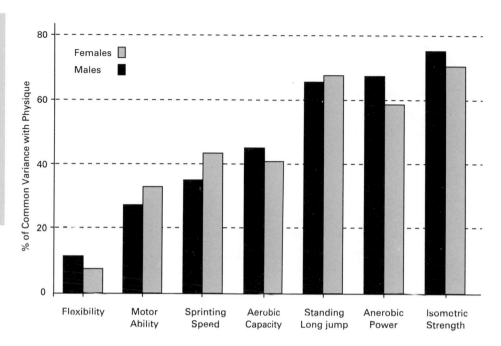

Figure 1.3. The percentage of common variance of various measures of physical performance that is accounted for by the subject's physique. Isometric strength is the fitness variable most highly related to physique, 70–80 per cent of the variations being attributable to differences in body size and shape.

Factor analysis of physique

Differences in the physique of athletes can also be studied by a second statistical technique known as **factor analysis**. Figure 1.4 shows the physique factors that were isolated in an analysis of 116 sportsmen who were involved in different activities. Each of the 12 factors shown on the right of the diagram represents a characteristic of physique that distinguishes one group of athletes from another. The results reveal the existence of three separate factors for body fat, in addition to independent factors related to trunk length, thigh length, leg length, shoulder width, hip width, trunk depth, trunk muscle-and-bone, and leg muscle. Three findings from this study are of significance:

(1) The existence of the twelve factors shown in the diagram.

(2) The fact that muscle development is dependent upon bone sizes.

(3) The existence of three independent fat factors.

This means that different individuals tend to accumulate fat in different parts of the body and tend to lose and gain fat in different places and at different rates (see also Figure 2.38).

Physique is a major determinant of athletic performance whose importance is frequently overlooked. The extent to which it can be modified is extremely limited, but it is possible – and desirable – to steer young athletes into activities in which they stand some chance of ultimate success. This happens much too rarely. The author is only too well aware of excellent junior athletes who never made it at the much more competitive senior level because they were simply of the wrong shape.

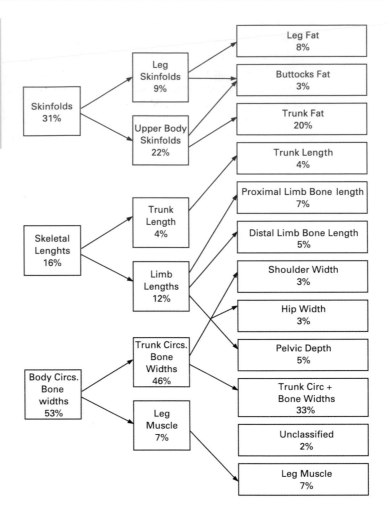

Figure 1.4. Factor analysis of the physiques of successful sportsmen. The analysis produced 12 independent physique factors. (Redrawn from Watson 1984c: see text for explanation.)

Physique and athletic performance: Summary

1 Physique is a term used to denote variations in both body shape and body size. Because of the complexities of the human body it is not possible to provide a single measure of a person's physique. **Somatotype** is a measure of body shape. A large number of different anthropometric measurements are used to quantify the size of various body segments.

2 Physique is largely genetically determined and beyond the individual's control. The size and shape of the skeleton are fixed at conception. Modifications to the amount of fat and muscle are possible but only within genetically determined limits.

3 Many physical performance variables, such as aerobic and anaerobic capacity, are influenced by physique. About three-quarters of the variance in the strength of adolescents can be accounted for by variations in physique.

4 Only about half the somatotypes that occur in the general population are found in high-level performers at traditional sports. When body size *and* shape are considered, champion athletes exhibit a very limited range of physiques.

5   With many activities a high level of performance is associated with a particular kind of physique, e.g. top-level shot putters, marathon runners and sprinters have physiques that are distinctive but different from each other.

6   Discriminant analysis is a statistical technique that is able to extract from a large number of measurements those that produce the best 'discrimination' between two or more groups of athletes.

7   Discriminant analysis shows that most sports are associated with a small 'range' or 'family' of physiques that favour success, rather than a single, unique, physique.

2 | COMPONENTS OF PHYSICAL FITNESS

In this chapter the biological basis of the various components of physical fitness are considered. Particular emphasis is placed on aspects relating to the effects of training, and some of this material is further developed in Chapters 3 and 4.

Flexibility
The biological basis of flexibility

Most machines require a rigid framework upon which to operate. In the human body this is provided by the skeleton which acts like a series of girders against which the muscles contract and develop force. Many man-made machines are expected to produce only a single kind of movement and so require few movable joints. The human body is capable of an enormous repertoire of different movements and has only a few immovable joints but a large number that are capable of different kinds of motion. Some – e.g. the knee and elbow joints – are designed to move mainly in one

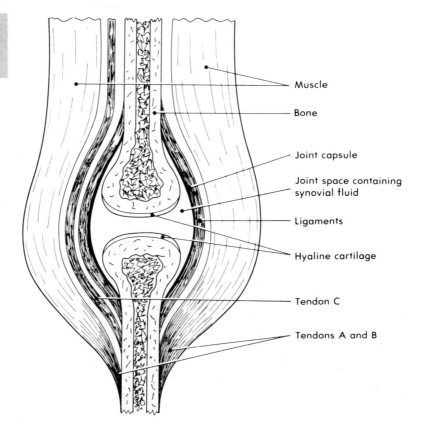

Figure 2.1. Diagram illustrating the general features of a movable joint.

Muscle

Bone

Joint capsule

Joint space containing synovial fluid

Ligaments

Hyaline cartilage

Tendon C

Tendons A and B

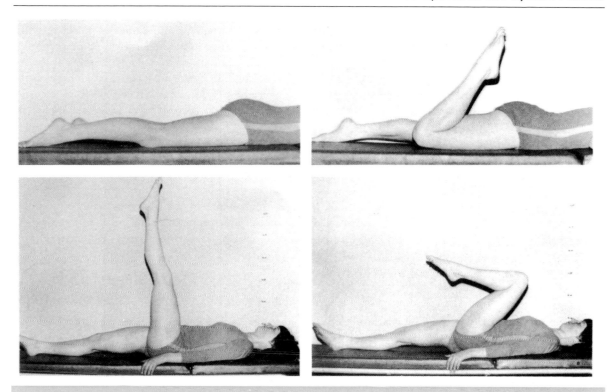

Figure 2.2. *Top:* Flexion of the knee is limited by contact between the soft tissue of the calf and thigh. *Bottom:* In contrast, hip flexion is limited by the length of the hamstring group of muscles. This constraint is reduced when the knee is flexed and the hip joint can then be moved much further.

plane. These act in a similar manner to the hinge on a door. Others are capable of movement in several directions. Typical examples are the joints found at the hip and shoulder. The structure of a generalised joint is illustrated in Figure 2.1.

Where two bones come in contact they are covered by a layer of **hyaline cartilage**, a tough, smooth material which reduces friction. The **joint space** is enclosed by the **joint capsule**, a tissue which secretes **synovial fluid**. This is a thick, slippery liquid containing the complex carbohydrate, **hyaluronic acid**, which keeps the joints lubricated. The joint capsule is surrounded by ligaments. These are strong fibrous tissues which prevent the joint being pulled apart; they influence the range of movement. The knee joint has strong ligaments at the side and back but none at the front. This is reflected in the type of motion possible. The shoulder joint has much looser ligaments which allow a wider range of movement including rotation. Over the ligaments there is a layer of muscle or tendon. Tendons join muscle to bone and may be short, like A and B in Figure 2.1, or long enough to traverse several joints, such as C, or those that connect the forearm muscles to the finger bones.

Joint motion is limited by a number of factors. Disease and injury can cause changes which include damage to the cartilage, deposits of solids in the joint space, inflammation of the capsule, or a deficiency of synovial fluid. These conditions frequently make any degree of movement painful and difficult. In the healthy individual the range of movement is usually limited by bone structure, the properties of the ligaments, the length of muscles or tendons, or the intervention of soft tissue. Extension of the knee is limited by the length of ligaments at the rear, while flexion is stopped by the contact of soft tissue in the calf and thigh. In contrast, hip flexion is usually limited by the length of the hamstring muscles. The difference is illustrated in Figure 2.2.

The length of muscles and tendons and the suppleness of ligaments are not fixed quantities. Where these two factors limit joint motion – which they do in the majority of cases – flexibility can be improved through training that alters the properties of these tissues. Ligaments and tendons both contain various forms of a non-elastic protein called **collagen**. This is mixed with varying amounts of other proteins such as **elastin** which has more elastic properties than collagen. Tendons are relatively non-elastic and resistant to stretch. Ligaments have a different chemical composition that makes them more pliable. Tendons and ligaments are collectively known as **connective tissue**.

Individual muscle fibres, bundles of fibres and whole muscles are all surrounded by their own connective tissue. Thus the force-developing part of muscle has connective tissue both in parallel with it and in series (the tendons at either end form the series component). The extensibility of muscle depends to a large extent upon the degree of elasticity of these tissues.

It has been shown experimentally that flexibility training decreases the stiffness of tendons (Wilson *et al.* 1992). The elastic properties of the muscle–tendon unit mean that when it is stretched energy is stored in it. This energy is released as force when the muscle–tendon unit shortens and is additional to the force produced by muscular contraction (see also Figure 2.11). This source of energy is of great importance in

Figure 2.3. Series and parallel elastic components associated with skeletal muscle. The contractile elements of muscle are covered with connective tissue which constitutes a parallel elastic component. The elastic tissue in the tendons is in series with with muscle. Further elastic elements are contained in the ligaments that surround joints. The elastic components store energy when the muscle is stretched. This is released during shortening of the muscle and is additional to that produced by the contractile elements.

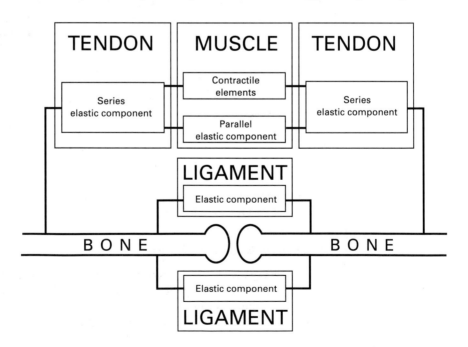

activities as diverse as running and weight-lifting (Bosco *et al.* 1987; Wilson *et al.* 1992).

One other factor which influences the extensibility of muscle is the presence of reflexes (see diagram and explanation on page 17). Length detectors inside muscles and tension detectors inside tendons are capable of either initiating or inhibiting muscular contraction. This can occur in muscles that are being stretched and in those on the opposite side of a joint that oppose the stretch.

It follows from the above that flexibility is strongly influenced by two factors: (1) the properties of the connective tissue in muscles, ligaments and tendons and (2) reflexes initiated in muscles and tendons. Training programmes that are intended to bring about improvements in flexibility must be carefully designed in order to bring about favourable changes in these two factors. The characteristics of such programmes are discussed in Chapter 4.

Specificity of flexibility

Flexibility is a property of individual muscles and joints. As such it is specific to particular types of movement. Thus it is possible, and very common, for an individual to have a very high level of flexibility in one area of the body and to be very poor in others. The same principles applies to flexibility training. Stretching a particular muscle group will have little or no effect on the level of flexibility in other parts of the body.

The importance of flexibility

Flexibility is one of the major components of physical fitness. It is important for a number of reasons, the three principle ones being: (1) to allow an adequate range of movement, (2) to avoid posture defects and (3) to avoid sports injuries.

Adequate movement for sport

A few sports require a spectacular range of movement in almost all the joints of the body. Gymnastics is the most obvious example. Many other activities require good flexibility in a much more limited number of movements. Poor flexibility can prevent a particular activity being carried out at all – for example, a sprint start or a full squat – or may make performance at an activity less efficient. A rower with poor hip flexion will lose power because of a shorter stroke. A boxer with poor ankle flexibility will have a reduced reach. These are just two examples. In many sports optimum performance requires a high level of flexibility in a number of joints.

Elasticity of the muscle–tendon unit

Elastic energy that is stored in the muscle–tendon unit when a muscle is stretched is an important source of energy for physical activity. This kind of energy is of particular importance during such rhythmic activities as running and jumping. It is likely to be influenced by flexibility but the relationship has not been fully investigated.

Injury prevention

The most common injuries in sport are pulled muscles and overuse injuries. Both these conditions are associated with a lack of flexibility. (See Chapter 6 for a more detailed discussion.) For most sports, injury-prevention requirements are (1) an adequate level of flexibility in all the major joints of the body and (2) a high level in those joints that are placed under particular stress by the activity.

Posture

Many posture defects are due to the tightness of muscles. These conditions are often associated with an increased risk of sports injury.

Adverse effects of excessive flexibility

Too much flexibility is less commonly a problem than too little, but the range of movement of a joint needs to be suited to the activity being undertaken. Javelin throwers and butterfly swimmers need excellent shoulder flexibility. In soccer and rugby, players require only an adequate level and in these sports it is probably more important to build up the strength of the muscles round the shoulder joint to protect it from sprain and dislocation. An unstable joint with loose ligaments can predispose to injury, but this condition is likely to be caused by factors other than flexibility training (Alter 1988).

General levels of flexibility

It is often stated that children have a naturally high level of flexibility that gradually declines with age; and that females are naturally more flexible than males. At the moment there is no definite scientific evidence that either of these generalisations is accurate. Alter (1988) suggests that the higher level of flexibility often found in females may be due to the type of activities undertaken by them, and to gender stereotyping: high levels of flexibility are still considered 'un-masculine' by some sections of the sporting community. This view is supported by the results of a study of Irish children between the ages of 6 and 13 who had no organised physical education classes. In this untrained group it was found that there were no significant differences in flexibility with either age or gender (Watson 1990).

Strength

In the present context strength is the maximum force that can be developed during muscular contraction. Force is measured in the same units as weight – often in lb or kg. Sometimes lb-wt is used instead of lb and kg-wt or kp instead of kg. The latter terms are more correct, but for measurements made on the earth's surface there are no practical differences between the two types of unit.

Muscle

There are three types of muscle in the body, each with slightly different properties. **Cardiac muscle** occurs in the heart and is especially suited to short, regular contractions. The gut and blood vessels contain **smooth muscle** which can operate with the minimum of intervention from the nervous system. The third type is that which moves the bones of the skeleton and is known as **skeletal** or **striated muscle**, from its appearance under a microscope. Skeletal muscle is the only type under voluntary control, being operated mainly by the conscious part of the brain. In this book the word *muscle* is used to mean skeletal muscle unless another type is specified.

The gross structure of skeletal muscle can be observed in the lean portion of a joint of meat. It consists of reddish fibres separated by **connective tissue** which is non-contractile. At each end this tissue forms the tendons which join the muscle to bone and transmit the force of contraction.

Connective tissue also isolates the fibre from its neighbours so that each is capable of contracting independently. Muscle also contains several different kinds of nerve, and blood vessels which supply oxygen and nutrients and remove waste products.

The nerves that initiate muscular contraction are known as **motor neurones** (Figure 2.4). Most control several muscle fibres which contract simultaneously when the nerve is stimulated. The muscles fibres controlled by a single nerve are known as a **motor unit**. Where very precise movement is necessary, such as in the muscles which control the direction of the eyes, each motor unit consists of only a few muscle fibres. In the muscles of the legs and back, motor units may consist of more than 100 fibres. The individual fibres making up a motor unit are widely scattered throughout a particular muscle. Any given portion of a muscle may contain fibres from 20 to 50 different motor units (Burke and Edgerton 1975).

A muscle fibre either contracts maximally or not at all. It is not possible to vary the force of individual contractions of a single fibre but this can be done in a whole muscle in one of two ways: by varying the number of motor units involved in the movement, or by changing the rate at which contraction occurs. These mechanisms are known, respectively, as **spatial** and **temporal summation** and are illustrated in Figure 2.5.

Although the contraction of skeletal muscle is generally initiated by the conscious part of the brain there is also a degree of automatic control. This is often overlooked but it has an important influence upon coordination and the development of strength. The athlete makes the decision to lift a weight or kick a ball with the conscious part of his or her brain, but the details of motor unit involvement are determined at lower levels of the brain and in the spinal cord. The upper brain acts like a managing director making a policy decision. The detailed execution of this is left to many other individuals who have specialised knowledge of the working of different departments. The overall success of the policy will depend upon the performance of all these individuals. A similar situation occurs with muscular contraction. The nervous system must learn to utilise the available equipment most effectively if maximum strength is to be developed. This process appears to take place in the initial stages of strength training. Several studies have shown that neurological changes take place (e.g. Komi *et al.* 1978) and that at the start of training strength increases without a corresponding change in muscle size (Lesmes *et al.* 1978). This is presumably due to better utilisation of the existing tissue by the nervous system.

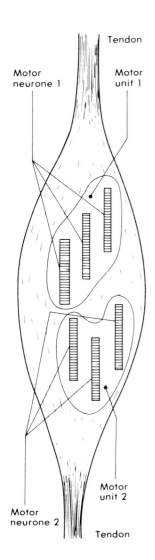

Figure 2.4. Two motor units distributed inside a muscle.

Tendon

Motor neurone 1

Motor unit 1

Motor unit 2

Motor neurone 2

Tendon

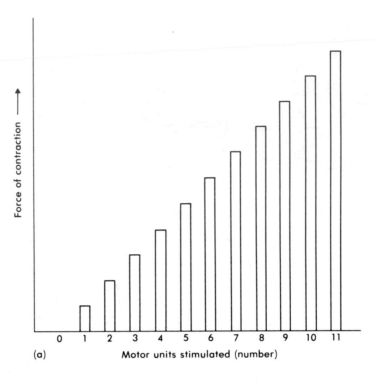

(a)

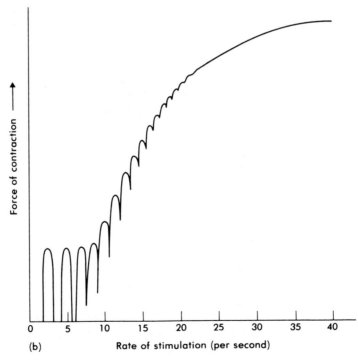

(b)

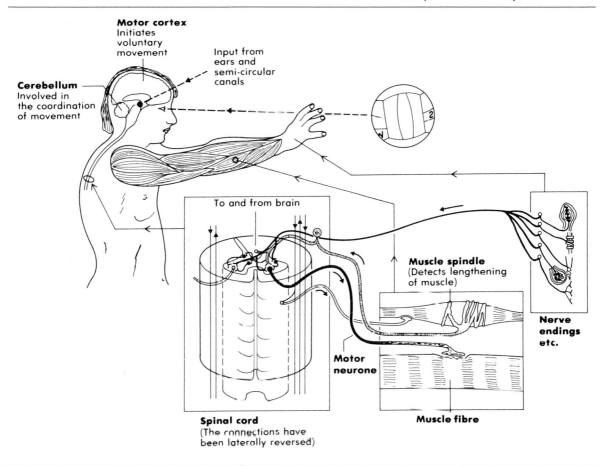

Figure 2.6. Some of the factors controlling the contraction of skeletal muscle during physical activity. The brain receives sensory information from a variety of sources including the eyes, ears and semi-circular canals, stretch receptors in muscles and tendons, nerve endings in joints and skin. Much of this information is processed in the spinal cord and lower brain and never reaches the level of consciousness.

These subconscious mechanisms are influenced by information from several sources, including the muscles themselves. Some of the neural outputs from muscle and other sources are illustrated in Figure 2.6.

Nerve endings in muscle detect compression, lack of oxygen, excessive tension and other conditions likely to lead to damage. Endings in tendons are sensitive to stretch – an indication of excessive muscle tension. These outputs are fed into the spinal cord and brain, along with information from other sources, and may limit or inhibit muscular contraction. The output from tendons has a direct inhibiting effect upon the motor neurones of the muscles that are causing the tension. This normally prevents the muscle contracting with its maximum force. In exceptional circumstances, such as an extreme emergency, these constrains may be removed. There have been a number of reports of mothers managing to lift huge weights in order to save a trapped child. In laboratory studies exposure to hypnosis, drugs and rifle shots have been shown to produce supra-normal peaks of strength (Ikai and Steinhaus 1961).

In sporting situations acts of strength are seldom the work of single muscles. Usually, several muscles cooperate in the direct development of force, and many others are involved indirectly in stabilising the body. The nervous system has a considerable role in the development of strength and this can be optimised through training and practice.

Types of muscular contraction

The term **contraction** is applied to a muscle whenever it is stimulated and consumes energy in developing a force. Rather confusingly, the muscle does not necessarily become shorter in the process. The type of contraction where shortening does occur is known as **concentric** contraction. Sometimes a muscle *contracts* but is unable to overcome a greater opposing force and the muscle gets longer. This type of contaction is termed **eccentric**. It is frequently used to resist the force of gravity as when an individual steps off a chair or lowers a fragile television set onto a table. Occasionally a muscle contracts against the resistance of an immovable object or meets an exactly equal opposing force. In this situation no movement occurs and the contraction is said to be **isometric** because the muscle does not change its length.

Figure 2.7. *Left*: most man–made machines operate against a rigid framework provided by immovable joints. *Right*: in man rigidity is provided by the isometric contraction of opposing sets of muscles. In this illustration isometric contraction maintains the stability of the legs and trunk while a weight is being moved with the arms. (courtesy E.J.M. O'Sullivan)

Isometric contraction would appear a somewhat pointless phenomenon but it is actually of great importance as the only means of providing rigidity to the body. The skeleton is a freely movable framework which is stabilised by the contraction of opposing muscles on opposite sides of joints. A heavy weight can be lifted with the arms only if the spine and leg joints are stabilised by isometric contraction (Figure 2.7). In an isometric contraction no force is wasted in overcoming inertia or tissue resistance, so that a greater force can be developed than in an isotonic contraction.

An **isotonic** contraction occurs if a muscle contracts while maintaining constant tension. It takes place if an isolated muscle is used to lift a weight. Isotonic contractions are rare when a muscle is in position in the body even if a constant weight is raised. This is because the changing length of lever arms varies the resistance applied to the muscle.

Mechanism of muscular contraction

Muscle fibres are composed principally of two proteins – **actin** and **myosin** – with smaller amounts of two others – **tropomyosin** and **troponin**. It is the interaction of these four substances that is responsible for the contraction of muscle and the consequent development of force.

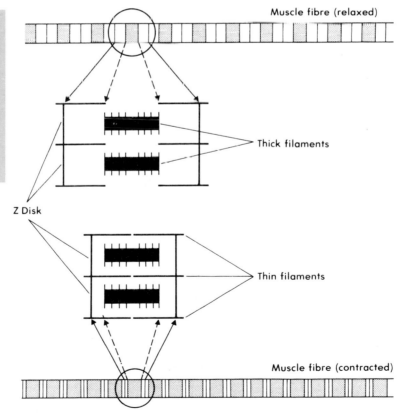

Figure 2.8. The ultra-structure of muscle: *Above*: the microscopic appearance of a skeletal muscle fibre in the relaxed state. The striations are due to the overlap of the thick and thin filaments. *Below*: the changes that occur when the muscle contracts.

Muscle fibre (relaxed)

Thick filaments

Z Disk

Thin filaments

Muscle fibre (contracted)

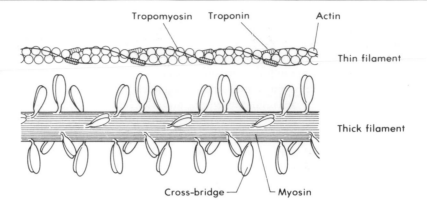

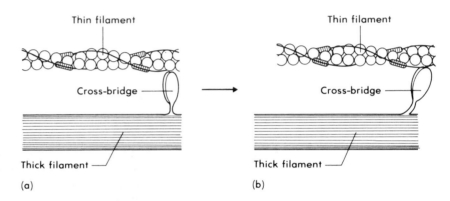

Figure 2.9. *Above*: structure of the thick and thin filaments in skeletal muscle. *Below*: Action of the cross-bridges during muscular contraction (see text).

When seen under a microscope, skeletal muscle has a characteristically striped appearance. The bands are known as **striations**. This is due to the overlap of two different kinds of protein filament, as illustrated in Figure 2.8. During the process of contraction the thinner filaments slide over the thicker ones making the muscle shorter and altering the appearance of the striations.

The thick filaments are made up of myosin and contain a series of projections known as **cross-bridges**. The thin filaments are composed principally of actin with small amounts of the other two proteins which play a part in the initiation and control of the contraction process. The necessary energy for contraction is obtained from a high-energy compound, adenosine triphosphate (ATP), which is considered in some detail in the section on endurance. Muscle contracts by the following process. ATP is joined to the myosin cross-bridges which then attach themselves to the actin of the thin filaments. Energy from the ATP enables the cross-bridges to 'flick over' to a different angle, which normally results in movements of the thin filaments. If the muscle is prevented from shortening, an isometric contraction occurs. The process is illustrated in Figure 2.9.

Tension is developed at points where the myosin cross-bridges intereact with the actin filaments. It is clear from Figure 2.8 that the number of such interactions will vary with the position of the two filaments and hence the length of the fibre. As a result, the maximum tension that can be produced by a muscle depends upon its resting length. This is known as the **length–tension relationship** which is illustrated

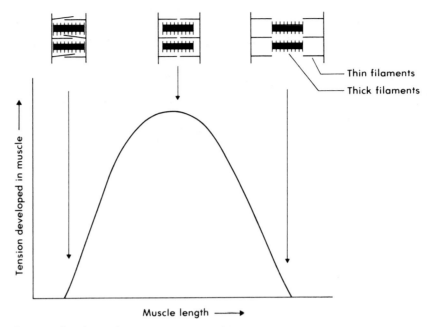

Figure 2.10. The length–tension relationship of skeletal muscle.

Thin filaments

Thick filaments

Tension developed in muscle

Muscle length ⟶

for an isolated muscle in Figure 2.10. When in place in the body the maximum resting length of most muscles corresponds to that which produces maximum tension.

When in place in the human body the thick and thin filaments of skeletal muscle are surrounded by connective tissue which constitutes series and parallel elastic components (see Figure 2.3). These tissues store energy when the muscle is stretched beyond its resting length. This energy contributes to the tension developed by the muscle (Table 2.1), and is additional to that generated by interaction of the thick and thin filaments.

The length–tension relationship of muscle, together with its associated connective tissue, is shown in Figure 2.11.

Force–velocity relationship

The maximum tension that can be developed in a contraction is influenced by the speed of muscle shortening. Figure 2.12(a) shows the relationship in an isolated muscle that is stimulated electrically. The force is maximum when the speed of contraction is zero, i.e. when the contraction is isometric so that no change in length takes place. If

Table 2.1. Angle at which maximum tension is developed in various joints.

Action	Joint	Angle at which maximum tension is developed
Forearm flexion	Elbow	120°
Forearm extension	Elbow	Minimum angle
Thigh flexion	Hip	90°
Knee flexion	Hip	90°
Shoulder extension	Shoulder	60°

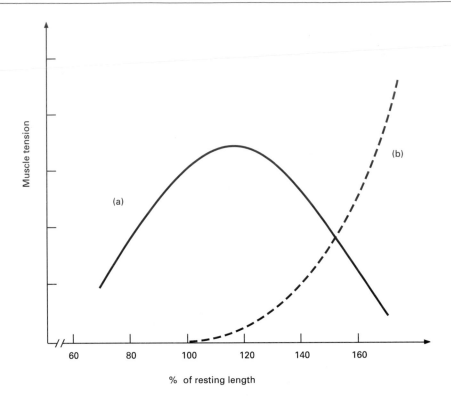

Figure 2.11. *Upper diagram*: the length tension relationship of (a) the contractile elements of skeletal muscle and (b) isolated series and parallel elastic components. *Lower diagram*: curve (c) is produced when curves (a) and (b) are combined. The muscle produces the greatest tension when it contracts from a stretched state because of the energy stored in the elastic components.

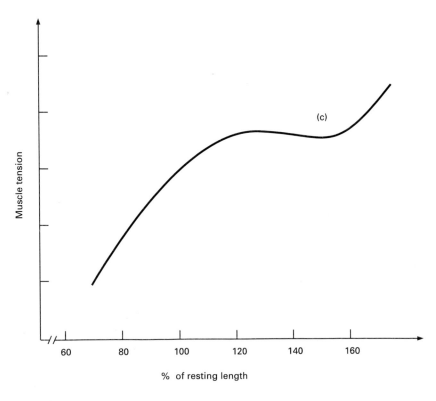

Figure 2.12. Force–velocity relationship of skeletal muscle. (a) A muscle removed from the body. (b) *In situ* muscle. (c) Curves for one weight-lifter and one jumper. At low speeds of contraction the weight-lifter produces the greatest force but the jumper is stronger at high speed.

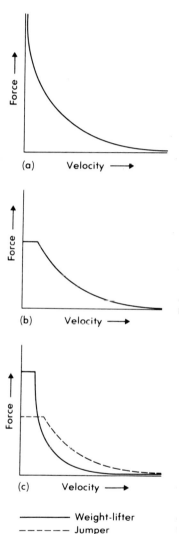

(a)   Velocity ⟶

(b)   Velocity ⟶

(c)   Velocity ⟶

——— Weight-lifter
– – – – Jumper

movement *does* occur the force developed decreases as the speed increases. It is thought that this is due to the rate of chemical reactions in muscle being influenced by the mechanical force (Wilkie 1968). Davies (1971) suggests that when a muscle contracts at high speed only a few of the myosin cross-bridges have time to react with actin and, therefore, the tension developed is low.

It is only recently that the force–velocity relationship has been studied in muscle groups operating in position in the human body. The form of the relationship is shown in Figure 2.12(b). At the higher velocities curves 2.12(a) and 2.12(b) are identical, but in intact muscle the maximum tension is considerably reduced at the lower speeds. This is thought to be due to inhibition in the nervous system that is designed to prevent the overload of tendons (Perrine and Edgerton 1978). The relationship is modified by changes in muscle temperature. A rise in temperature results in an increase in the force developed at a given speed of contraction and in the maximum speed of contraction. Binkhorst *et al.* (1977) report that a 5 degC rise in muscle temperature may result in 10 per cent increase in speed and maximum power output. This is one of the reasons why performance may improve after a warm-up.

The force–velocity relationship of muscle has important implications for sport. Many activities take place at high speed so that performance is influenced by the force that muscles can develop when contracting rapidly. This is not necessarily related to the force that can be produced in a static contraction. It is possible for an individual to have a high level of static strength while being unable to produce much force at high speed. This is illustrated in Figure 2.12(c). The force–velocity relationship is probably influenced by the individual's motor unit distribution (see Chapter 3) but it can be modified by suitable training (Thorstensson *et al.* 1977). Lesmes *et al.* (1978) have demonstrated that when a muscle is trained at constant speed, strength is increased at the training and lower speeds but not at higher speeds. This work means that it is necessary to specify the speed of contraction when describing an individual's strength. For example, in Figure 2.12(c) the weight-lifter is stronger than the jumper at low speeds but the jumper has the greater strength when the speed of contraction is high. The study of strength at different speeds of contraction has generated a term for contraction taking place at constant speed: **isokinetic contraction**. See Chapter 4 for a discussion of methods of strength training.

Applications to sport Strength is the maximum force that can be developed during muscular contraction. The human body is capable of a multitude of different muscle actions. It follows that there is an equally large number of types of strength: there is no overall measure of this aspect of physical fitness. Many movements appear to be attributable to isolated

STRENGTH

Arousal and motivation

Coordination of contractions of prime movers

Synchronisation of motor units in individual muscles

Cross–sectional areas of the prime movers

Muscle fibre type and biochemical properties

Inhibition from muscle spindles tendon organs, etc.

Length of muscles, Joint angles, etc.

Type of muscular contraction

Speed of contraction

Energy from series and parallel elastic components

Stabilisation of body: isometric contraction

Resistance from joints, soft tissue, fat, etc.

muscle groups known as **prime movers** – e.g. the arm and shoulder muscles in throwing events. However, these muscles can develop force only if other parts of the body are held rigid by the isometric contraction of supporting muscles in the legs and trunk. Thus, force development is not exclusively a characteristic of the prime movers. The situation is made more complex by the fact that many actions actually consist of a rapid series of contractions in different parts of the body – e.g. the legs, thighs, hips, trunk, shoulders, arms and forearms in a shot-put. And the force developed is also influenced by muscle length and the type and speed of contraction. The influence of these, and some other factors, on strength are summarised in Figure 2.13.

Strength has a vital influence on performance in activities involving speed and power: sprints, jumps, middle distance track, swimming, cycling, rowing, gymnastics, most team and individual sports. One of the most convincing demonstrations of the effects of strength on performance is from a study on swimmers (Sharp *et al.* 1982). When both stroke-action and speed of movement were replicated the common variance between strength and swimming speed over 25, 100, 200 and 500 metres was 81, 74, 72 and 58 per cent respectively. Four weeks of strength training produced a 19 per cent increase in power which resulted in a 4 per cent improvement in swimming speed.

It is more difficult to demonstrate such an effect in land-based activities where the speed of movement is much higher and the action may be more complex. High levels of isometric strength increase the stability of the body and may offer protection from injury, particularly in body contact sports. However, high levels of dynamic strength seem to increase the risk of the athlete sustaining an intrinsic injury (see page 205).

Although of great importance, strength is an extremely complex phenomenon. Its expression in practical sporting situations is still poorly understood and much remains to be learned about its relationship to athletic performance.

Muscle damage and muscle soreness

Everyone who takes part in sport is aware that exercise – particularly unaccustomed exercise – can result in muscle soreness. In the last few years a good deal of research has been devoted to investigating this topic.

Soreness is caused predominantly by eccentric contraction of muscle. If bench-stepping is carried out using the left leg to raise the body and the right one to lower it, it is the right leg that develops soreness, not the left leg. The characteristics of exercise-induced muscle damage have been reviewed by Clarkson *et al.* (1992) as follows:

1 Soreness is delayed for 24 hours. It reaches a peak after 2–3 days and then declines, disappearing after 8–10 days.
2 Strength declines by as much as 50 per cent and is not fully restored after 10 days.
3 Swelling of the muscle occurs.
4 The range of motion of the effected joint is reduced.
5 The damage to muscle is reversible but actual physical damage occurs. This can be demonstrated in two ways.
6 Proteins, such as **creatin phosphokinase**, leak from the damaged muscle and can be detected in the athlete's blood.
7 The ultrastructure of the muscle may be disrupted. When viewed under an electron microscope the Z-band may be damaged. This is known as **Z-band streaming** (Friden and Lieber 1992).
8 The performance of one bout of eccentric exercise produces an adaptation of muscle that protects it from further damage during subsequent exercise. This protection appears to last for 6 to 10 weeks.

9 Muscle damage is greater in middle aged and older subjects than in 20 and 30 year olds.

Endurance

In everyday language the term 'endurance' is used to describe the durability of an object or an individual's ability to tolerate circumstances that are less than pleasant. In sport it is usually used in the context of the ability to sustain some form of physical activity. This implies that the athlete operates like many mechanical engines which are able to develop maximum power until they finally break down or run out of fuel. In the case of the human machine the situation is less straightforward. The power that can be developed depends upon the duration of the activity. This becomes apparent when the relationship between race length and running speed is examined. There is no particular achievement in being able to run continuously for four minutes; but it is very much harder to do so at a pace which results in a mile being covered. Superficially this may appear to be a matter of speed rather than endurance, but in fact endurance *is* very much involved. A 4-minute mile requires a speed of 6.7 metres per second ($m\,s^{-1}$). It is relatively easy to maintain this pace over 100 metres – the distance would be covered in about 15 seconds, 50 per cent slower than the current world record. A successful miler must maintain this speed for almost 4 minutes which requires the development of half a horsepower over this period. While it is easy to work at this rate for a few seconds, very few individuals can develop such power over a period of several minutes. Endurance thus amounts to more than the ability to continue physical activity; it involves continuing to work at a rate that is high in relation to the duration.

Energy sources

Maximum power output (Figure 2.14) varies with duration because different energy sources are involved. Some provide power at a high rate but are quickly exhausted; others last for much longer but are capable of supporting only a low work rate. There are similarities with a space vehicle that is powered by a multi-stage rocket. The energy available to a well-trained human, from the various sources, are listed in Table 2.2. The size of each energy source is inversely related to the maximum rate of power output. High-energy phosphate compounds provide energy at the greatest rate but the total amount available is so small that exhaustion occurs in a few seconds. At the other end of the scale the body can have vast stores of fat but the rate of utilisation of this fuel is so low that it is normally used as an energy source only during light or moderate activity. Endurance is primarily about the ability to generate energy at an appropriately high rate. The biological mechanisms by which this occurs are considered below.

Energy for muscular contraction

All the energy used by the human is obtained from foodstuffs, carbohydrates being the most important type. Glucose is one of the simplest carbohydrates. It is a compound of carbon, hydrogen and oxygen that has a great deal of energy locked into the

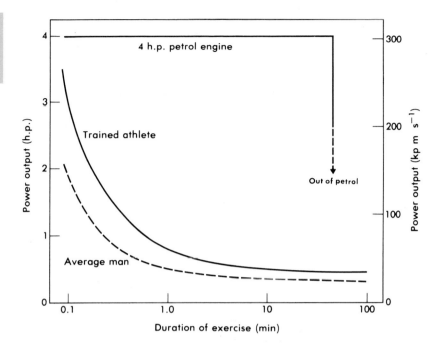

Figure 2.14. The power output available during activities of various durations.

Table 2.2. Energy available to a well-trained athlete from various sources. Values in kcal and *litres of oxygen*.

Source		Total energy available	Maximum rate of utilisation (min^{-1})	Time before the source is exhausted at maximum rate of utilisation
↑ AEROBIC ↑	Oxidation of fats	30 000 / *6 000*	12 / *2.5*	40 h
	Oxidation of glycogen	3 000 / *600*	25 / *5*	2 h
← ANAEROBIC →	Glycogen→ Lactic acid	40 / *8*	40 / *8*	1 min
	From high-energy phosphate compounds	15 / *3*	90 / *18*	10 s

chemical bonds holding the atoms together. This energy was obtained from the sun during the process of photosynthesis. When glucose is combined with oxygen it is converted back into carbon dioxide and water and the energy in the chemical bonds is released, sometimes as heat, occasionally in a form that can be used to produce muscular contraction. The energy available is known as the **free energy**. In the case of glucose this amounts to approximately 400 kcal per 100 g, about the amount used during one hour of moderately heavy physical activity. If glucose is burnt it is converted into carbon dioxide and water and all the energy is released as heat. It cannot be converted into muscular work and in order to provide energy in a useful

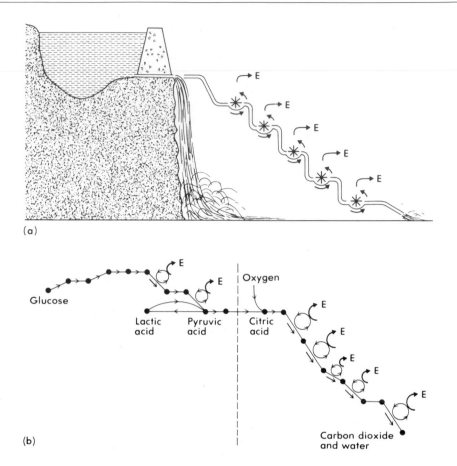

form the body allows the reaction to proceed in a series of steps. A small amount of energy is released during each step (Figure 2.15) and is transferred to other chemicals that are used during the contraction of muscle. The most important of these is adenosine triphosphate (ATP).

The stepwise process occurs due to the intervention of other chemicals known as **enzymes**. These play a vital role in the regulation of all aspects of body chemistry and an introduction to their mode of action will assist in the understanding of several aspects of physical fitness.

Enzymes   All the energy in foodstuffs and other compounds is locked up in the chemical bonds between atoms. Energy is released when these bonds are broken; it must be taken in before new bonds can be formed. When foodstuffs are converted into carbon dioxide and water the amount of matter remains unchanged but as the bond energy of the products is lower than that of the starting materials, energy is released and becomes available to the body. Unfortunately, it is often difficult to get the process under way. A lot of energy may be needed to do this. Before sugar or petrol can be burned, energy must be supplied in the form of a flame or spark. This kind of stimulus is not available in the body and in any case it would serve no useful purpose if the chemical energy in food-stuffs was converted into heat.

The principal role of an enzyme is to assist in the transition from one chemical state to the next, helping this to occur without a massive input of energy. Part of the enzyme enters into a loose chemical combination with one or both of the reactants. It assists in the breaking of existing chemical bonds and in the formation of new ones. Once this process has occurred the enzyme is released, unchanged, and can be re-used. Substances that act in this way are known as **catalysts** (Figure 2.16).

An enzyme is not consumed in the reaction it catalyses and in theory its concentration will remain unchanged. In practice enzymes slowly deteriorate and must eventually be replaced. In some ways an enzyme is similar to the oil in a car engine which is not burned as a fuel but eventually has to be renewed (Figure 2.17).

Almost all the reactions that take place in the body proceed via the aid of a catalyst. A different catalyst is required for each transition. If the reaction proceeds in stages several different enzymes may be involved in one relatively simple process. Some enzymes are known by common names that have been in use for a considerable time. An example is **trypsin**, which is involved in the reactions occurring during the digestion of protein. Others are known by longer names that describe the particular chemical reaction catalysed. During muscular contraction ATP must be combined

Table 2.3. Names of some enzymes and enzyme-like substances important in muscle and energy metabolism.

Name	Common abbreviation	Code	Plays a part in
Glycogen synthase		EC 2.4.1.11	Metabolism of glycogen
Phosphorylase		EC 2.4.1.1	Metabolism of glycogen
Phosphoglucomutase	PGM	EC 2.7.5.1	Metabolism of glycogen
Hexokinase	HK	EC 2.7.1.1	Glycolysis
(Phosphohexokinase)	PHK		Glycolysis
Phosphofructokinase	PFK	EC 2.7.1.11	Glycolysis
Lactic dehydrogenase	LDH or LD	EC 1.1.1.27	Lactic acid metabolism
Citrate synthase	CS	EC 4.1.3.07	
		EC 4.1.3.28	Citric acid cycle
Succinate dehydrogenase	SDH	EC 1.3.99.1	Citric acid cycle
Malate dehydrogenase	MDH	EC 1.1.1.40	Citric acid cycle
Cytochrome a	Cyt a		Respiratory chain
Cytochrome c	Cyt c		Respiratory chain
Cytochrome oxidase	Cyt ox		Respiratory chain
Lipase	L		Fat metabolism
Alpha-glycerophosphate dehydrogenase	AGPR or AGPD	EC 1.1.1.72	Fat metabolism
Beta-keto-thiolase	BKT	EC 2.3.1.16	Fat metabolism
Acid hydrolase			Protein metabolism
Beta-glucoronidase			Protein metabolism
Carbonic anhydrase		EC 4.2.1.1	Transport of CO_2 in blood
Myosin ATP-ase			Muscular contraction
Ca^{2+} activated ATP-ase	Ca ATP-ase		Muscular contraction
Mg^{2+} activated ATP-ase	Mg ATP-ase		Muscular contraction
Myokinase	MK	EC 2.7.4.3	Muscular contraction
Creatin phosphokinase	CPK	EC 2.7.3.2	
(Creatin kinase)	CK		Muscular contraction

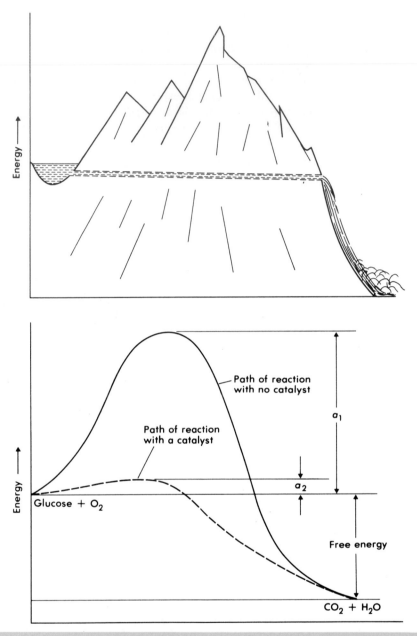

Figure 2.16. Role of the catalyst in a chemical reaction. Without the catalyst the energy a_1 must be input before the reaction can start. This is the activation energy. With a catalyst the activation energy is only a_2.

with part of the myosin component of muscle. The enzyme that catalyses this reaction is known as **myosin ATP-ase**. **Succinate dehydrogenase** is an enzyme that catalyses the removal of hydrogen from succinic acid, a step in the conversion of foodstuffs into carbon dioxide and water. The main processes involved in energy metabolism are

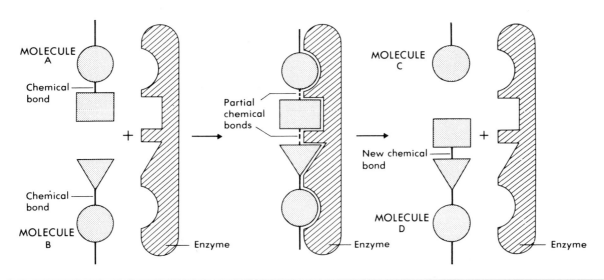

Figure 2.17. Action of an enzyme catalyst. Molecules A and B enter into a loose chemical combination with specific sites on the enzyme. This disrupts one of the bonds in molecule A and forms a partial bond with part of molecule B. As a result, part of A is transferred to B and two new molecules, C and D, are formed.

summarised in Figure 2.18 and a few of the important enzymes are listed in Table 2.3. Some enzymes have several different forms or work in conjunction with other substances known as **co-enzymes**. For example, there are several different **iso-enzymes** of lactate dehydrogenase. In the discussion which follows all these substances are referred to as *enzymes*.

Figure 2.18 outlines the main processes involved in the breakdown of carbohydrates and fats. Carbohydrates are stored in the liver and skeletal muscle as **glycogen** – an insoluble form of glucose. This process has a limited capacity, however, because the build-up of lactic acid eventually makes it necessary for the physical activity to be discontinued.

When oxygen *is* available, pyruvic acid is converted into other compounds and metabolised in the **citric acid cycle**, together with the products of fat and protein breakdown. A complex series of reactions occurs resulting in the formation of carbon dioxide. The process is coupled with another series of reactions, known as the **respiratory chain**, in which water is produced. The free energy of each step is slightly lower than that of the preceding one and energy is extracted and used for the formation of ATP. The energy transfer is considerable, producing about eighteen times as much ATP as occurs during glycolysis. A large number of enzymes are involved in the citric acid cycle and respiratory chain. The components of the latter are in fact a series of enzyme-like substances involved in the transfer of energy from the citric acid cycle to ATP. The whole process takes place in microscopic parts of the cell known as **mitochondria**. These are thus responsible for the major part of the energy production in muscle and other kinds of tissue. It has been shown that the capacity to use oxygen is related to the mitochondrial content of muscle, and that

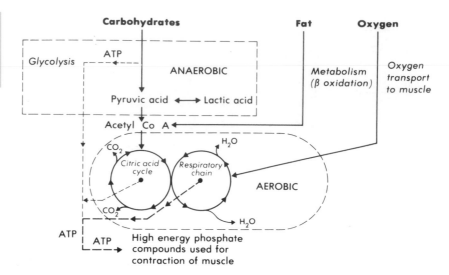

both are increased by suitable kinds of endurance training (Barnard *et al.* 1970; Ingjer 1979).

During physical activity ATP is used to provide energy for muscular contraction. Several enzymes take part in this process and in the interconversion of other high-energy phosphate compounds that are also involved.

The rate of a particular chemical reaction is often influenced by the concentration of the principle enzyme involved. This has implications for physical activity because a higher concentration of a key enzyme may allow energy to be produced at a faster rate. The influence of the concentration of the enzymes listed in Table 2.3 on various aspects of physical performance has been investigated. In many cases it has been shown that athletes have a higher concentration of these enzymes than non-athletes. For example, Costill *et al.* (1976) found that successful runners had about three times the concentration of succinate dehydrogenase in their leg muscles as untrained subjects. This enzyme is involved in the citric acid cycle and an increase in concentration would be expected to benefit performance in middle- and long-distance running. It has also been shown that an increase in enzyme concentrations is one of the effects of training. For example, Thorstensson *et al.* (1975) demonstrated a 36 per cent increase in creatin phosphokinase – an enzyme involved in the release of energy from creatin phosphate – after sprint training.

Particular energy sources

The various mechanisms by which muscle can obtain energy were shown in Figure 2.18: (1) from high-energy phosphate compounds; (2) glycolysis; (3) aerobic metabolism of muscle glycogen; and (4) aerobic metabolism of fats and other energy sources. The approximate contribution of each to total power output is illustrated in Figure 2.19.

An energy source has two important characteristics: the maximum rate at which power can be developed and the duration of its effective operation. It is obvious that an increase in the former will raise the total power output. Figure 2.19 shows that an

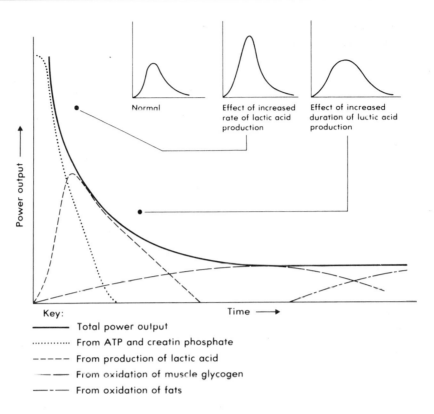

Figure 2.19. Contribution of the various energy sources to total power output. The effect of changing the characteristics of one of the sources is illustrated. Raising either the maximum power output or the duration of operation results in an increase in the total power available.

Key:

——————— Total power output

.... From ATP and creatin phosphate

– – – – From production of lactic acid

—— — From oxidation of muscle glycogen

—— –— From oxidation of fats

increase in duration can also have a similar effect. Endurance is thus influenced by both the capacity and maximum power of the various energy sources.

High-energy phosphate compounds

When a muscle contracts and develops force the energy is supplied from the breakdown of adenosine triphosphate (ATP). No other energy source can fulfil this function. ATP consists of an adenosine residue joined to three phosphate groups by relatively high energy bonds. When the last of these is broken its bond energy becomes available for muscular contraction and the molecule is split into two parts: adenosine diphosphate (ADP) and a free phosphate group (P). The reaction can be reversed if energy is available from other sources, such as the metabolism of foodstuffs, and ATP is then manufactured from ADP and P.

The reaction shown in Figure 2.20 is used as a means of accepting or donating energy. It always occurs in conjunction with a second process that either receives energy from ATP, or provides it, so that ATP is manufactured from ADP and P. ATP is produced during the metabolism of foodstuffs but is used up during the contraction of muscle. In practice these two processes occur simultaneously, ATP acting as a temporary store of energy.

In the resting state aerobic metabolism normally converts almost all muscle ADP and P into ATP. The muscle is provided with an energy store which can be used for contraction irrespective of any other process taking place. The release of energy from

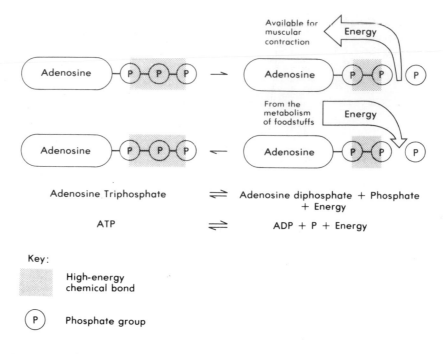

Figure 2.20. ATP as a store of energy. Energy is taken in during the breakdown of foodstuffs and released during muscular contraction.

ATP is catalysed by enzymes known as **ATP-ases**. It has been shown that the concentration of these substances is increased by sprint training (Wilkerson and Evonuk 1971; Thorstensson *et al.* 1975). In certain circumstances it is possible to obtain energy from adenosine diphosphate (ADP). Two molecules of ADP combine to form one molecule of ATP which is then used in the normal way. The process is catalysed by the enzyme **myokinase**, the concentration of which is increased by high-intensity training (Thorstensson *et al.* 1975).

2 adenosine diphosphate $\rightarrow$ adenosine monophosphate + adenosine triphosphate

$$2ADP \rightarrow AMP + ATP$$

A further quantity of energy is stored by a second high-energy phosphate compound, **creatin phosphate**. This consists of a combination of creatin and phosphate that can split into these two parts with the release of energy from the chemical bond:

creatin phosphate $\rightleftharpoons$ creatin + phosphate + energy

$$CP \rightleftharpoons C + P + energy$$

Creatin phosphate is capable of receiving energy only from ATP, and ATP is the only substance its energy can be donated to. It is produced during periods of rest when plenty of energy is available from the metabolism of foods. It is consumed during exercise when ATP is in short supply.

The sole function of creatin phosphate is to act as an extension of the ATP energy store. It is energetically more favourable to employ two different high-energy phosphate compounds rather than a larger amount of ATP. This minimises unfavourable thermodynamic effects which would otherwise reduce the energy available. The roles of ATP and creatin phosphate are summarized in Figure 2.23.

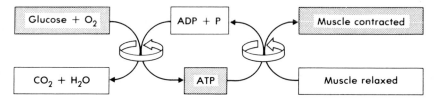

Figure 2.21. Transfer of chemical energy from glucose to ATP and then from ATP to muscle.

Key:

☐ (shaded) High energy   ☐ Low energy   ↻ Energy transfer

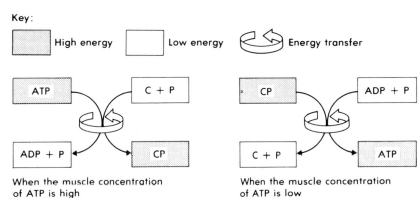

Figure 2.22. Transfer of chemical energy from ATP to creatin phosphate.

When the muscle concentration of ATP is high

When the muscle concentration of ATP is low

Figure 2.23. Summary of the roles of the various high-energy phosphate compounds.

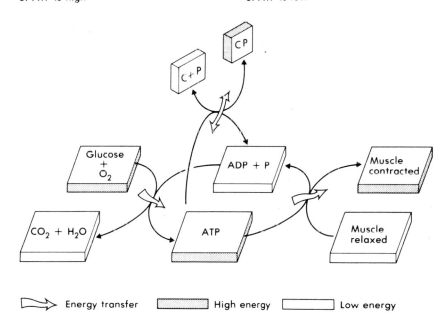

⇨ Energy transfer   ▨ High energy   ☐ Low energy

Of the mechanisms available to the human the high-energy phosphate process provides energy at the highest rate, but it has by far the lowest capacity. The maximum rate of output approaches $100\,\mathrm{kcal\,min^{-1}}$ but at this rate of working the stores are exhausted in only a few seconds. There are variations in both the capacity and power output of the ATP–creatin phosphate system between different individuals and before and after training. A large capacity will allow the individual to work at a relatively high rate for a longer period. It would assist a 200 or 400 m runner because he would be able to complete a greater proportion of the race before having to switch over to other mechanisms that provide energy at a lower rate. However, it would be of more doubtful value to a shot-putter, because the activity is so short. In this case it would be an advantage if the energy from ATP and creatin phosphate could be released at a higher rate.

Training has been shown to affect the concentration of both high-energy phosphate compounds and the enzymes involved in their metabolism. For example, increases in ATP concentration of 25 and 15 per cent have been reported (Karlsson et al. 1972; Houston and Thomson 1977). Some studies have also shown an increase in the creatin phosphate reserves (Eriksson et al. 1973) while others report no change (Karlsson et al. 1972; Houston and Thomson 1977). Several authors have demonstrated increases in the metabolism of high-energy phosphate compounds (Staudte et al. 1973; Thorstensson et al. 1975, Costill et al. 1979).

The capacity of the ATP–creatin phosphate system can be expressed in terms of the volume of oxygen needed for the production of an equivalent amount of ATP. Several studies indicate that the effective capacity of the store is equivalent to between 1 and 2 litres of oxygen (Margaria et al. 1933; Margaria et al. 1964; Roberts and Morton 1978). This energy can be used by muscle in a few seconds – even when working flat out the circulation could not supply oxygen to muscle at this rate. The stores can also be used to supplement the energy obtained aerobically. At the end of a middle-distance race a runner may be pumping 5 litres of oxygen to the muscles each minute. Energy in the ATP–creatin phosphate stores can be used to supplement this during the final burst of speed.

Lactic acid system: anaerobic glycolysis

The lactic acid system is a second method of producing energy for muscular contraction. It involves the conversion of glycogen into lactic acid – a process that results in the formation of small amounts of ATP. As oxygen is not required for this conversion, it is an **anaerobic** process – often known as **anaerobic glycolysis**. It can provide energy at a higher rate than the aerobic system and is the major source of energy in intense activities that last for more than a few seconds. In a race lasting for a minute, 70–90 per cent of the energy is derived from anaerobic processes: in a 4-minute event the contribution is between 30 and 40 per cent.

Figure 2.24 illustrates the basis of the lactic acid system and its relationship to the contraction of muscle. All the major components are situated in the muscle cell, close to the contractile filaments, so that the process can occur quickly and without intervention from any other part of the body. Muscle glycogen is converted into pyruvic acid with the manufacture of ATP from ADP and P. This is the process of glycolysis illustrated in Figure 2.18. The reaction involves the removal of hydrogen from glycogen, and under aerobic conditions this is achieved by combining it with oxygen. When oxygen is in short supply the hydrogen is joined onto pyruvic acid and lactic acid is formed. This process does not itself release energy but is essential for energy production because without it no glycolysis could occur under anaerobic conditions. Unlike ATP and creatin phosphate, lactic acid is a by-product of a process that produces energy, not the source from which energy is obtained. Although the production of lactic acid indicates that glycolysis has occurred its presence is undesirable because in high concentration it prevents muscle contraction from taking

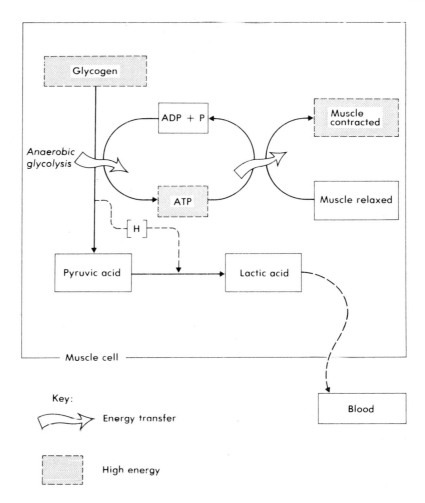

Figure 2.24. The metabolism of lactic acid (see text for details).

place. It does this because lactic acid releases hydrogen ions which lower muscle pH. This state of affairs inhibits the making and breaking of bonds between actin and myosin cross bridges and results in a significant reduction in the power output of the muscle. Fatigue and a considerably reduced work-rate results.

Removal of lactic acid

The lactic acid produced by muscle finds its way into the bloodstream and is carried round the body. The concentration is easily estimated and is often used as a measure of the energy produced from anaerobic glycolysis. It will be seen later that such scores are difficult to interpret. The lactate concentration of blood continues to rise for a few minutes after exercise has ceased, due to the time taken for transport from the muscle cell into blood. Blood lactate concentration then declines but remains elevated for approximately one hour.

There are a number of different ways that lactic acid can be removed from blood: (1) Conversion back into glycogen or glucose. This process requires the input of both

Figure 2.25. Lactic acid is produced when oxygen is in short supply. Its role is as a carrier of excess hydrogen atoms. During exercise, lactic acid diffuses from the site of production to other parts of the body where it is combined with oxygen. The removal of lactic acid from a muscle cell is thus equivalent to supplying extra oxygen to it.

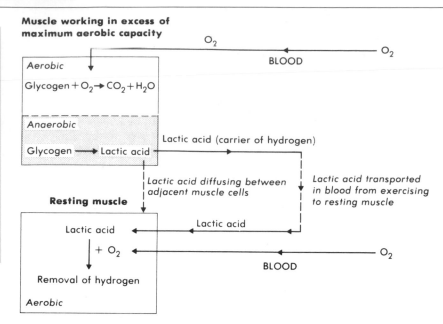

oxygen and energy. (2) Oxidation to carbon dioxide and water. This process actually releases energy but oxygen is required. It can take place only in tissues where oxygen is plentiful – usually the heart, resting muscle, or during recovery. (3) A small amount of lactic acid is excreted in urine and sweat (Minaire 1973).

Lactic acid is removed during exercise. Since it is effectively a carrier of excess hydrogen the removal process effectively amounts to a transport of hydrogen away from overworked muscles to a part of the body where oxygen is plentiful. This process has two important consequences: (1) a greater production of power from anaerobic glycolysis, which occurs because lactic acid is being continually removed so that more can be produced before the concentration of hydrogen ions reaches a toxic level; and (2) lactic acid can be produced on a continuous basis to supplement the power obtained from aerobic metabolism. The transport of lactic acid *from* a muscle has the same effect as transport of additional oxygen *to* it.

During exercise lactic acid is removed at several times the rate that occurs at rest (Depocas *et al.* 1969; Issekutz *et al.* 1976). The most important sites are skeletal muscle, where it is oxidised to carbon dioxide and water, and the liver, which converts it into glycogen. Between 52 per cent (Depocas *et al.* 1969) and 80 per cent (Minaire 1973) is oxidised by muscle, and the liver appears to account for between 3–4 per cent and 25 per cent (Issekutz *et al.* 1976). Other tissues, including heart muscle and kidney, are capable of removing small amounts of lactic acid (Keul *et al.* 1972; Nishiitsutsuji-Uwo *et al.* 1967). During exercise there appears to be an increase in blood flow and oxygen uptake in muscle, even in those not directly involved in the activity. Muscles switch from the utilisation of fats (the fuel used at rest) to carbohydrates, mainly lactic acid. Ahlborg *et al.* (1975) suggest that 46 per cent of fuel used by resting muscle may consists of lactic acid. The ability to remove lactic acid from blood effectively is clearly of considerable advantage to the athlete. The factors which influence the rate at which this process occurs are not yet fully understood and are the subject of considerable

Figure 2.26. The removal of lactic acid. An explanation of the processes is given in the text.

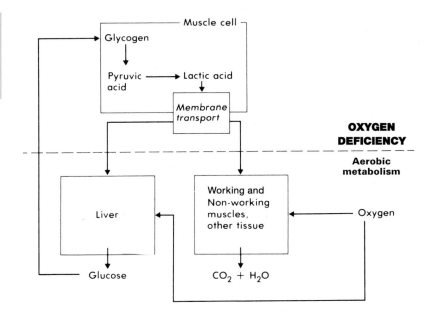

controversy (Brooks 1986; Davis 1986). The removal of lactate during exercise is summarised in Figure 2.26.

Poortmans and Jeanloz (1978) have shown that removal of lactate by non-exercising muscle stops soon after the end of the activity. For this reason the recovery from an accumulation of lactic acid is slower during rest than during light or moderate physical activity (Belcastro and Bonen 1975; Stamford et al. 1978). This is one of the reasons why recovery from heavy physical activity is faster if the individual jogs or 'warms down' than if he or she rests completely. Suitable training can increase the capacity of the lactic acid system. After a few weeks of such training maximum blood lactate concentrations rise (Eddy et al. 1977; Houston and Thomson 1977), which is presumably due to an increased capacity for lactate production. After two or three months of training maximum blood lactate values tend to fall. This is due to an increase in the capacity for lactate removal and buffering (Eddy et al. 1977; Parkhouse and McKensie 1984).

Anaerobic threshold

The trigger that starts anaerobic glycolysis is unknown and is currently a matter of considerable speculation. It is apparently not a sudden process that begins only when muscle ATP stores are exhausted, or when the tissue runs out of oxygen, because the build-up of lactic acid is very gradual. It begins at very low levels of work and slowly increases with the intensity of exercise. The conversion of glycogen into lactic acid takes place at the same time as aerobic metabolism and provides some of the energy requirements during aerobic exercise. This is possible because lactic acid is removed on a continuous basis, as described above. It is important to appreciate that the concentration of lactic acid in an athlete's blood is not simply a reflection of the

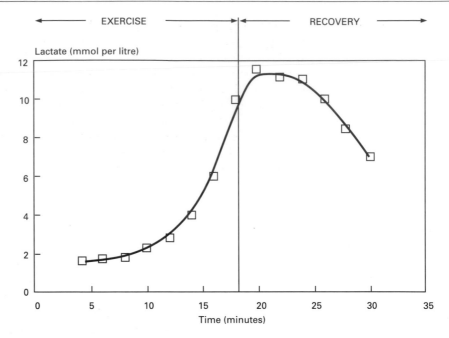

Figure 2.27. A typical plot of blood lactate concentration during 18 minutes of exercise followed by a period of rest. In this example the point of inflexion occurs at a lactate concentration of just over 2 mmol per litre.

amount of lactate being produced. It actually represents the balance between lactate production and lactate removal.

At a certain intensity of exercise the production of lactate begins to exceed its rate of removal. At this point the exercise becomes predominantly anaerobic and the concentration of lactic acid builds up inside the muscles. Eventually the hydrogen ions from the lactic acid cause such a drop in pH that the muscle is no longer able to contract and the athlete is forced to stop exercising.

The point at which the lactic acid begins to build up is known as the **anaerobic threshold**. At intensities of work below this the athlete is normally able to work for an extended period of time: above it, exercise is usually possible for only a few minutes. A graph of blood lactate concentration plotted against work load is often presented as two straight lines which intersect at a concentration of 4 mmol per litre. This figure is then called the anaerobic threshold. This picture is too simplistic. A more typical lactate–time plot for one subject is presented in Figure 2.27.

The figure illustrates a number of points. Firstly, that plots of lactate concentration at increasing work loads are more typically curves than two intersecting straight lines. This makes it difficult to estimate where the build-up of lactate begins. When only a few readings are taken the point of inflection of the curve becomes impossible to determine. Secondly, Figure 2.27 shows that the point of inflection may not necessarily be at 4 mmol per litre. In the graph illustrated it occurs at under 3 mmol per litre. Lactate tests are often carried out on athletes in the belief that an intensity of exercise that produces a lactate concentration of 4 mmol per litre is the optimum for endurance training. This approach is again too simplistic as there are considerable individual variations in lactate concentration at the anaerobic threshold. Other research suggests that a work load that produces 4 mmol of lactic acid per litre of blood is not an appropriate training intensity for many athletes. It is too high for some and too low for others.

Conditioning produces changes in the anaerobic threshold. After endurance training it occurs at a higher work load and at a greater percentage of the subject's maximum oxygen uptake. This is illustrated in Figure 4.11, in which lactate concentration is plotted against work intensity expressed as a percentage of $\dot{V}_{O_2max}$ for both a trained and an untrained subject. The shift in the anaerobic threshold that occurs with training is one of its most useful features. The phenomenon is much more sensitive to the effects of endurance training than changes in aerobic capacity, which are extremely small in athletes. It is the most practical way of monitoring the effects of endurance training in sportsmen and women.

In some laboratories an attempt is made to determine the anaerobic threshold from measurements of the respiratory function of the athlete during exercise – the so-called **ventilatory anaerobic threshold** (Davies *et al.* 1986). The basis of this determination is as follows. As soon as metabolism becomes significantly anaerobic two changes in respiration occur: (1) air intake is increased in excess of metabolic requirements in order to blow-off carbon dioxide and reduce the acidity caused by the accumulation of lactic acid, and (2) the ratio of carbon dioxide used to oxygen consumed may be altered. However, both the theoretical basis of the ventilatory anaerobic threshold and procedures for its laboratory determination have been questioned and the concept is not yet clearly established (Gaesser and Poole 1986).

The concept of the anaerobic threshold is often poorly understood, even by some who operate both lactate and ventilatory testing machines. This has often resulted in athletes being provided with poor, and sometimes misleading, advice on how they should train. Although the analysis of blood lactate can provide useful information to the athlete the interpretation of such data is extremely difficult and requires great experience and skill. It is therefore important that all athletes and coaches likely to utilise lactate testing and ventilatory anaerobic threshold testing should understand the concept of anaerobic threshold, and its limitations, for themselves.

Aerobic production of energy

The aerobic system produces energy by combining carbohydrates, fats and some protein with oxygen. Carbon dioxide and water are formed as by-products. The free energy of the starting materials is transferred to ATP which is used for muscular contraction. This process takes place inside the muscle and it is necessary to transport oxygen there before the reactions can take place. In terms of total energy production this system is by far the most important. It is used exclusively at rest and during moderate forms of continuous activity. It also serves to replenish the other energy systems when they are exhausted. During exercise it is used for activities which last for more than a minute or so. Maximum power is less than with the other two systems but energy can be provided for very much longer. In activities that last more than about 2 minutes it is the capacity of the aerobic system that limits the work output. The system is complex and has a number of separate parts. As a result it is possible to distinguish several components of aerobic endurance which serve to limit performance under different conditions.

The basis of the aerobic production of energy is illustrated in Figure 2.28. It is clear that the process is more complex than the other methods of energy production, and more than just muscle is involved. The bulk of energy comes from reactions occurring

41

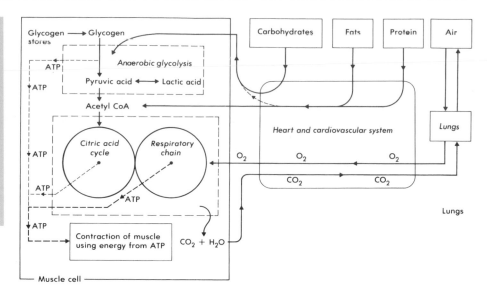

Figure 2.28. Summary of processes occurring in the aerobic production of energy. The raw materials are oxygen, muscle glycogen, other carbohydrates, fats, and occasionally the breakdown products of protein. All except muscle glycogen must be taken into the muscle cell by the cardiovascular system.

in the citric acid cycle and respiratory chain. Acetyl CoA and its derivatives are combined with oxygen and for this process to occur there are three principle requirements: a source of fuel (usually acetyl CoA), oxygen, and an adequate concentration of the enzymes of the citric acid cycle and respiratory chain. Any of the three is capable of limiting the amount of energy available from aerobic metabolism and so may affect athletic performance.

The fuel is perhaps the most straightfoward of the three requirements. Acetyl CoA, or related compounds, can be produced from any of the three major foodstuffs – carbohydrates, proteins or fats. The production is most rapid when it takes place from the carbohydrate glycogen, which is stored in muscle. There is usually enough for about 1 hour or so of heavy physical activity, and as long as adequate muscle glycogen is available energy can be produced at a high rate. As soon as the muscle glycogen stores are depleted other fuel must be taken to the muscle by the bloodstream, and this process limits the rate at which energy can be produced. Small amounts of carbohydrate are available in other parts of the body and derivatives of fats and protein can also be used as fuel. These sources are important at rest and during long periods of light or moderate activity, but they do not allow production of energy at the high rate possible from muscle glycogen. Since we have defined endurance as 'the ability to continue working at the highest possible rate' the availability of glycogen obviously has an influence on endurance.

A supply of oxygen is the other requirement. As long as adequate muscle glycogen is available, oxygen transport limits the rate of energy production from aerobic metabolism. Oxygen must be taken from the air to the part of the muscle where the chemical reactions occur. The process involves several different stages which are summarised in Figure 2.29.

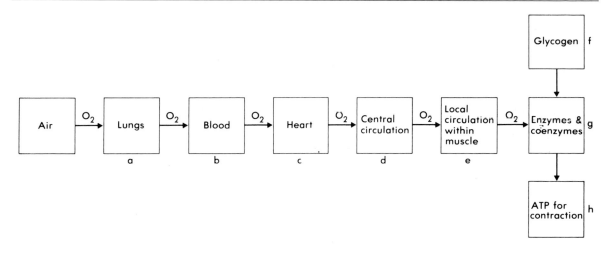

Figure 2.29. Stages in the aerobic production of ATP for muscular contraction. The efficiency of the process depends on factors peculiar to individual muscles as well as the characteristics of the cardio-respiratory system.

Table 2.4. Maximum oxygen uptake of untrained individuals and different types of athlete (males).	Subjects	$\dot{V}_{O_2max}$ (litre min^{-1})	$\dot{V}_{O_2max}$ per kg body weight (ml kg^{-1} min^{-1})
	Cross-country skiers	5.42	78.3
	Long-distance runners	5.19	78.1
	Speed skaters	5.58	72.9
	800 m runners	5.04	69.8
	Cyclists	4.88	67.1
	Canoeists	5.25	66.1
	Sprinters	4.33	57.1
	Untrained	3.14	38.2

Air enters the lungs where the oxygen diffuses into the bloodstream and combines loosely with haemoglobin. The blood is then pumped into the arteries by the heart and finally into capillaries which run adjacent to the muscle cells. Oxygen then dissociates itself from haemoglobin and diffuses into individual cells, to the mitochondria, where the citric acid cycle and respiratory chain are located. Enzymes catalyse the chemical reactions which result in oxygen being used up so that energy can be released. The first four of these stages (a, b, c and d) are centrally located and therefore common to all muscles in the body. The remainder are situated in individual muscles. Aerobic capacity is usually measured in terms of **maximum oxygen uptake**. This is the number of litres of oxygen that the individual can consume in 1 minute of maximum exercise and is often abbreviated to $\dot{V}_{O_2max}$. Maximum oxygen uptake is influenced by size as well as the efficiency of aerobic processes, so that it is often expressed in terms of the uptake of oxygen per kilogram of body weight. Typical values for various types of athlete are given in Table 2.4.

An individual's maximum oxygen uptake depends partly on the capacity of the central cardio-respiratory system and partly on the characteristics of individual muscles. The features of each link in this chain are considered below.

Components of the cardio-respiratory system

Lung function

It is the function of the respiratory system to bring air into contact with blood. This process provides oxygen and removes carbon dioxide. The latter effect is of particular importance during very strenuous exercise when a significant amount of the work is anaerobic. This is because the body's only short-term defence against the drop in pH that is caused by the build-up of lactic acid is to 'blow off' from the blood large amounts of the acidic gas carbon dioxide. This process requires that very large amounts of air are moved in and out of the lungs quickly and cost-effectively.

At the high speeds that occur during maximum exercise, the flow of air into and out of the lungs is turbulent and requires the expenditure of a considerable amount of energy which is provided by the respiratory muscles. It is commonly assumed that the diaphragm and intercostal muscles are responsible for all this work, but the reality is much more complex. A very large number of muscles interact in producing the movements in the abdomen, chest and back that propel air in and out of the lungs. Their role is so poorly known that the principal muscles involved in the process of respiration are presented below:

Diaphragm	Subcostalis
Internal intercostals	Levatores costarum
External intercostals	Serratus posterior superior
Abdominals	Serratus posterior inferior
Scalenus group	Erector spinae
Sternocostalis	Iliocostalis
Intercostalis internae	Quadratus lumborium

The respiratory muscles use up oxygen as they move gases in and out of the airways. Their consumption increases exponentially at high flow rates and a point is eventually reached where the increase in their oxygen intake equals the increase in the oxygen content of the air that is delivered to the lungs. This is known as the 'break point' of exercise.

Figure 2.30 illustrates the increase in the oxygen consumption of the respiratory muscles as the ventilation rate rises. The graph also shows that the consumption varies between different types of individual. Certain chronic respiratory diseases result in an enormous increase in the work of breathing. In contrast, the respiratory systems of successful endurance athletes are of above-average efficiency, delivering a larger amount of air to the lungs for a given oxygen consumption. This is presumably one of the reasons for the increased **economy** of effort of successful runners, cyclists and swimmers in comparison to untrained individuals. Training may increase the efficiency of the respiratory system but this matter has not yet been investigated.

The function of the respiratory system can be evaluated in a number of ways, the chief of which are summarised below.

Figure 2.30. The oxygen cost of breathing is plotted on the vertical axis against minute volume on the horizontal axis for an average subject, an athlete and a person with lung disease. In comparison with the normal subject the respiratory muscles of the athlete uses less oxygen to move a given volume of air while the consumption of the person with lung disease is greatly increased.

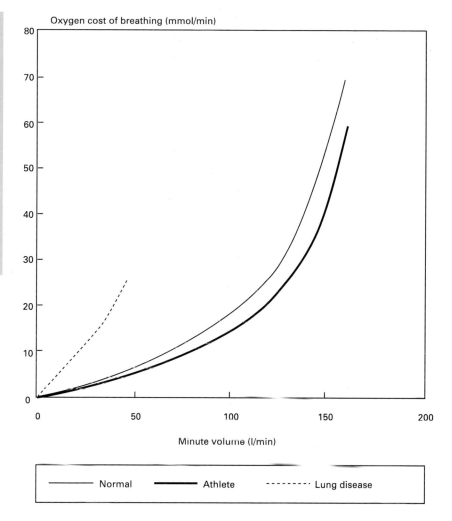

Vital capacity or forced vital capacity (FVC) Not all the air that is contained in the lungs can be expelled during breathing. The volume that remains in the lungs after a maximum expiration is known as the **residual volume**. The volume that *is* expelled from the lungs in a maximum expiration that immediately follows a maximum inspiration is called the **vital capacity**. If the air is expired from the lungs forcefully, the volume is then known as the subject's **forced vital capacity**.

FEV_1 This is the volume of air that the subject can expel from his or her lungs in one second of maximal expiration. FVC and FEV_1 can be measured using relatively simple equipment and, for this reason, are often included in studies on athletes.

Peak expiratory flow rate (PEFR) This is the maximum rate of air flow that the subject can achieve during expiration. It can be estimated using very simple equipment, available from pharmacists. However, these devices are far from ideal for the measurement of the high flow rates achieved by athletes.

MVV_{15} This is the amount of air that the subject can expire during 15 seconds of maximal breathing.

Expiratory minute volume ($\dot{V}_E$ max)   This is the volume of air expired in one minute of maximum exercise.

The last two measurements require more complex equipment, normally available only in a laboratory. A large number of other respiratory measurements are also possible, including inspiratory flow rates and estimates of the compliance of the lungs. However, these are seldom used in the context of the evaluation of athletic performance.

Dead space   This is the part of the respiratory system where air is not in contact with capillary blood so that no gaseous exchange occurs. It consists mainly of the volume of the air passages but is increased in certain respiratory diseases when the capillary blood flow is compromised.

The traditional view of the role of lung function in sport is that it does not limit athletic performance in normal individuals. This view is too simplistic and requires modification in the light of advances in knowledge in this field. In our experience at least 15–20 per cent of athletes suffer from abnormalities of breathing which places a significant restriction on their ability to undertake endurance work. Usually this is unknown to the individual but in the majority of cases can be corrected if diagnosed. In other athletes the development of lung function improves economy which, in turn, results in better performance.

Lung function is most critical in situations where the ventilation rate is maximal and the athlete is operating close to the respiratory break point. It is of less importance in very long endurance events like the marathon which is run at only about 75 per cent of $\dot{V}_{O_2max}$ so that breathing is not stressed. It is not surprising, therefore, that lung function appears of greater importance in middle-distance running events and sports such as rowing, than in the true endurance sports (Yamakawa and Ishiko 1966; Secher 1983; Maughan 1990). This point is illustrated by some results obtained in our own laboratory, shown in Figure 2.31.

Figure 2.31 shows that while the lung function of marathon runners is only average, rowers and middle-distance runners have higher than normal values for FVC and MVV_{15}: the difference is greater the higher the level of competition.

Some factors which have been found to be associated with a reduction in the lung function of athletes are listed in Table 2.5. These include physique, stiffness of the shoulders, spine and trunk, and posture defects of the same areas of the body.

Blood   The volume and composition of blood have an important influence on aerobic capacity. Oxygen is carried in a loose combination with haemoglobin which is contained in the red blood cells. When the concentration of this pigment falls below the normal level, oxygen transport is reduced in direct proportion to the reduction in haemoglobin concentration. The influence of diet on this factor is discussed later.

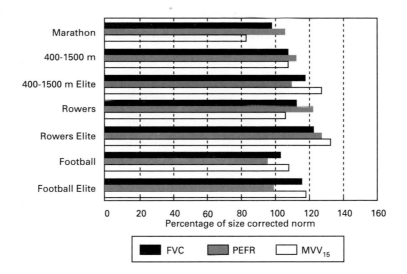

Figure 2.31. Forced vital capacity (FVC) peak expiratory flow rate (PEFR) and MVV_{15} of various groups of athletes. All scores are given as a percentage of the size and age corrected norms for the general population. The graph illustrates that élite athletes have better lung function scores than average competitors and that lung function scores tend to be highest in individuals who are involved in 'middle-distance' type events.

Haemoglobin concentration may be temporarily reduced soon after the start of a training programme. This occurs because blood volume increases at a faster rate than the production of new red blood cells. Eventually the amount of haemoglobin increases so that its concentration is similar to that at the start of training. The extra blood volume is an advantage because it increases the efficiency of the heart's pumping action. This occurs for two reasons: first, the output of blood per beat is increased; second, the extra volume allows this to be achieved with a lower rate of flow so that less energy is wasted through turbulence (Falch and Strømme 1979). Blood volume becomes reduced during dehydration, and this will decrease the efficiency of oxygen transport. The situation is likely to occur during exercise in a hot environment when a great deal of sweating takes place.

Cardiovascular function

The heart and major blood vessels limit the amount of blood that can be pumped round the body each minute. This quantity is known as the **cardiac output** ($\dot{Q}$). Maximum cardiac output is influenced by the individual's size, the state of training and the volume of the heart. A non-athletic individual could have a maximum cardiac output of 20 litres of blood per minute while in a well-trained endurance athlete the figure might be as much as 35. A greater cardiac output allows more oxygenated blood to be pumped to the muscles and increases the capacity for the aerobic production of energy. Cardiac output depends upon the number of times the heart beats each minute (**heart rate**) and the volume of blood pumped with each beat (**stroke volume**):

$$\text{Cardiac output} = \text{Heart rate} \times \text{Stroke volume}$$

Oxygen transport is therefore facilitated if the individual has a high maximum heart rate and a large maximum stroke volume. The high cardiac output of the endurance athlete is due to the latter factor. The maximum stroke volume is likely to be almost

Subjects	FVC	MVV$_{15}$
History of significant respiratory illness	5	8
Mesomorphy above 4.5	8	1
Poor flexibility of the spine, shoulder or trunk	15	12
Significant kyphosis	18	21
Significant abducted scapulae	12	12
Significant scoliosis	8	11
Chronic respiratory illness	26	35

Table 2.5. Percentage reduction in lung function scores of groups of athletes identified in the left-hand column of the table. All scores are expressed as a percentage of the age and size adjusted norms for the subjects

0.2 litre while in the untrained non-athlete it could be only just over 0.1 litre. There are a number of reasons for this difference. Endurance athletes have larger hearts, probably due to genetic factors. Also, their heart muscle is able to develop a greater force of contraction so that a greater volume of blood is expelled with each heart beat. This may be partly due to the effects of training on the contraction of heart muscle but it is mainly due to changes in the circulation. Trained individuals have a larger blood volume and a more efficient return of blood to the heart (**venous return**). This causes a greater stretch of the heart muscle during the filling phase of the cardiac cycle and results in more force being developed when the heart muscle contracts. Contrary to popular opinion, training seems to have little, if any, effect upon the heart size of adults (Ekblom *et al.* 1968; Wolfe *et al.* 1979). The increase in stroke volume is due to the effect described above.

It is often not appreciated that the circulation has an important influence upon stroke volume and cardiac output. The diameter of the arteries and veins is under neural control and this influences both the resistance to blood flow and the rate of return of blood to the heart. This, in turn, affects the degree of stretch of cardiac muscle, and that has an important influence upon stroke volume and cardiac output. The heart is thus the servant of the circulation as well as its master. The relationship between these variables has been extensively investigated by Guyton and his colleagues (Guyton 1963, 1968). Part of the response to endurance training consists of an increase in blood volume and adaptations in the control mechanisms that regulate blood vessel diameter and blood flow. These changes occur relatively soon after the start of training and are sometimes mistaken for an increase in the size and efficiency of the heart.

In contrast to the situation with stroke volume, there is no clearly established difference between the maximum heart rate of athletes and non-athletes, or trained and untrained individuals. If the maximum heart rate could be raised this would increase cardiac output. But training does not have this effect – it may even cause a slight decrease in maximum heart rate. The literature is not clear on this point. Moffatt *et al.* (1977) quote five studies in which training was found to have no effect upon maximum heart rate and five others in which a slight decrease was observed.

From the arteries the blood travels into capillaries that run inside the body of the muscles, close to individual cells. There is a certain amount of dispute in the scientific literature as to whether endurance training increases the number of capillaries in muscle. Part of the difficulty arises because the older investigations were undertaken using the light microscope which does not distinguish clearly between capillaries and certain other types of tissue. More recent studies, using the electron microscope, confirm that endurance training does increase the ratio of capillaries to muscle fibres (see Ingjer 1979 for details).

Oxygen diffuses from capillary blood into individual muscle cells where it enters into the chemical reactions that lead to the release of energy. It is only at this point that fuel supply and oxygen finally come into contact. The process takes place in many small steps each of which makes a contribution to the production of ATP. Many different enzymes are involved and the concentration of some of these seems to limit the rate at which the uptake of oxygen can occur. Several recent investigators have found that maximum oxygen uptake is significantly related to the concentration of enzymes of the citric acid cycle and respiratory chain. For example, Costill *et al.* (1976) found a correlation of 0.79 between $\dot{V}_{O_2max}$ and the activity of succinate dehydrogenase and Vihko *et al.* (1978) report that $\dot{V}_{O_2max}$ is related to the activity of several enzymes of the citric acid cycle and respiratory chain. One of the effects of endurance training is to increase the concentration of these enzymes and co-enzymes (Baldwin *et al.* 1972; Holloszy 1967; Barnard and Peter 1971). This allows greater oxygen utilisation and results in an increase in the individual's maximum oxygen uptake. These studies show that $\dot{V}_{O_2max}$ is influenced just as much by oxygen utilisation inside muscle as by the ability of the cardiovascular system to pump this gas round the body. The chemical events that take place inside the muscle cell actually have an important influence upon the amount of oxygen transported by the blood. This statement may cause surprise because most people see oxygen transport as a process whereby the gas is forcefully pushed into muscle by the lungs and heart, somewhat like the injection of a drug with a hypodermic syringe. In fact the process is closer to the sucking action of a vacuum cleaner. This occurs largely because of the chemical properties of haemoglobin, which are outlined below.

Haemoglobin is the red pigment found in blood. It has the property of being able to combine with oxygen when plenty of this gas is present, but of releasing itself from the combination when oxygen is scarce:

Haemoglobin + oxygen $\rightleftharpoons$ oxyhaemoglobin
when oxygen is plentiful $\rightarrow$
$\leftarrow$ *when oxygen is scarce*

The percentage of haemoglobin molecules that are combined with oxygen depends upon the concentration of oxygen in the atmosphere that surrounds the haemoglobin. For example, in the lungs about 98 per cent of all haemoglobin molecules are combined with oxygen. If the concentration of oxygen is reduced to half this value only just over 80 per cent of the haemoglobin remains combined. The relationship is shown graphically in Figure 2.32.

The concentration of free oxygen is shown along the bottom of the graph. It is expressed as the partial pressure of oxygen, which in the lungs is about 104 mm of mercury. The left-hand axis shows the percentage of haemoglobin molecules that are combined with oxygen. This ranges from about 98 per cent at the partial pressure found in the lungs, down to 0 per cent when the oxygen concentration is zero. The

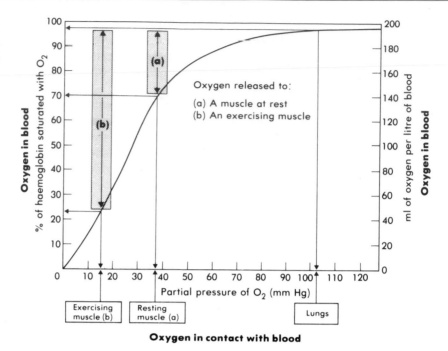

Figure 2.32. The oxygen–haemoglobin dissociation curve.

right-hand axis shows the volume of oxygen that is joined to the haemoglobin contained in 1 litre of blood.

Figure 2.32 shows that at the partial pressure of oxygen found in the lungs about 98 per cent of haemoglobin is combined so that 1 litre of blood carries nearly 200 ml of oxygen. (a) If this is transported to a muscle where the partial pressure is between 30 and 40 mm Hg, only 70 per cent of the haemoglobin remains combined and 18 per cent gives up its oxygen to the muscle. (b) If the muscle is using oxygen rapidly so that the partial pressure is reduced to about 15 mm Hg, only just over 20 per cent of the haemoglobin remains combined and about 75 per cent gives up its oxygen to the muscle. The amount of oxygen delivered by the blood thus depends upon the demands of the tissue. One litre of blood supplies about 50 ml of oxygen to muscle (a) while to (b) the same blood donates nearly 150 ml. When the blood is returned to the lungs the haemoglobin once again becomes 98 per cent saturated so that it again contains about 200 ml of oxygen per litre. The process requires the passage of oxygen from the lungs into the bloodstream. A litre of blood returned from muscle (a) will absorb 50 ml of oxygen while the same volume of blood from muscle (b) will take in 150 ml. This example makes it clear that the metabolism of muscle not only controls the release of oxygen from blood but also influences the amount that is taken into the bloodstream in the lungs.

During exercise three additional factors increase the transfer of oxygen from haemoglobin to muscle: raised muscle temperature, acidity due to carbon dioxide production, and the presence of 2,3-diglycerophosphate – a compound involved in the metabolism of carbohydrates. These three factors facilitate the release of oxygen from haemoglobin making more of the gas available to muscle. Ramsey and Pipoly (1979) have shown that lactic acid reduces 2,3-diglycerophosphate concentration. This has the effect of reducing the capacity of the aerobic system and may be a

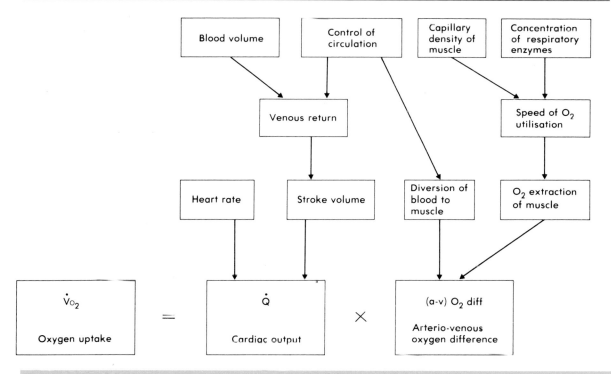

Figure 2.33. Factors which influence cardiac output, (a-v) O_2 difference and thus $\dot{V}_{O_2max}$.

problem in poorly trained individuals who produce lactic acid at low levels of energy expenditure.

It should now be clear that the volume of oxygen delivered to muscle is influenced by the amount removed from blood as well as by the rate of blood flow. The volume of oxygen removed from blood is the difference between the volume that is contained in 1 litre of arterial blood and the volume returned to the lungs in the veins. This quantity is known as the arterio-venous oxygen difference, (a-v)O_2 diff. For example, in Figure 2.32 the following applies to the blood flow to muscle (a):

Oxygen in 1 litre of arterial blood	Oxygen in 1 litre of venous blood	Oxygen removed from 1 litre of blood
180 ml	140 ml	40 ml

Thus the (a-v)O_2 difference is 40 ml O_2 per litre of blood.

When a muscle is working hard it can remove almost all the oxygen from the blood supplied to it. However, not all blood flow goes to working muscle, some is directed to tissues which extract little oxygen. The average (a-v)O_2 difference for the whole body depends upon how effectively blood can be diverted to the muscles that are active. There are several physiological mechanisms which help achieve this (for details see Guyton 1991), and their effectiveness is probably increased by training. A well-trained endurance athlete can extract the major portion of the oxygen contained in arterial blood, his (a-v)O_2 difference being over 150 ml of oxygen per litre of blood.

In an earlier section we saw that the capacity for the aerobic production of energy is measured as the individual's maximum oxygen uptake. It should now be clear that this is determined both by the rate of blood flow (cardiac output) and the degree of oxygen extraction (arterio-venous oxygen difference):

Oxygen uptake = Rate of blood flow × Degree of oxygen removal from blood (arterio-venous oxygen difference)

$$\dot{V}_{O_2} = \dot{Q} \times (a\text{-}v)O_2 \text{ diff.}$$

A high maximum oxygen uptake will result from a high cardiac output and a large $(a\text{-}v)O_2$ difference. Some of the factors which influence these two variables are shown in Figure 2.33. Several recent studies confirm that the ability to transport oxygen is influenced by the characteristics of muscle as well as by the action of the heart. Muscles that have undergone endurance training can extract more oxygen from blood than others. Thus rowers attain a greater maximum oxygen uptake while rowing than when they run on a treadmill; cyclists have a higher $\dot{V}_{O_2max}$ while cycling than when running or undertaking any other kind of activity. It has also been shown that training has a specific effect on oxygen uptake. Swim-training increases the maximum oxygen uptake when swimming but not during running; run-training has a greater effect on the $\dot{V}_{O_2max}$ measured during running than on the $\dot{V}_{O_2max}$ measured during swimming. These studies are considered in more detail in the section on endurance training in Chapter 4.

Economy of running and other aerobic activities

It might be expected that in such aerobic activities as running and swimming there would be a direct relationship between the athlete's performance and his or her maximum oxygen uptake – the athlete with the best performance would be expected to have the highest maximum oxygen uptake. In fact this is far from being the case. Top performers at endurance activities sometimes have only moderate levels of maximum oxygen uptake (Figure 2.34).

One of the reasons for this lack of association between performance and aerobic capacity is differences in the **economy** of different individuals. The economy of a runner is measured as the volume of oxygen used per minute when running at a constant, submaximal speed. For example, Daniels *et al.* (1984) reported oxygen uptakes of between 43.2 and 53.8 ml per kg per minute for 13 experienced distance runners when running at 4.13 metres per second. Runners with a low oxygen uptake at a given speed have a high **running economy** and have less need for a high maximum oxygen uptake.

Economy is task-specific and athletes who are economical at running are not necessarily economical at walking or stepping. It is generally assumed that running economy is related to running style, and that individuals with poor techniques also have poor economy. Children have poor running economy which seems to increase naturally with age (Krahenbuhl and Williams 1992). The majority of studies have found that training improves running economy but this has not been a universal

Figure 2.34. Summary of various factors that contribute to performance in endurance events. A high maximum oxygen uptake is not the only factor that is important.

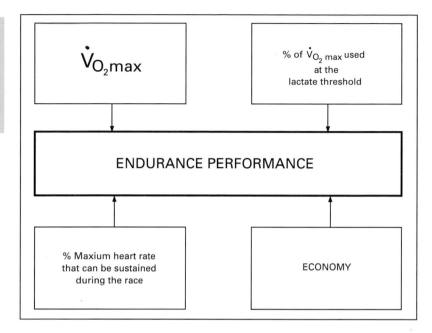

finding (Morgan and Craib 1992). Females normally have a lower running economy than males.

Swimming economy has also been extensively studied. In contrast to the situation in running, women have better swimming economy than men (Prendergast *et al.* 1977; Chatard *et al.* 1990). It has been demonstrated that the following factors are associated with a high level of swimming economy:

- a high level of swimming performance
- long arms
- use of the arms rather than the legs in a stroke
- high buoyancy.

Other factors that may have an effect but have not yet been fully investigated include: flexibility and hand surface area. The shaving of body hair reduces drag and increases swimming economy in male subjects (Sharp and Costill 1989).

Cycling economy has also been investigated. Coyle *et al.* (1992) studied a group of competitive cyclists and found that their most economical subject was 37.1 per cent more efficient than the least economical. They conclude that in cycling, economy is mainly a function of the percentage of Type I fibres in the athlete's muscles.

Long-term endurance   Some sports involve a prolonged period of physical activity – long-distance running, canoeing, skiing and cycling are examples. In such activities endurance can be influence by one or more of a large number of different factors. The more important include: the supply of nutrients, cardiovascular function, the ability to regulate body temperature, water and electrolyte loss, tissue breakdown and injury, resistance to fatigue.

Cardiovascular function

During prolonged exercise there is a gradual decline in the subject's stroke volume and a corresponding increase in heart rate (Saltin and Stenberg 1964; Rowell 1974). It is not known for certain whether this is due to fatigue of the heart muscle, or to other causes. Maher *et al.* (1978) suggest that it is probably due to changes occurring in the circulation which lead to a pooling of blood and a decrease in the venous return to the heart.

Temperature regulation

Physical activity results in a massive generation of heat. When working hard an athlete produces about as much heat as a one-bar electric fire. If steps were not taken to remove this energy a fatal rise in body temperature would soon occur. In fact body temperature does not remain completely constant. At the start of exercise it rises from a resting value of 36 to 37 deg C up to a new level which is closer to 39 deg C. At the end of a marathon run in cold conditions rectal temperatures ranging from 35.6 to 39.8 deg C, with a mean of 38.3 deg C, have been reported (Maughan 1990). At an ambient temperature of 19 deg C values as high as 41.9 deg C occur (Maron *et al.* 1977). The moderate elevation of temperature that takes place during exercise appears to make the body more efficient. However, it is close to the upper limit that can be tolerated and a number of physiological processes come into operation to ensure that temperature rises no further. It is important that the athlete facilitates these processes by the wearing of appropriate kit and ensuring an adequate level of hydration.

There are two principal mechanisms for heat loss. Large quantities of blood are diverted to the skin where energy is lost from the body by convection, conduction and radiation. This process requires the diversion of blood away from the working muscles so that their oxygen supply is reduced. This results in a corresponding drop in work output. The other mechanism involves the production of sweat which evaporates, taking heat away from the body. The latter process is more efficient in that it involves the diversion of less blood away from working muscle. Endurance training appears to reduce the temperature at which sweating begins so that more of the cardiac output is reserved for the transport of oxygen to the tissues (Gisolfi 1973; Henane *et al.* 1977; Nadel 1979). A similar but more pronounced effect occurs in the process of acclimatisation to a hot environment (Wyndham 1967). Sweat consists of water and certain salts. These are obtained from plasma, the watery part of blood. Thus sweating results in a reduction in blood volume and a loss of electrolytes from the body. If much water is lost, venous return and cardiac output are compromised and the blood supply to muscle is reduced. When the subject becomes dehydrated sweating is reduced and eventually stops altogether. Body temperature then rises and the individual succumbs to heat stroke. There is an increased risk of heat stroke in children and old people (Drinkwater and Horavath 1979). During long periods of activity fluid losses should be replaced as they occur and the athlete obviously should not begin the activity in a state of partial dehydration. Other ways in which the athlete can minimise the problem of heat dissipation are through endurance training, acclimatisation to heat, and wearing the minimum of clothing appropriate to the activity; natural fibres generally allow for better evaporation of sweat. When the

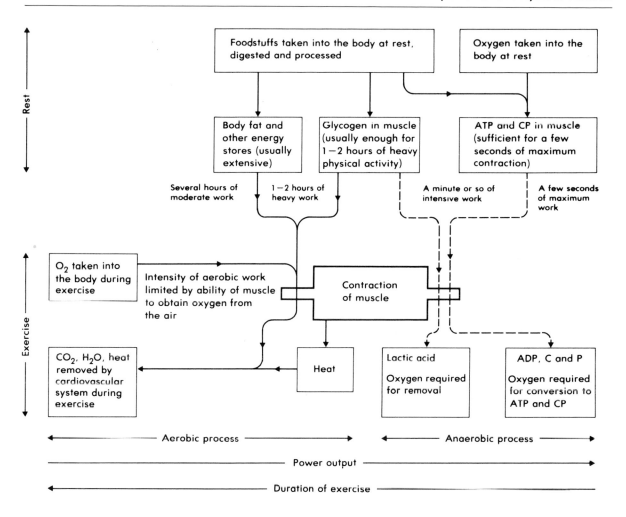

Figure 2.35. Summary of energy metabolism during exercise of different intensities. The top half of the diagram illustrates processes occurring at rest; the lower half shows those taking place during exercise. Going from left to right, the activity becomes shorter but of greater intensity.

relative humidity is high, the evaporation of sweat is reduced. If the environmental temperature is also high heat cannot be lost from the body by conduction or convection and any form of prolonged activity will inevitably lead to heat stroke.

Prolonged exercise may also be limited by several other factors. Fatigue in the nervous system is a likely candidate. This is not meant to imply that the individual simply stops trying. Changes in the function of the nervous system may prevent the activity being continued or indicate that it must take place at a considerably reduced rate

It is likely that tissue damage also has an important effect. Enzymes and other chemicals leak from muscle, and this may be responsible for a decline in power output with time. Strenuous exercise can increase the urinary excretion of protein up to one hundred times (Poortmans and Jeanloz 1978); some of this may be due to simple leakage, but there is evidence that tissue breakdown also occurs (Williams and Ward 1977). The various mechanisms concerned with energy production are summarised in Figure 2.35.

Speed

The term 'speed' is applied to a variety of different phenomena that occur in sport: fast reactions, a burst of rapid movement, the ability to run continuously at high speed. **Reaction time** is a property of the nervous system and depends upon the speed at which information is processed. A burst of rapid movement involves the translation of reaction into motion. It requires acceleration of the body, or part of it, and the continuation of movement at high speed.

In mechanical terms, speed is the distance covered in a given time:

$$\text{Speed} = \frac{\text{Distance}}{\text{Time}}$$

It is measured in terms of distance per unit time, for example: miles per hour (mph); feet per second ($ft\,s^{-1}$); metres per second ($m\,s^{-1}$).

Acceleration specifies how rapidly speed is changed. A car that can go from rest to 60 mph in 20 seconds has greater acceleration than one that takes 60 seconds. Acceleration is thus speed/time:

$$\text{Acceleration} = \frac{\text{Speed}}{\text{Time}} = \frac{\text{Distance}}{\text{Time}} \times \frac{1}{\text{Time}} = \frac{\text{Distance}}{(\text{Time})^2}$$

Acceleration is measured in terms of distance per second squared. For example: metres per second squared ($m\,s^{-2}$); feet per second squared ($ft\,s^{-2}$). For example, the acceleration due to the earth's gravitational field is approximately $9.75\,m\,s^{-2}$. Consider the case of a runner who starts at rest and accelerates at a rate of $3\,m\,s^{-2}$. After 1 second, the speed will be $3\,m\,s^{-1}$. During the course of the next second, the speed will again increase by $3\,m\,s^{-1}$ so that at the end of 2 seconds the runner's speed will be $6\,m\,s^{-1}$. After 5 seconds the speed will be $15\,m\,s^{-1}$.

Acceleration does not occur unless a force is applied to an object. In the case of a runner this is provided mainly by the muscles of the legs. The amount of acceleration is influenced both by the mass of the body and the force applied to it. The relationship is specified in Newton's second law of motion which can be stated as:

$$\text{Acceleration} = \frac{\text{Force}}{\text{Mass}}$$

The acceleration will be doubled if the force causing it is doubled, but is halved if the mass of the object increases two-fold. In sporting situations acceleration will be improved by increasing the force available from muscular contraction and by reducing the weight of the object to be moved.

In throwing events the weight of the projectile is fixed and acceleration can be improved only by applying greater force. In running, jumping and all other activities involving movement of the body there is generally some room for weight reduction through the removal of non-essential tissue such as fat. The gains in acceleration will be proportional to the decrease in body weight. Sprinters should not be tempted to lose weight by becoming dehydrated. This will have an adverse effect on the ability to develop force. The force available for acceleration is not usually the same as that developed by the muscles. Losses due to joint friction and tissue viscosity must be subtracted. In some individuals excess fat in the arms and thighs makes these limbs 'tight' and results in considerable loss of muscular force. It is difficult to measure this effect and, as far as is known, it has never been systematically studied. In the author's view, limb-tightness does have an adverse effect upon performance.

The force–velocity relationship of muscle is also relevant to acceleration. It was shown earlier that the force developed by a muscle depends upon its speed of contraction. A high level of static strength will assist the athlete in the initial phase of motion. But if the acceleration is to be maintained, it is also necessary that adequate force is developed when the speed of contraction is high (for further details see the section on strength earlier in this chapter).

In running there is no clear-cut distinction between acceleration and moving at constant velocity. Once top speed has been reached it is still necessary to accelerate the limbs, which are stationary twice in each cycle of movement. Considerable energy expenditure is also required to move the body up and down and to overcome tissue and air resistance.

The ability to run at high speed is, to a large extent, a matter of skill, and much of this is inherited rather than acquired. Improvements in speed are possible through training but tend to be smaller than the gains common with many other aspects of fitness.

Children who excel at sprinting are more likely to be successful at team sports than middle and long-distance runners (Table 2.6) However, in most games the requirement is for extremely short bursts of acceleration to be repeated frequently throughout the match, and such sports are often termed **multiple sprint** activities. In some high-speed sports such as speed skating and sprint cycling, turbulent air flow may be a problem, and aerodynamic kit and equipment are necessary for optimum performance.

Figure 2.36. The relationship between acceleration, speed and distance covered. (a) Acceleration occurs at 3 m s^{-2} for 5 s and then drops to zero. (b) After 5 s the speed is 15 m s^{-1} and then remains constant. (c) After 5 s the distance covered is about 38 m; 112 m after 10 s.

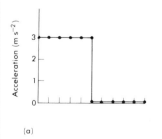
(a)

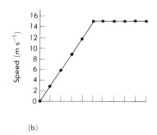
(b)

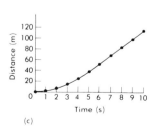
(c)

Type of athlete	Number of Subjects	Membership of school teams (places per athlete)*	Membership of country teams (places per athlete)*
Sprinters	20	3.5	0.5
		2–8	0–3
Middle- and long-distance runners	15	1.5	0
		0–4	0–0
Field athletes	16	2.1	0.2
		1–5	0–2

Table 2.6. Places on school and county teams (athletics excluded) of juveniles attending an athletics coaching course in Norwich, 1972.

*Mean and range of scores.

Power

Power is about the rate at which work can be done. In athletic situations it is closely related to the development of strength and speed. In physical terms, work is done when an object is moved against the resistance of an opposing force:

$$\text{Work} = \text{Force} \times \text{Distance}$$

It is easy to calculate the work done when an object is moved through a vertical distance because the motion is opposed by gravity. If a 200 lb man steps onto a chair 1.5 ft high the work done is 200×1.5 ft lb, or 300 ft lb. On the metric system work is often measured in kp m. The above action would involve moving 90.91 kg through 0.4572 m and be equivalent to 41.56 kp m of work. These calculations are of the useful work done. Some work is wasted in overcoming tissue and joint resistance. In activities like running there is usually no overall vertical movement although oscillations occur during each stride. These contribute to the work done; so does motion against air and tissue resistance. These factors make it impossible to make a direct calculation of work output, except during vertical movement when the useful work is large compared to that wasted.

Power output can be optimised by reducing some of the wasted force. Well-designed footwear and other equipment will increase traction and allow more force to be usefully applied. Tissue resistance and extraneous weight should be reduced to a minimum. Maximum power output is increased when muscle temperature is raised (Binkhorst *et al.* 1977).

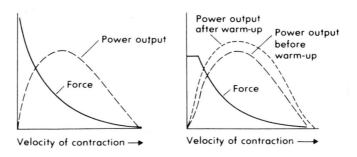

Figure 2.37. *Top*: force and power output for an isolated muscle. *Bottom*: the situation for a muscle in position in the body before and after warm-up.

Power is the amount of work done in unit time. Therefore:

$$\text{Power} = \frac{\text{Work}}{\text{Time}} = \frac{\text{Force} \times \text{Distance}}{\text{Time}}$$

Since speed is distance/time, power is also equal to force × speed.

In the section on strength it was shown that the force developed by a muscle depends upon the speed of contraction. This means that the power output also depends upon speed. This is illustrated in Figure 2.37. Since power = force × speed, power is zero when either the speed of contraction is zero (an isometric contraction) or the force developed is zero. These are the conditions at the extreme left and right of each graph. Power output rises at intermediate combinations of force and speed and reaches a maximum at about one-third of the maximum speed. In the human, neural mechanisms limit the force developed at low speeds and this results in a corresponding decrease in power output.

Maximum power can be developed for only a few seconds because the energy stores in muscle are rapidly depleted and other, less efficient, sources must then be employed. Intensive exercise increases the size of these stores so that high power output can be maintained for a longer period. This is considered in more detail in the section on endurance.

The so-called **power events** are activities such as jumps, sprints and throwing events. They consist of activities where the athlete's body is propelled – jumping and sprinting – or an external object is projected – a hammer or shot. In the latter type of activity a high body weight is an advantage, provided it is also accompanied by dynamic strength and speed. This is because the momentum of the body can be transferred to the projectile. Weight is not an advantage in sprinting because the body is the object which must be accelerated.

Fat

Fat is used by the muscles as a fuel during light and moderate physical activity. Endurance training improves the capacity to utilise fats as the intensity of exercise increases, thus sparing muscle glycogen reserves. However, even over the duration of a marathon the amount consumed is very small in relation to the reserves of even the thinnest athlete. Fat insulates the body against heat loss and helps prevent hypothermia developing in activities that take place in a cold environment. Its chief disadvantage is that it adds unproductive weight to the body. This increases energy expenditure and reduces the ability to accelerate. Fat on the lower limbs reduces anaerobic power output during work with legs (Watson 1984b). Fat also has an adverse effect on dissipation of the heat produced during strenuous physical activity (Haymers et al. 1975). Obese individuals find it more difficult to work in a hot environment and have a greater susceptibility to heat stroke.

Fat is stored inside the muscles and in deposits on various parts of the body. The latter is sometimes referred to as 'adipose tissue'. The tendency to accumulate body fat is a genetic trait and is strongly related to somatotype (see Watson 1979). Some individuals possess biochemical pathways that are able to dissipate excessive calorie intake, while others convert it all into fat and become obese.

Excessive amounts of body fat are associated with an increased risk of a number of different kinds of pathology. The *distribution* of fat in the body also varies between individuals and is influenced by age, gender, race and developmental factors. This is illustrated by the factor analysis of physique, presented in Chapter 1, in which three independent fat factors were identified, and by Figure 2.38.

The importance of an appropriate level of body fat to athletic performance is illustrated in Table 2.7. Top-level performers in almost all sports have levels considerably below the average for the general population. A minority of footballers appear to be an exception to this generalisation, although they are not typical of their team-mates. In endurance sports a low level of fat is essential.

Body weight Weight is influenced by the mass of all the individual body tissues and as such is far too general a measure to give much information about physical condition. The components likely to show the greatest fluctuations are water, fat and muscle but the weighing machine does not distinguish between any of these. Even weight *changes* are not particularly informative because a loss in one tissue may be masked by a gain in another.

Following a single session of intensive exercise body weight drops, due almost entirely to water loss through sweating. Significant dehydration is dangerous, being likely to lead to heat stroke; mild dehydration degrades performance by reducing blood volume and upsetting water–electrolyte balance. After exercise the water is quickly replaced; saunas and sticky games of squash do not result in a lasting reduction in body weight.

Following a few days of exercise the body weight usually rises. This is due mainly to retention of water. During longer periods of activity weight is reduced in some

Figure 2.38. The distribution of fat on different parts of the body. The graph shows that there is a wide variation in the thickness of skinfolds on different sites in this typical group of athletes. For example, the contribution of the abdominal skinfold varies between 10 and 30 per cent of the total skinfolds measured on the six sites. Thus there is wide variation in the distribution of fat in different individuals.

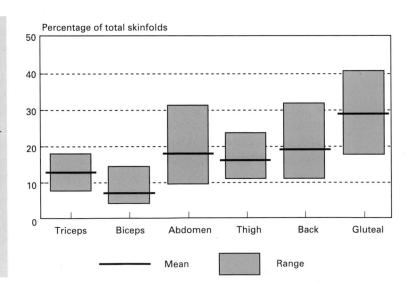

Subjects	Males	Females
Runners:		
Marathon	4.7–7.5	15.2–19.2
Middle distance	6.9–11.4	15.5–18.7
Sprint	5.4–15.4	17.5–20.5
Discus	12.8–17.2	18.2–29.3
Cyclists	6.8–10.7	15.4–18.0
Swimmers: – élite	5.0–10.8	14.6–24.1
Triathlon	5.5–8.2	12.6–17.8
Basketball	7.1–10.6	20.8–26.9
Gymnasts	4.6–10.5	9.6–17.0
Rowers	6.5–11.8	14.8–23.4
Tennis	8.9–16.1	20.3–25.4
Soccer: Brazil	10.7	
UK league	8.9–19.8	
Rugby	10.6–19.5	
American football	9.4–14.4	
Gaelic football	6.8–22.4	
Mean for 20- to 30-year olds	15	25

Table 2.7. Levels of body fat reported in the literature for selected groups of athletes. All scores are expressed as a percentage of body weight.

individuals through loss of fat. In a group who exercised for one month Watson (1973) found that subjects who began with little fat gained weight, while those who were fat at the start of training lost weight because their fat loss was greater than their gain in non-fat tissue.

Posture

Posture and body mechanics

The human body can be viewed as a number of segments that are arranged on top of one another. The upper segments are supported by the lower ones. Thus the weight of the head and trunk is carried by the spine, hips, knees, ankles and feet. This arrangement is most stable when the centre of gravity of each segment is placed vertically above the one underneath it. If a segment is displaced, additional strain is placed on the ligaments which hold the bones in place, and the body is then less stable.

In practice, the human body is not a rigid structure but is held upright by the isometric contraction of muscle on opposite sides of the body. Misalignment of the segments increases the force that is required to keep the body vertical and to move it during physical activity. Thus additional stress is placed on ligaments and muscle groups when postural problems occur.

A large number of different posture and body mechanics defects have been described. Those that are of greatest significance in the context of sport and physical activity are summarised below.

Kyphosis Excessive forward curvature of the upper part of the spine. This is often due to weak muscles of the upper back and tight, inflexible muscles on the chest.

Forward head An excessive forward curvature of the neck.

Abducted scapulae   Shoulder blades which protrude from the subject's upper back. This condition is due to weakness of the muscles illustrated in Figure 2.39.

Asymmetric shoulders   This condition is due to uneven development of the muscles around the shoulders.

Asymmetric back   Uneven development of the muscle of the back.

Figure 2.39. *Left*: cross-section through the trunk at the level of the shoulder. *Right*: abducted scapulae due to weakness of the muscles illustrated in the left-hand diagram.

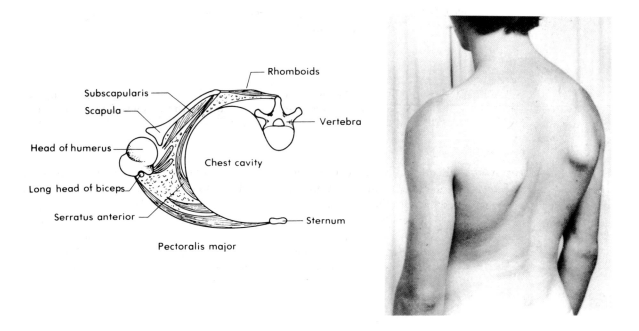

Scoliosis   A side-ways curvature of the spine. In 'C' scoliosis there is a single curve. In 'S' scoliosis there are two opposing curves (Figure 2.40).

Lordosis   An excessive hollow in the lumbar region of the back with a corresponding protrusion of the abdomen. The hips are normally rotated forward in lordosis.

Poor chest mechanics   Poor elevation of the rib cage.

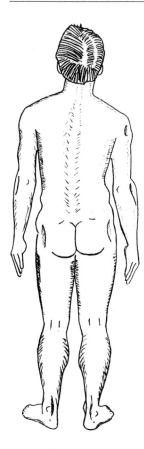

Hyper-extended knees   Knees which extend (move backwards) too far.

Bow legs (genu varum)   An abnormally large space between the knees.

Knock knees (genu valgum)   Lack of a space between the knees.

High 'Q' angle   When the angle between the direction of pull of the quadraceps muscle and the direction of the patella tendon is greater than 10 degrees (see Figure 6.6).

Tibial torsion   The bones of the leg twisted in an outward direction so that the toes point outwards when the knee caps are facing straight ahead.

Ankle deviation   The ankles twisted either inwards or outwards.

Low foot arches (pes planus)   Flat feet.

High foot arches (pes cavus)   Only the heels and the balls of the feet touch the ground when the subject stands normally.

Figure 2.40. Scoliosis due to unequal leg lengths. In this individual the left leg is slightly shorter than the right. This has caused a left 'C' scoliosis and a drop in the right shoulder.

✳ Causes of posture defects

Body mechanics is influenced both by the shape of bones and by the properties of the ligaments and muscles that hold them in place. Bone structure is the principal factor responsible for the shape of the legs and feet, and most major deviations of posture are caused by hereditary factors or diseases that are largely beyond the individual's control. Gross scoliosis and major twisting and bending of the legs are examples of serious posture problems caused by defects of bone structure. Scoliosis may be due to problems in the spine itself or to unequal leg length. This places one hip higher than the other, which causes the spine to bend to one side. The forces produced during exercise are then unequally distributed and the chances of sustaining a sports injury are considerably increased.

In contrast, many minor deviations of posture are due to problems of muscle development. Abducted scapulae and kyphosis are common in children when the upper back and shoulder muscles are weak – especially if those on the chest are tight at the same time (Watson 1990). Lordosis is often due to over-development of the psoas muscle, caused by too much kicking – especially if the hamstring muscles are weak (Figure 2.41). Asymmetric development of the muscles of the shoulders and back can cause deviations of the spine and moderate forms of scoliosis known as '*functional scoliosis*'.

The extent to which sports participation leads to the development of posture defects has not been adequately investigated but a number of studies suggest that the

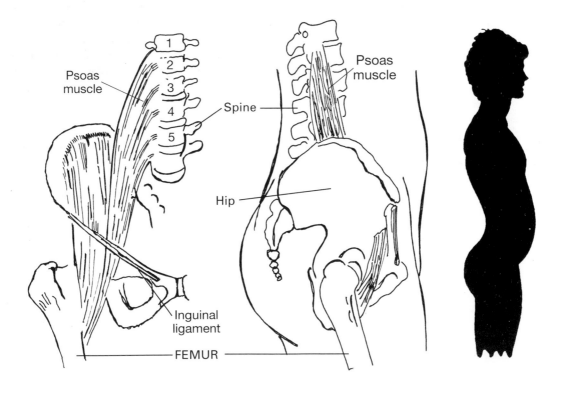

Figure 2.41. Specialisation in one sport can lead to the development of posture defects. This example shows how kicking activities can produce lumbar lordosis. The psoas muscle is used in the early phase of kicking. Its origin is on the lumbar spine so that over-development pulls the lumbar spine forwards causing lumbar lordosis.

two *are* linked. An above average incidence of lordosis has been noted in players of the kicking games soccer, rugby and Gaelic football: and mild scoliosis is common in asymmetric sports such as hurling, tennis and rowing (Watson 1982). This work points to the need for all athletes to undergo a well-rounded training programme that results in even development of every muscle group in the body. Muscles that are under-used in a particular sport may need to be developed during training if posture problems are to be avoided.

Consequences of poor posture

This is another topic that has not yet been adequately studied, partly due to the difficulties of conducting proper research. There are a considerable number of different posture defects, all of which have the capacity to cause problems in different athletic situations. Effects of poor posture that have received attention include:

1 *Psychological problems*. Posture defects are associated with a poor self-image.
2 *Breathing*. Work in our laboratory has shown that certain posture defects (e.g. kyphosis, abducted scapulae and poor chest mechanics) are associated with reduced scores on lung function tests. It is well known clinically that scoliosis has the same effect (see page 48).
3 *Mechanical inefficiency*. The misalignment of the segments of the body is likely to result in mechanical inefficiency that will increase the energy cost of activities such as running and swimming. So far the matter has not been empirically investigated.
4 *Sports injuries*. The excessive stresses that are caused by posture defects leads to an increased risk of a number of different sports injuries. The topic is considered in detail in Chapter 6.

Nutrition; fluid and electrolyte balance
Food intake

Diet provides the raw materials necessary for energy production. It is also the source of chemicals used in the manufacture and replenishment of structural components of the body, and the various biochemical pathways.

Along with water the principal components of diet are proteins, carbohydrates and fats but several accessory food factors – vitamins and minerals – are also necesssary, bringing the total number of essential dietary constituents to around 40. A deficiency of any one of these can have noticeable effects. Proper diet is particularly important for sportspeople, because a high level of physical activity increases the turnover of such substances as proteins and minerals. Exercise frequently results in the leakage or degradation of enzymes in muscle and other tissues and of red blood cells. Damage to connective tissue is also common. Sportspeople must therefore ensure an adequate intake of the precursors of these items, notably protein, iron and other minerals, and vitamins. The nutritional requirements of the athlete are complex and space permits only a few general comments to be made.

Protein

Protein is the source of amino acids from which the body synthesises new protein. Animal protein from lean meat, poultry and fish contains all the essential amino acids required by the body. Protein from vegetable sources may lack one or more essential amino acid. However, this difficulty can be overcome if a wide variety of different vegetable proteins are included in the diet. The daily requirements for protein are small: 1 g of animal protein per kg of body weight for sedentary adults; 2 g per kg for athletes who are involved in heavy training programmes. The large amounts of protein consumed by some body-builders are unnecessary and undesirable.

Carbohydrates

Carbohydrate intake is of interest because of its influence on the concentration of glycogen in skeletal muscle. This fuel is used during heavy physical activity. After 40–90 minutes of such exercise muscle glycogen stores become exhausted and the capacity to undertake very intensive work is reduced. On the other hand, heavy physical activity can be continued for a longer period if the concentration of glycogen in muscle is raised. This situation can be achieved by a special procedure known as 'glycogen loading'. The athlete first empties his or her muscles of glycogen by an hour or so of heavy physical activity. For the next three days a diet containing no carbohydrate is consumed. This is followed by three days on an almost exclusively carbohydrate diet containing little protein and fat. The procedure is capable of increasing muscle glycogen stores two- or three-fold and, although there may occasionally be undesirable side effects, may be of considerable benefit in long-endurance events.

The training programmes undertaken by many athletes are capable of producing a progressive depletion of muscle glycogen stores, as is illustrated in Figure 2.42.

During heavy daily training a carbohydrate intake of 65–70 per cent of the total calorie intake may be necessary in order to maintain muscle glycogen at an optimum level. This should consist of polysaccharides (starches) rather than sugars.

The assimilation of carbohydrates results in the release of the hormone insulin which may, in turn, inhibit the utilisation of muscle glycogen. Some investigators have found that the ingestion of sugars within 30 minutes of heavy physical activity

Figure 2.42. The effects of training for 2 hours per day for three days on a normal diet (solid lines) and a high carbohydrate diet (dashed lines). On the normal diet muscle glycogen concentration gradually declined over the three-day period. The normal dietary intake of carbohydrates was not sufficient to replenish the glycogen losses caused by training. On a high-carbohydrate diet muscle glycogen levels were maintained. (Data from Costill and Miller 1988.)

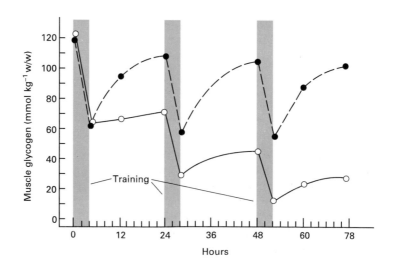

reduces endurance (Foster *et al.* 1979), but this has not been a universal finding and several more recent investigations have come to the opposite conclusion.

Vitamins and minerals   Vitamins are essential for normal body function although they are required only in minute amounts. Many appear to act as co-enzymes in various metabolic processes. A number of the B group vitamins act in this way in various parts of the citric acid cycle and respiratory chain. Vitamin C is necessary for the synthesis of collagen, an important component of connective tissue. It is also involved in the production of red blood cells and has many other functions that are not yet understood.

Many athletes believe that vitamin and mineral supplements improve their performance. Despite several well-controlled (double-blind) investigations such an effect has never been demonstrated experimentally. It is possible that the vitamin intake of some athletes is less than optimal. This is more likely if they are consuming a high carbohydrate diet or if the range of foods eaten is restricted or consists of pre-cooked or badly prepared food. In such circumstances a *small* supplement of vitamins will do no harm and may be beneficial.

Health foods   Health foods come in a variety of guises. Some are no more than low-fat or low-sugar versions of normal foods. Others are more exotic and contain a number of natural substances whose value as foodstuffs has never been scientifically demonstrated. Health foods may or may not be more healthy than a normal diet but there is no evidence that they are an aid to athletic performance.

Water and electrolytes   Water does not undergo chemical breakdown in the body but a certain amount must be excreted each day in order to remove harmful waste products. Water is also lost during breathing and sweating. Insensible perspiration occurs at all times. During exercise in a hot enviroment the water loss is considerable and may amount to one gallon, or more, per hour.

Water balance is monitored by osmoreceptors situated in the brain. When water is lost plasma becomes more concentrated. This is detected by the osmoreceptors: a sensation of thirst is produced and the water excretion of the kidney is reduced. The opposite occurs if excess water is ingested and it is soon excreted as urine. This mechanism normally maintains water balance in humans. It is inadequate only when sweating is excessive. The sensation of thirst may then be delayed and dehydration can result. This is a serious situation for two reasons: blood volume is reduced, leading to a fall in stroke volume and reduced efficiency of the heart; sweating then stops in order to conserve blood volume, and the athlete succumbs to heat stroke.

Anyone involved in strenuous physical activity needs to ensure an adequate level of hydration and an appreciation of the physiological principles involved in attaining this.

After being swallowed, liquids are temporarily stored in the stomach. They then pass to the small intestine where they are absorbed into the bloodstream; little or no absorption occurs in the stomach. A number of different factors influence the speed with which these processes occur. Exercise of an intensity less than 75 per cent of $\dot{V}_{O_2max}$ does not delay the emptying of the stomach; but above this level gastric emptying is slow. This means that it is possible to absorb liquids during long races, but not during shorter, more intensive, activities. Gastric emptying is more rapid if liquids are cool but it is slowed down by high concentrations of electrolytes and carbohydrates. Concentrations of up to 8 per cent of carbohydrates can be tolerated during exercise although gastric emptying is slower than with more dilute solutions.

In contrast to the situation in the stomach, fluids are better absorbed in the intestines if they contain small quantities of carbohydrates and sodium (Gisolfi *et al.* 1990). Since this will not inhibit gastric emptying the ideal water-replacement drink for consumption during exercise is a dilute solution of carbohydrate and sodium. This will provide the optimum replacement of water. In events lasting for more than 1 hour, muscle glycogen stores become depleted and replacement of carbohydrate improves performance (Maughan 1990). However, drinks containing carbohydrate should probably not be consumed before or during the early stages of long events since they may inhibit the metabolism of fats.

Gisolfi and Dutchman (1992) have provided an excellent summary of the literature on this topic.

Other issues

Altitude: Exercising and training

At altitudes above sea level the atmosphere becomes less dense. The percentage of oxygen remains unchanged but the partial pressure declines in line with the atmospheric pressure and at 10 000 feet both are 69 per cent of their sea-level values. The thinner air offers less resistance to the motion of the human body and performances in short, anaerobic activities such as the long jump and sprints improve slightly. Altitude has the opposite effect on endurance activities. The lower partial pressure of oxygen results in less haemoglobin combining with oxygen. Due to the shape of the oxygen–haemoglobin dissociation curve (see page 50) the saturation does not fall to the same extent as the pO_2. But at 10 000 ft only 90 per cent of the haemoglobin is able to combine with oxygen. This results in a corresponding decrease in oxygen transport to the muscles and in endurance performance.

On first moving to high altitude the individual may suffer from breathlessness, depression and acute or chronic mountain sickness. After a while the body begins to adapt or **acclimatise**. There are short-term changes in breathing. Then after two to three weeks the number of red cells and the haemoglobin that they contain begins to rise. These increases are half developed in four weeks but take many months for completion. Other changes also occur, including an increase in 2,3-diglycerol phosphate concentration, which enhances the release of oxygen to the muscles.

The above is the basis for altitude training which became popular in runners, swimmers, rowers and other endurance athletes following the Mexico Olympics. Altitude training still has some advocates but the predicted benefits do not seem to translate into increases in maximum oxygen uptake and performance in endurance activities (Adams *et al.* 1975).

Caffeine   Caffeine has a number of effects that are of interest in the context of endurance sports. It increases the level of free fatty acids in the blood (LeBlanc *et al.* 1985), it also increases the endurance of the respiratory muscles (Supinski *et al.* 1986) and results in a sparing of muscle glycogen stores (Erikson *et al.* 1987). These changes ought to result in an increase in endurance performance and a number of studies have reported such results. Ivy *et al.* (1979) found that caffeine ingestion resulted in a 7.4 per cent increase in work production during a 2-hour cycle ride, and Costill *et al.* (1978) reported that subjects who received caffeine could cycle for 15 minutes longer than a group of untreated controls. Other studies have failed to confirm these results (Knapik *et al.* 1983b; William 1986).

The precise effects of caffeine on endurance performance remain to be established. Dodd *et al.* (1991) suggest that it may have a more marked effect on individuals who are 'caffeine naive', while in habituated subjects the effects are either absent or less marked.

Blood doping   Blood doping consists of removing blood from an athlete and then re-introducing it some time later. After the initial removal, the athlete's blood volume is restored to normal in a matter of hours, although the concentration of haemoglobin is reduced. This also returns to normal after an interval of several weeks. In blood that is stored in a frozen condition, the red cells are preserved; they deteriorate if the blood is merely refrigerated (Williams *et al.* 1981; Glenhill 1982).

The process of blood doping is illegal in many sports and can now be detected, but it does result in a significant increase in physiological variables associated with endurance and in endurance performance. In 1500 m runners the re-introduction of 400 ml of previously frozen blood increased the number of red blood cells, the concentration of haemoglobin and maximum oxygen uptake by about 10 per cent. Performance in the 1500 m increased by about 1.5 per cent (Brien and Simpson 1988).

Bicarbonate loading   Bicarbonate is a normal constituent of blood where its function is to maintain acid-base balance by absorbing hydrogen ions. It functions by being converted into water and carbon dioxide, the latter product being removed by the lungs. Hydrogen ions are produced in large quantities during anaerobic exercise as a by-product of the formation of lactic acid. It might, therefore, be anticipated that additional bicarbonate would assist in maintaining a normal blood pH during intensive exercise, so improving endurance performance.

Bicarbonate may be partially neutralised by acid in the stomach if it is taken orally. It is excreted by the kidney and large amounts will have harmful effects. Thus the quantity of bicarbonate consumed and the timing of the intake are important. It has been found that a dose of between 300 and 400 mg of bicarbonate per kg of body weight, consumed 1 to 2 hours before competition, can have a positive effect on performance in intensive events lasting for a minute or two (Wilkes *et al.* 1983; Goldfinch *et al.* 1988). Track times over 400 and 800 m were improved by 3 and 2 per cent respectively. The negative side of bicarbonate loading is that it has unpleasant side-effects and is poorly tolerated by the majority of athletes.

Bone and connective tissue

Weightlessness and immobilization of a limb result in increased excretion of calcium and loss of bone density and mass. This effect is not reversed by exercise performed lying down and it seems that the anti-gravity muscles must be active in order to counteract the problem (Stone 1992). A positive relationship has been demonstrated between the level of physical activity undertaken and bone density and mass in both males and females (Chow et al. 1986; Pollock et al. 1986). Bone in the dominant arm of tennis and baseball players has been shown to have greater mass, density and mineral content than that of the opposite arm (Watson 1974; Jones et al. 1977). Some research also suggests that childhood exercise favourable affects bone density in adult life (McCulloch et al. 1990).

Demineralisation of bone is a particular problem in postmenopausal women. Various studies have demonstrated that exercise can help to reduce this effect if it is sufficiently strenuous. Chow et al. (1986) found that aerobics combined with low-intensity strength training was more effective than aerobic training on its own.

It also seems likely that physical training alters the properties of tendons and ligaments so that they become larger, stronger and more resistant to injury (Stone 1992).

3

PRINCIPLES OF TRAINING, WARM-UP, MOTOR UNIT TYPES, SOURCES OF INFORMATION

Principles of training

If you regularly take your car up the motorway at high speed one of two things will eventually happen. The machine will either expire in a noisy disintegration of half-shafts, big ends and cylinder head gaskets; or its top speed will gradually decline as the engine loses its tune and begins to wear. If you run at high speed yourself the result is likely to be different. A catastrophic disintegration is still possible but provided that you remain intact your top speed will slowly increase. This improvement is due to the effects of training. The human body differs from a mechanical engine in that it is able to modify itself in response to stimuli that occur during training. This process is known as **adaptation**.

The body is capable of responding only to certain stimuli. Weight-lifting leads to the development of larger muscles, and running produces a greater stroke volume of the heart. But high-jumping does not result in an increase in leg length or interval training to a higher maximum heart rate, although both these changes would be advantageous. They do not occur because the body has no biological mechanism capable of bringing them about. Some of the biochemical and physiological adaptations that occur in response to specific forms of training are considered in Chapters 2 and 4.

Overload

A training effect occurs when a part of the body is worked harder than normal. This situation is referred to as **overload**. Biological changes then occur and fitness is increased. Within certain limits the magnitude of the training effect depends upon the degree of overload. For example, if the muscles are used to lift weights only slightly heavier than those normally encountered, the training effect is small. If heavier weights are used the strength gains are much more pronounced.

There is a definite intensity of effort below which no training effect occurs. This varies from person to person depending mainly upon the individual's initial level of fitness, as is illustrated in Figure 3.1.

As the training proceeds the individual becomes stronger and 75 kg is no longer 75 per cent of his or her maximum lift. The individual will now need to train with a heavier weight if the strength gains are to continue at the same rate as before. This is illustrated in Figure 3.2. The situation with other aspects of fitness is similar. As the individual's fitness increases the absolute intensity of the exercise must be increased in order to maintain the overload.

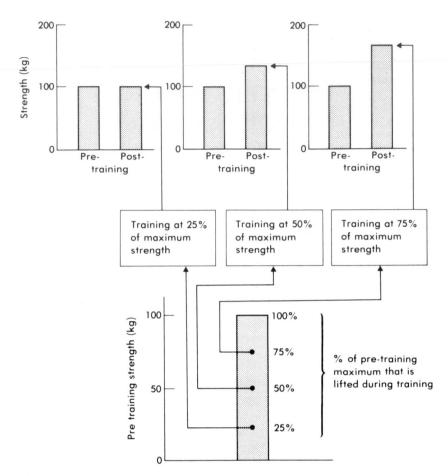

Figure 3.1 The overload principle. The bottom portion of the diagram indicates that 100 kg could be lifted prior to training. Using 75 per cent of this as the training load (75 kg) produces considerable overload and a large increase in strength results (*right-hand diagram*). 50 kg produces less overload and a lower increase in strength (*centre*). Training with 25 kg produces negligible overload and negligible gains in strength occur (*left*).

Progression   The organisation of the increases in training duration, frequency and intensity that the athlete undertakes is known as **progression**. This must be carefully gauged if the programme is to be effective. Increases that are too large or too sudden over-stress the athlete and inhibit the process of adaptation, or result in injury and other problems. Sudden change in the type of training should also be avoided. New methods of training should be introduced gradually and must be appropriate to the fitness status of the athlete.

Specificity   The effects of training are confined to those parts of the body actually subjected to overload. Thus, running does little or nothing to improve arm strength and weight-lifting does not increase flexibility. Furthermore, strength training affects only the muscles actually involved in the exercise, and gains in strength are confined to the movements that were used during training. Training effects are so specific that after isometric exercise the gains in strength are confined to the joint angles used during contraction and there may be little or no increase in the capacity for isotonic work. Increases in anaerobic capacity are also confined to the muscles actually trained.

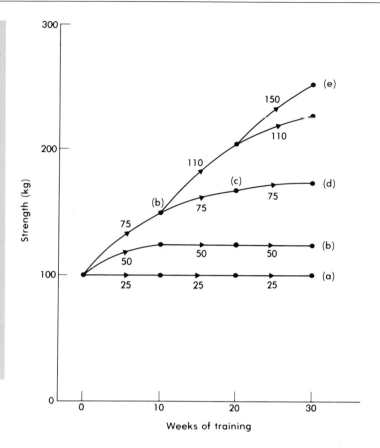

Figure 3.2 The effects of training with different percentages of the maximum lift. The subject's initial strength is 100 kg. Training with a weight of 25 kg produces no overload and strength does not increase however long the subject trains (a). If the subject trains by lifting 75 kg, strength is gained more rapidly than when 50 kg is used (b) and (c). If he or she continues to train with 75 kg the gains become slower (c) and eventually stop altogether (d). For maximum increases the training load must be increased to keep pace with the gains in the subject's strength (e).

Endurance fitness is slightly more general in that the heart and major blood vessels service all the tissues, but even here there is a great deal of specificity because of adaptations that are unique to the muscles active during training. All types of aerobic training have similar effects on blood volume and cardiac function – the 'central effects'. But the 'peripheral' effects are confined to the muscles actually trained. Thus exercise involving running does not lead to optimal increases in maximal oxygen uptake during swimming where a different set of muscles is involved.

As a general principle, training is most effective when carried out in a manner that simulates the athlete's competitive activity as closely as possible.

Cross-transfer   Despite the remarks of the previous section, some cross-transfer effects of training do occur. This is because the different organs and tissues of the body are not completely separate and the effects of one type of training are not entirely confined to one part of the body. Endurance training is not a good method of developing the strength of the legs. However, an individual who undertakes such exercise regularly will develop greater leg strength than a person who takes no exercise at all.

The term **cross-transfer** was originally used to describe the strength gains occurring in a limb when the opposite one is trained. The phenomenon was first noted as long

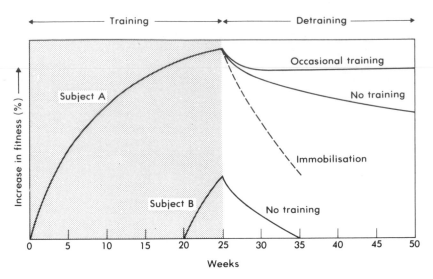

Figure 3.3 The acquisition and reversal of fitness. Subject A trains for 25 weeks. This results in a large increase in fitness. The rate of reversal of these gains depends upon the subsequent level of activity. Quite small amounts of further training may result in the gains being retained. Subject B aquires small fitness gains over a period of five weeks. These are soon reversed when the training is stopped.

ago as 1894 (Scripture *et al.* 1894). In a typical study it was found that the untrained arm increased in strength by 8.9 per cent following exercise that produced a 12.6 per cent increase in the trained arm (Shaver 1975). The effect is usually attributed to motor impulses arriving at the muscles of the inactive as well as the exercising limb. These cause isometric contractions in the muscles of the limb that is not being trained (Rasch and Morehouse 1957). The cross-transfer effects of training are usually much less than the primary result and for optimum gains in fitness it is essential that training programmes are tailored to the requirements of particular sports.

Reversal   The effects of training are not permanent and when physical activity is discontinued fitness drops towards the pre-training level. The regression is usually less rapid than the initial increase and a given level of fitness can often be retained with a much lower level of training than was required for its development. Differences in the activity level of different individuals make it difficult to quantify the rate of reversal of training. After short training programmes strength seems to be lost at a rate of 0.3–1 per cent of the gains each week (Muller and Hettinger 1954; McMorris and Elkins 1954); that is, if the individual resumes his or her normal pre-training activity. If the limb is totally immobilised the losses may be up to 5 per cent *per day* (Muller 1970). This vast difference illustrates the importance of the level of post-training activity on the maintenance of strength. Berger (1965) has shown that one set of maximum contractions per week is enough to maintain strength. With a normal level of activity losses are often negligible during the first week. After this there is a more rapid decline for 4–6 weeks, then the losses become more gradual.

Endurance fitness also declines when training is stopped. The drop is gradual and the higher the level achieved the longer the effects persist. Smith and Stransky (1976) found that an 8 per cent gain achieved over 7 weeks, disappeared 7 weeks after training was discontinued. In another study 10–14 per cent gains in $\dot{V}_{O_2max}$ were reversed after 7 weeks (Pendersen and Jorgensen 1978). In contrast, a group of champion oarsmen who had trained for a considerable time retained about half their increase in $\dot{V}_{O_2max}$ 18 months after the end of training (Hagermann *et al.* 1975).

But even very high levels of endurance fitness eventually decline. A group of champion middle-distance runners, whose maximum oxygen uptake was once 41 per cent above average, had values only 14 per cent above average 25 years later. Most of these individuals were still doing some running. The $\dot{V}_{O_2max}$ of two who had become sedentary was below the average for their age group (Robinson *et al.* 1976). Some features of the reversal of training are summarised in Figure 3.3. For a further discussion of the reversal of training see Chapter 4.

Interference

When strength and endurance training are carried out simultaneously it seems that the increases in strength are less than would have occurred if the strength training had been carried out on its own (Hickson 1980; Hortobagyi *et al.* 1991; Hennessy and Watson 1994). This negative interaction between different forms of training is known as **interference**. Other research suggests that endurance training also interferes with the development of speed and power (Hennessy and Watson 1994). The effects of interference seem to be less marked during the initial phases of training, but it is a particular problem when high levels of fitness need to be developed.

Interference is a phenomenon of considerable importance because most sports require the development of several components of fitness simultaneously. Its effects may be reduced by the careful **periodisation** of the athlete's training programme (see Chapter 4). The precise physiological mechanism of interference is not known at present although the following suggestions have been offered:

1   The opposing demands placed on cellular adaptation.
2   Over-training.

Rest and recovery: Avoidance of over-training

The biological changes that result from training take place during the recovery period between training sessions. Training periods that are too long or too intense, and recovery periods that are too short, inhibit these adaptations and may even result in tissue breakdown. Adequate recovery from exercise and the avoidance of over-training are thus vital elements in the development of fitness.

What can be achieved through training?

Performance is improved by training but it is important to realise that there are upper limits to what can be achieved. These are set by the opportunities available (environmental factors) and by the genetic endowment of the individual. Such effects have been most widely studied in relation to the development of aerobic capacity. The maximum possible improvement for a sedentary individual appears to be between 25 and 35 per cent, considerably less for someone who is already semi-trained (Astrand and Rodahl 1986; Shephard 1969). The range of maximum oxygen uptake scores found in the general male population is shown in Figure 3.4; scores for

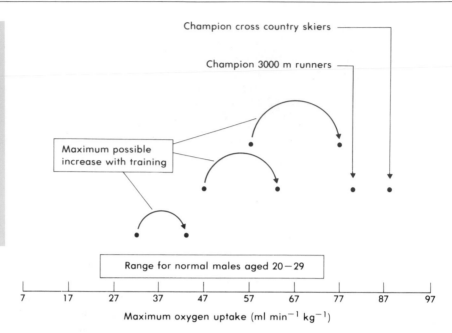

Figure 3.4 Changes in maximum oxygen uptake that are possible with training. The normal range for males is shown at the bottom of the diagram. Gains are limited to 20–30 per cent of the initial value. Thus, even with maximum amounts of training it is not possible for most individuals to achieve the values necessary for top-level performance.

champion endurance athletes are also given. The effects of a 35 per cent improvement on various values is indicated. It is clear that an average sedentary individual cannot expect to raise his maximum oxygen uptake to the level of a champion endurance athlete however hard he trains. He is in with a chance of a medal only if he has an untrained value of about $60 \, \text{ml} \, \text{min}^{-1} \, \text{kg}^{-1}$ or above. This is largely a matter of genetic endowment.

Genetic influences on performance and the effects of training

Physical performance is capable of being influenced by only two factors: genetic and environmental. In the context of sport by far the most important environmental factor is that of training. Although it has long been realised that the effects of training are often relatively small, the genetic influences on athletic performance are not particularly well documented, largely because they are so difficult to measure. Until recently research has been confined to training studies carried out on pairs of monozygotic (identical) twins and other members of the family unit.

As a result of these studies it is now known that the genetic endowment of an individual influences not only his or her fitness *per se* but also the changes that take place as a result of a programme of training – the so-called **trainability** of the individual. For example, Bielen *et al.* (1991) found that 47 per cent of the ability to increase end-diastolic volume with training was contributed by hereditary factors. Bouchard (1991) found that genetic factors contributed 25 per cent of the variance of fat mass but that the habitual level of physical activity was also influenced by genetic factors so that the overall genetic contribution was 40 per cent of the variance. It has also been suggested that genetic mediation of the effects of training are of great importance during aerobic training and may account for 40 per cent of the differences in individual response (Malina and Bouchard 1986).

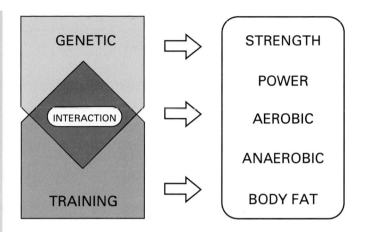

Figure 3.5 Genetic and environmental factors in sport. Fitness variables such as strength, power, aerobic capacity, anaerobic capacity and body fat content are influenced by both training and genetic factors. These two factors also interact. This means that genetic factors influence the outcome of training as well as the individual's initial level of fitness.

More recently, sequence variations in mitochondrial DNA has been used to study genetic differences in variables such as $\dot{V}_{O_2max}$ and its response to training (Dionne *et al.* 1991). This is an area of research that is likely to expand considerably in the next decade as technique improve and become more accessible (see Figure 3.5).

The upper limit of many performance variables is determined by characteristics that are not influenced by training. The way that some of these influence the potential for four athletic events is illustrated in Figure 3.6.

Figure 3.6 Structural factors favourable to performance in four different athletic events; long-distance running, high jump, sprinting, shot-put.

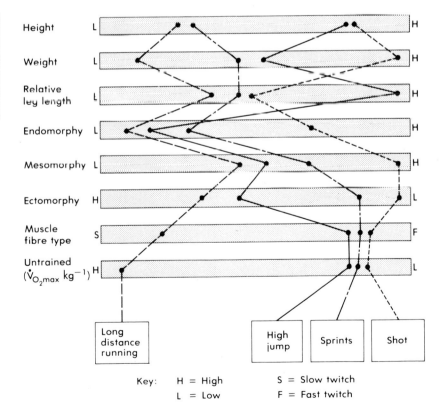

Factors affecting the outcome of training

The rate of improvement in fitness in response to training may be influenced by a number of factors, including: the initial level of fitness, the parameters of the training programme, and the age of the subject.

Initial level of fitness

The initial level of fitness has a critical influence on the gains possible through training. Figure 3.7 shows pre- and post-training scores for 16 youths who undertook exactly the same programme of interval training. The individuals with the lowest pre-training scores increased their physical working capacities while those who were fittest at the start of the study demonstrated no improvement. This is because the training did not produce overload in the fitter subjects who had previously undertaken other forms of endurance training.

The influence of initial fitness level on the rate of improvement often causes considerable difficulties when interpreting the results of training studies. If you devise a new type of training programme and test it on discharged hospital patients you will probably get spectacular results. Many of the claims for commercial training programmes and equipment are based on just this type of study. They frequently give very disappointing results when used with athletes who are already in reasonable condition.

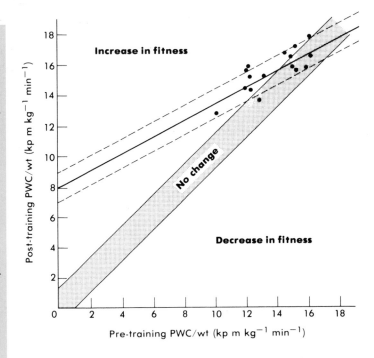

Figure 3.7 The effects of initial level of fitness on the outcome of a training programme. Sixteen subjects undertook interval training for a period of five weeks. Their post-training physical working capacities are plotted on the vertical axis against the initial value on the horizontal axis. All individuals with a physical working capacity of 12 units or less increased their physical working capacity as a result of the training. The majority of those with a pre-training score of 14 units or above failed to improve. (Data from Watson and O'Donovan (1977b.)

The parameters of training

The parameters of a programme of training include: intensity, duration (the duration of each training session), frequency, length (the number of weeks of training) and periodisation (how the various phases of the programme are organised). Each has an important influence on the outcome of training, as is discussed individually in Chapter 4.

Age and level of physical maturation

Pre-puberal children do not respond to training in the same way as adults. To some extent this is due to biochemical differences including the level of certain hormones. But of even greater importance is the influence that growth and maturation exert on most physical performance variables. Strength, aerobic capacity and power are all strongly influenced by size and by the child's ability to coordinate the actions of various parts of the body. These characteristics develop rapidly, but unevenly, during childhood and adolescence. Their influence on most physical performance variables is so great that many of the effects of training become obscured. This is particularly so during the part of adolescence when growth is greatest – the **adolescent growth spurt**.

In some sports, notably swimming, endurance training is commonly undertaken at an extremely young age. There is no conclusive evidence that this has especially beneficial or long-lasting effects. There is also no evidence for a 'critical period' when endurance training is especially beneficial (Rowland 1992). Despite a large number of studies, the effects of training on the maximum oxygen uptake of children remains a matter of dispute. In young runners, endurance training seems to have a greater influence on running economy than on aerobic capacity (Krahenbuhl and Williams 1992). The maximum oxygen uptake per kg of body weight of the average child hardly changes between the ages of 5 and 14 despite a considerable increase in running performance.

When training children, great care must be taken not to inflict physical or psychological damage. With the majority of individuals in this age group attention to motor development and the introduction of a wide range of different skills is generally preferable to intensive physical training.

Modified forms of strength and endurance training can be of benefit to the child athlete if he or she is psychologically ready for them. However, special precautions must be taken. Modified adult programmes are definitely *not* suitable for young children.

Warm-up

A period of preparatory activity undertaken before the start of exercise is known as **warm-up**. A warm-up of an appropriate nature enhances physical performance by producing a number of physiological changes in the body, including:

1 Rise in core and muscle temperatures
2 Facilitation of neuromuscular function

3 Increase in joint mobility and flexibility

4 Increase in muscle blood flow

5 Increase in aerobic metabolism

6 Increase in the amount of oxygen extracted from blood

7 Decrease in the production of lactic acid

8 Increase in utilisation of fats for aerobic metabolism

9 Decrease in utilisation of muscle glycogen

10 Increase in maximum power output

11 Increase in economy of movement.

(Gutin *et al.* 1976; Hetzler *et al.* 1986; Skinner *et al.* 1986; Robergs *et al.* 1991.)

Flexibility
A short period of light stretching is capable of increasing the range of motion of joints, by its effect on the connective tissue in muscles, ligaments and tendons. Strenuous exercise without stretching seems to have a similar effect.

Power output
The power output of muscle is increased when its temperature is raised (Binkhorst *et al.* 1977). This effect is illustrated in Figure 2.37, p. 58. The effect occurs for three reasons: (1) muscle viscosity is reduced; (2) the speed of conduction of impulses by nerves is increased (Zuntz *et al.* 1906); and (3) the rate of chemical reactions inside muscle is increased. It is necessary to raise muscle temperature by at least 2 degC before these effects become apparent: a strenuous warm-up lasting several minutes is thus required in order to optimise power output.

Coordination
Coordination improves after a few minutes of practice. Activities involving fine motor skills should therefore be rehearsed during warm-up.

Aerobic metabolism
An adequate warm-up increases the rate of aerobic metabolism at the start of exercise. This decreases the contribution of anaerobic processes, thus minimising the accumulation of lactic acid. This is illustrated in Figure 3.8, which shows the effect of a warm-up consisting of 15 minutes of strenuous running on the metabolism of a well-trained athlete.

The warm-up produced five changes: (1) muscle temperature rose by more than 3 degC; (2) oxygen intake rose more sharply at the start of exercise and (3) reached a higher maximum value; (4) as a consequence of (2) and (3) less energy was obtained from anaerobic processes so that the concentration of blood lactate was lower; and (5) the heart rate increased more rapidly. The physiological changes that produce these results are many and complex. Hormones that are secreted into the bloodstream enhance cardiac function and cause blood to be diverted to the working muscles.

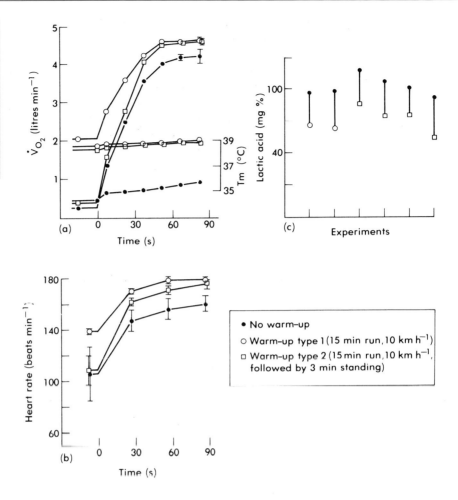

Figure 3.8 The effects of warm-up on oxygen uptake, blood lactate concentration, heart rate and core temperature during subsequent exercise. (Data from Martin *et al.* 1975, by kind permission of the authors.)

Activity of the autonomic nervous system has a similar effect. This results in a greater blood flow to skeletal muscle and a cardiovascular system that is more responsive to sudden demands. The increase in muscle temperature is also important: it reduces the affinity of haemoglobin for oxygen thus allowing more of this gas to be released to the muscles. It also increases the rate of chemical reactions inside muscle cells. All this results in more oxygen being extracted from a given volume of inspired air so that the cost-effectiveness of breathing is improved (Ingjer and Strømme 1979). There also seem to be psychological benefits that occur even if the warm-up is physiologically ineffective (Malarecki 1954).

In order to produce these changes the warm-up must consist of 15–30 minutes of heavy physical activity. This must be sufficiently strenuous to produce sweating. Passive warm-up by means of hot baths or showers has little if any effect (Ingjer and Strømme 1979). Only fit individuals are able to benefit. Apparently the poorly conditioned lack the cardiovascular and cellular adaptations necessary for an intensive warm-up to be effective. This is probably an academic point since only the well-trained will be capable of completing such a warm-up without becoming exhausted.

It is one of the reasons why a reasonable level of all-round fitness is necessary for all athletes, whatever their sport.

Economy of physical activity

The physiological changes outlined above result in the body using a lower volume of oxygen for a given amount of work. This is known as greater **economy**. (See Chapter 2 for a discussion of this topic.)

The transition from exercise to recovery

Recovery from physical activity is facilitated if the transition is made gradually. Lactic acid is removed more rapidly during moderate levels of activity than it is at rest and cardiac function is better maintained. During exercise much of the venous return to the heart is achieved by the action of contracting skeletal muscle on limb veins (the muscle pump) and by breathing (the respiratory pump). If physical activity is halted suddenly a great deal of blood remains in the limbs and cardiac function is seriously impaired. The cool-down period is an ideal time to undertake flexibility training.

Practical advice on warm-up

The previous section has demonstrated that the athlete's physiological state during exercise is different to that at rest. The warm-up needs to bring about these changes as efficiently as possible without introducing any extra risks, such as the possibility of injury. Cool-down is the reverse of this process and helps return the body to its resting state.

All forms of exercise should be preceded by a warm-up. This should normally consist of four phases, which in practice can be intermixed (Figure 3.9).

Phase 1: Whole body exercise Whole body exercise begins the increase in body temperature and initiates the biochemical changes that occur as a result of physical

Figure 3.9 Warm-up – the four phases of an effective warm-up: (1) whole body exercise carried out in order to raise core temperature; (2) stretching; (3) rehearsal of skills; (4) integration and the lead up to competition. After competition or training the intensity of exercise should be reduced gradually. The post-exercise period is an ideal time in which to undertake stretching exercises.

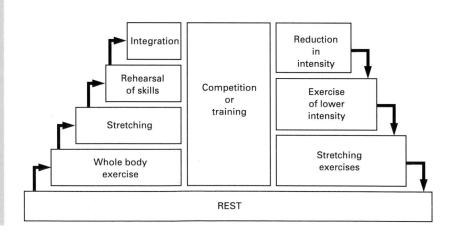

activity. It should begin very gently and then systematically increase in intensity. The mode of the exercise should be sports specific, i.e. running for the majority of activities, arm and shoulder work for canoeists, etc.

Phase 2: Stretching   Stretching exercises should be undertaken once the biochemical changes are underway and body temperature is increasing. Again, these should be sports specific and should address the muscle groups about to be used.

Phase 3: Skill rehearsal   Rehearsal of the skills that are about to be used in the activity, e.g. kicking, heading, etc., in soccer. Initially this should be carried out at a low level of intensity.

Phase 4: Integration and lead-up to competition   Sports-specific skills carried out at a gradually increasing intensity so that further biochemical and body temperature changes occur. Peak 'match-intensity' activity should be reached at this stage of the warm-up rather than a few minutes into actual competition.

Using the above principles, warm-up needs to be adapted to suit the exercise it is preceding. For high-level athletics the warm-up process may last an hour or more and will conclude at a high level of intensity. For recreational walking a gradual build-up of intensity and some lower body stretches is all that is needed.

The above principles of warm-up should also be incorporated into training sessions. These should begin and end at a low level of intensity with more vigorous work in the central phase.

An effective warm-up will allow peak performance to be achieved at the beginning of a competitive situation rather than some time into the event. It is also important in minimising the risk of injury.

Motor unit types: Muscle fibre types

Skeletal muscle consists of a number of different types of muscle fibre. These have distinct mechanical and chemical properties including the tension that can be developed during a maximum contraction, the time taken for contraction, the resistance to fatigue, and the concentration of different enzymes and other biologically active chemicals. In addition, different types of fibre are innervated by distinct varieties of motor neurone which have a crucial role in determining how the muscle fibre behaves. Thus, skeletal muscle consists of a number of different types of motor unit (see Chapter 2 for a description of motor unit). This distribution of motor unit types varies from individual to individual and has an important influence upon physical performance.

This is a confusing area because there are several ways of classifying muscle fibres. They can be grouped in terms of mechanical properties, such as twitch-speed, or by their biochemical and histological characteristics. There is a good deal of overlap between the systems because mechanical properties are, to a large extent, determined by the structure and biochemistry of the fibre. The best-known system classifies fibres as either 'red – slow-twitch fibres with high endurance' or 'white – fast-twitch fibres with low endurance'. It is actually possible to distinguish up to eight different types of

Table 3.1. Equivalent systems of classifying muscle fibres.	Motor unit designation	Slow twitch	Fast twitch, fatigue resistant (FR)	Fast twitch, fatiguable (FF)
	Biochemical designation	Slow twitch, oxidative (SO)	Fast twitch, oxidative, glycolytic (FOG)	Fast twitch, glycolytic (FG)
	Number designation	I	IIa	IIb
	Other designation	Slow twitch, Red	Fast twitch, Intermediate	Fast twitch, White

By courtesy of J. T. Fitzgerald.

Table 3.2.		IIb	IIa	I
	Motor neurone properties			
	Speed of conduction (m s^{-1})	85–114	84–113	75–99
	Mechanical properties			
	Twitch contraction time (m s^{-1})	20–47	30–55	58–110
	Maximum tension (g)	30–130	4.5–55	1.2–12.6
	Resistance to fatigue	Low	High	Very high
	Mean fibre area (μ^2)	5,290	2,890	1,730
	Biochemical properties			
	Myofibrillar ATP-ase	High	High	Low
	CP–ATP-ase	High	Intermediate	Low
	Glycolytic enzymes	High	High	Low
	Oxidative enzymes	Low	High	High
	Other features			
	Capillary supply	Poor	Abundant	Abundant
	Colour	White	Reddish	Reddish

fibre. Of these, three are of particular importance. These can be designated either in terms of their mechanical properties or their biochemical profile. A number designation is also frequently used. Classifications that are essentially similar are listed in Table 3.1, and the principal properties of the three types of fibre are given in Table 3.2.

Type I fibres (S or SO)

These are the classical 'red' muscle fibres. They contract relatively slowly, have low maximum tension and high endurance. They are rich in mitochrondria, oxidative enzymes and capillary supply and have a low concentration of myofibrillar ATP-ase and glycolytic enzymes (Burke and Edgerton 1975). They tend to contain a type of lactate dehydrogenase adapted for the conversion of lactic acid into pyruvic acid

(Peter *et al.* 1971); thus they specialise in removing the lactic acid produced by other types of fibre (see p. 37). They are used during activities involving low muscle tension (Milner–Brown *et al.* 1973).

Type IIb fibres (FF or FG)
These are the classical 'white' fibres and have properties that are practically the reverse of type I. They are used for 'strength' and 'explosive' type activities and are not activated during low-tension work (Warmolts and Engel 1973).

Type IIa fibres (FR or FOG)
These are intermediate type fibres. They have mechanical properties similar to type IIb but have a higher concentration of oxidative enzymes and a better blood supply. Consequently, they are considerably more resistant to fatigue. Type IIa fibres are red in colour and fast-twitch in mechanical properties.

The properties of a muscle fibre seem to be principally determined by the type of motor neurone innervating it (Guth 1968; Salmons and Vrbova 1969; Pette *et al.* 1973). Extraneous factors, such as training, can influence function only within the limits set by the basic fibre type. Not enough work has been done in this area to be categorical, but it seems that the effects of certain sorts of training may be restricted to particular fibre types. Strength training seems to cause hypertrophy of fast-twitch fibres (principally type IIb) with much less effect on slow-twitch fibres (type I) and the oxidative capacity of muscle (Gollnick *et al.* 1972; MacDougal *et al.* 1980). The cross-sectional area of fast-twitch fibres is increased but not the total number of fibres. Endurance training seems to have a different effect. Following six months of such a programme Gollnick *et al.* (1973) found a 24 per cent enlargement of the slow-twitch fibres with no significant change in the area of the fast-twitch type. It is well documented that endurance training increases the concentration of oxidative enzymes (see Chapter 2). It seems likely that an individual's capacity for oxygen uptake (maximum oxygen uptake) is considerably influenced by the percentage of slow-twitch fibres (type I) (Bergh *et al.* 1978).

Type IIa fibres (FOG) differ from the FG variety (type IIb) mainly in terms of enzyme concentrations. There is some evidence that endurance training can lead to a conversion of type FG fibres to FOG (Barnard *et al.* 1970). This does not amount to a change in mechanical properties since both are of the fast-twitch type. There seems to be no evidence to suggest that fast-twitch fibres can be converted to the slow-twitch type or vice-versa.

It has been demonstrated that strength and the speed of muscle contraction are related to the percentage of fast-twitch fibres (Thorstensson *et al.* 1976a). As might be expected, the relationship between strength and percentage of fast-twitch fibres is particularly marked when the speed of contraction is high (Coyle *et al.* 1979).

Also Bosco and Komi (1979) have shown that power output is influenced by muscle fibre composition. But the relationship is not an exact one. This is because of the influence of many other factors. Figures 3.10 and 3.11 illustrate results that are typical.

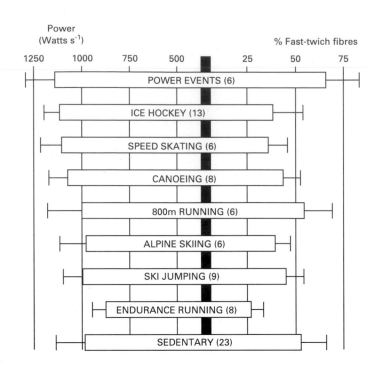

Figure 3.10 Power output and the percentage of fast-twitch fibres in the vastus medialis muscle of various groups of athletes. Power was measured using the Margaria power test and is plotted on the left-hand side of the diagram. The power-event athletes have the highest power output and the endurance athletes the lowest. The percentage of fast-twitch fibres is shown on the left of the diagram. Power athletes have the highest percentage and endurance athletes the lowest. In the other groups of subjects the relationship between muscle fibre composition and power output is much less obvious. (Data from Komi *et al.* 1977.)

Sources of information on the human response to exercise and training

There are a number of different ways of gathering information concerning the human response to exercise and training. As an aid to the study of this book some comments may be helpful. At the most basic level, information can be obtained in one of two ways: by scientific analysis and from the observations of the practitioners in sport – the athletes and their coaches. Both approaches have their place: each has different limitations. Some of these are considered in the discussion of sources of information below.

Common knowledge

Some facts are so well established that no justification is necessary. Basic details of human anatomy and physiology fall into this category.

Direct observation

Direct observation can occasionally establish something as a fact without recourse to any experimental justification. But only if the phenomenon is extremely clear-cut,

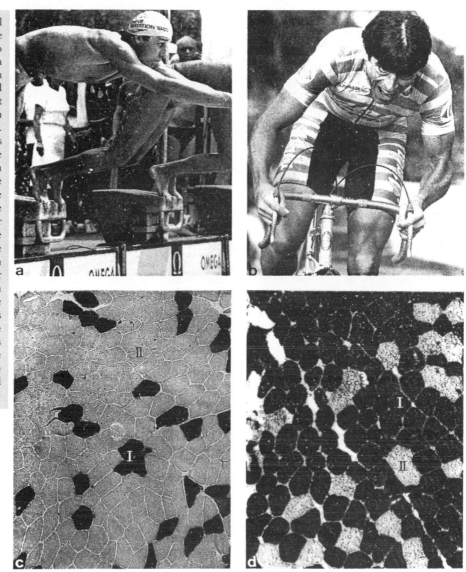

Figure 3.11 Typical muscle fibre type composition of two élite athletes: (a) a swimmer specialising in the 50 m front crawl sprint; (b) a cyclist specialising in endurance events. Sections of the vastus lateralis muscle of the two athletes are shown in (c) and (d). The muscle samples have been stained for the presence of myofibrillar ATPase. Type I muscle fibres stain dark while type II fibres remain unstained. It is clear from the illustration that the majority of the sprint swimmer's fibres are of type II, while the endurance cyclist's fibres are predominantly of type I. (From Billeter and Hoppeler 1992.)

straightforward, and in line with what is expected. An observation that the use of gloves for cold-weather running keeps the hands warm and makes the athlete more comfortable, can be accepted as a fact. A comparison of the effects of different gloves, or a study of their influence on core temperature, are more complex matters that would require an experimental investigation.

Predictions from basic anatomical and physiological principles

Principles of basic anatomy and physiology are sometimes used to make predictions about how the body will behave during exercise and training. Such forecasts are fraught with difficulties because the human body is such a complex organism. For example, whether the maximal contraction of a muscle will help or hinder a subsequent stretch is extremely difficult to anticipate because it is capable of being influenced by any, or all, of a large number of different factors. These include: the rise in muscle temperature, reflexes initiated by stretch receptors in the tendons that join the muscle to bone, reflexes initiated by length detectors in the body of the muscle, reflexes initiated by stretch and length detectors in muscles and tendons on the opposite side of the body that oppose the stretch, and information from the central nervous system. To be of any value to the athlete, theoretical predictions must always be verified by an empirical investigation.

Empirical studies carried out on animals or animal tissue

Many people have ethical objections to experiments on animals. This aside, species differences cause problems when attempts are made to extrapolate the results of animal studies to human beings. For example, the human is one of only a handful of species that cannot synthesise its own vitamin C. The problems are reduced in studies on the properties of isolated tissues, such as nerves, muscles and tendons. Even then, studies carried out on human tissue tend to be more convincing.

Empirical studies carried out on humans

The term **Empirical** means 'by trial or experiment'. It is beyond the scope of this book to discuss all the features of good experimental design, but one or two points can be made. A well-designed experiment must:

1   Have a clear, precise and restricted aim. A study of the effects of 10 weeks of a specified programme of stretching on the hip extension flexibility of 40-year-old females would be a feasible investigation. An attempt to prove that exercise improves health is far too broad to be capable of producing useful results.
2   Ensure that only the factors being investigated are allowed to influence the results of the experiment.
3   Ensure that the accuracy of the measurements taken is as high as possible and that the amount of experimental error is known.
4   Ensure that the subjects are typical of the section of the population that they are meant to represent.
5   Ensure that any numerical data is analysed using the appropriate statistical techniques.
6   Ensure that any conclusions drawn from the results can be fully justified.

A surprisingly small amount of the research that is published in books and journals meets the above criteria, and it is usually very difficult for the non-specialist to discriminate between the good, the not-so-good and the totally misleading. The best advice to the non-specialist is to keep to papers that are published in top-level journals. Expert screening will already have been carried out on such studies and there is a good chance that the results are reasonable.

The range of topics that have been investigated empirically increases each year. But there remain many issues of interest to the athlete on which hard and fast scientific information is not available. This is partly because of the difficulty of conducting valid empirical studies, especially into the practical type of issue that is of most concern to the practising athlete. While the optimum parameters of endurance training for sedentary individuals are known, much less information is available about how endurance athletes ought to train. Many other topics, such as the effects of warm up and flexibility training on the performance and susceptibility to injury of top-level athletes, have never been empirically determined and are still largely a matter of speculation.

With such matters it is necessary to rely on the experience of the practitioners. If their observations are analysed and made the basis of future scientific investigations our knowledge of the effects of exercise and training will continue to improve.

4 TRAINING METHODS

Strength   Most coaches and athletes agree that some form of strength training is necessary to prepare for sports participation. Strength training is used to develop the capacity to express strength and power and also to protect the athlete against injury. Many individuals also use resistance training methods as the main form of training for weight-lifting, power-lifting and body-building. Others engage in resistance training in the course of recreational, general fitness and health programmes. Resistance training has its own distinctive terminology and some of the more commonly used terms are explained in Table 4.1.

In the area of sport and athletic performance several types of strength are evident. These are outlined in Table 4.2. As noted in Chapter 2 (see Figure 2.12) force is

Table 4.1. Some terms used in resistance training.

Term	Meaning	Example
Lift	A practical way of moving a weight	The arm curl. The weight is moved by flexion at the elbows
Repetition	One execution of a lift or exercise against a resistance	Lifting and lowering a weight once
Number of repetitions	The number of repetitions performed consecutively	
Set	A group of repetitions followed by a rest or change of activity	Six arm curls followed by a rest would constitute one set. In theory there is no limit to the number of repetitions in a set. In practice a number between 1 and 20 is usually used
Repetition maximum (RM)	The maximum weight that can be lifted a specified number of times	If subject X can manage five repetitions with a 100 kg weight and no more, his 5 RM is 100 kg.
Training load or intensity	The weight or resistance employed. Often specified in terms of the RM	50% of 10 RM. This is half the weight that the individual can lift 10 times
Training volume	Volume is the product of the weight used, the total number of repetitions and sets performed	An individual executes 10 repetitions using 10 kg for three sets. The total volume for this exercise is 3000 kg.
Training frequency	The number of training sessions per week	
Training programme	A prescription specifying some, or all, of the parameters above	

Table 4.2. Types of strength.	Type	Meaning	Example
	Gross, maximum, static, isometric strength	The maximum force a muscle can exert	No movement occurs as in a rugby scrum and holding the strain in tug-o'-war
	Explosiveness or explosive strength	The maximum rate of force development	Start of a sprint. Start of a shot-put glide. Jumping from a stationary position
	Speed-strength	The greatest possible speed exerted on a set resistance	Javelin-throwing. Ball-throwing. Punching.
	Elastic or plyometric strength: (i) short ground contact	The development of force following a rapid and limited range of eccentric contraction	Sprinting. Take-off in long jump
	(ii) long ground contact	The development of force following a relatively large range of eccentric contraction	Take-off as in basketball jump shot. Fielding in ball games
	Specific strength	Force expressed in a manner similar to event or sport	Using harness pulls for sprinter. Under/over weight throwing implements
	Strength endurance	The ability to repeat muscular activity with a high rate of force	Maintaining high force output in sprinting for long periods

greatest when the speed of contraction is zero. This type of strength (isometric) is evident in several sports (rugby, archery, wrestling, judo) but it is also important in many explosive athletic movements where certain segments of the body have to be fixed or stabilised. This type of contraction occurs, for example, in the back muscles of a long jumper at take-off. Explosive power, as demonstrated at the start of a sprint and in the sudden change of direction of a games player, demands the greatest expression of force over a predetermined distance in a set time period. Speed-strength on the other hand, demands the expression of a set force as fast as possible.

The fast development of force in a limb or against an external object is important in sports such as boxing, karate, fencing and javelin-throwing; on the other hand, where a greater resistance has to be moved (i.e. a shot or a whole body movement), the maximum rate of force development in a set time period is essential. Further, when very heavy resistances have to be overcome, maximum dynamic and isometric strength are of paramount importance.

The capacity to express force or power repeatedly is also another type of strength. Strength endurance is not only required in sports such as boxing and distance running but also in sprinting or any sporting action lasting more than a few seconds.

Strength training adaptations

Initial gains in strength are attributed to neuromuscular adaptations (Sale 1992a). Consequently, it is not surprising to find increases in strength without accompanying muscular hypertrophy. Subsequent gains in strength are largely accounted for by

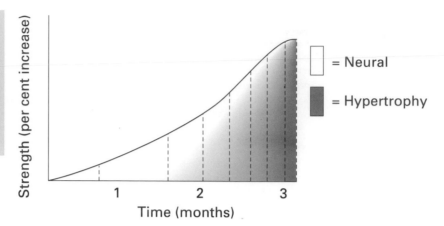

Figure 4.1. Time course of adaptations during strength training. Initial gains in strength are a result of neural adaptations while muscle fibres explains gains in strength as training progresses.

hypertrophy. In general, a positive relationship exists between muscle cross-sectional area and the force it can exert. This helps explain why individuals with the largest muscle masses are generally the strongest. However, it is possible for a muscle of a relatively smaller mass to exert greater force than a larger muscle. This can be explained by the contribution of neuromuscular factors to force expression see Figure 2.13. The activation of a greater percentage of motor units in a muscle will promote greater force development. Additionally, a greater firing rate and degree of motor unit synchronisation may allow a muscle of a given size to contract more forcefully. Intermuscular coordination also contributes to force development. This is especially relevant to the skilful use of power and relates to the timing and sequencing of different muscles during the execution of a skill.

The time course for neuromuscular and hypertrophy changes are outlined in Figure 4.1 and are typical of the adaptations occurring in beginners. While the same mechanisms of adaptation are associated with experienced strength-trained athletes they follow a different time course (Schmidtbleicher 1992). Experienced strength-trained athletes do not have the same potential for strength and power gains as beginners (Hakkinen 1985). When training programmes are continued for several months or years the upper limit for strength development is determined by the ability of the athlete to increase muscle size (Sale 1992a). Continued gains in muscular strength at the advanced stage have been shown to occur as a result of variation of the training stimulus (Schmidtbleicher 1992). Consequently, individually prescribed programmes with frequent variation in training stimulus need to be devised for the experienced athlete.

Consideration of other methods of training currently employed by the athlete is also of importance as endurance training can compromise strength gains (see Interference, page 75). Further, an assessment of the deficiencies of the athlete needs to be made so that an appropriate strength-training programme can be devised. Additionally, before designing a training programme the types of strength or power required in the sporting event need to be identified.

Generality in strength training

Gains in strength and power and in motor performance tasks have been reported following the use of most dynamic strength-training methods. Most methods are

Table 4.3. Strength training criteria for beginners.		
	Weight	Low to moderate
	Repetitions	Range 8–20 repetitions
	Sets	1–3 sets
	Rest	2–3 mins between sets
	Frequency	2–3 times per week
	Movement speed	Controlled
	Exercises	Structural★ and body part

★ A structural exercise refers to the use of several muscle groups and joints in the execution of a lift, e.g. squat.

Note: The athlete should learn the proper lifting technique for all exercises.

effective in producing gains in the ability to perform different types of strength for beginners provided that certain minimum criteria are employed (see Table 4.3). For example, Manning *et al.* (1990) reported isometric strength gains for inexperienced subjects training with constant and variable resistance methods. Silvester *et al.* (1984) reported similar gains in isometric leg strength between two groups training over 11 weeks with one set of 7–10 RM. However, the group that trained with greater frequency (i.e. three sessions per week) made greater improvements in the vertical jump as compared to the group that trained for two sessions per week.

The generality of strength training is further illustrated in a study by Hickson *et al.* (1988). These authors reported that strength training for either 3 or 5 days per week over 10 weeks enhanced short-term endurance in cycling and running for *trained endurance* individuals. No improvements were found in $\dot{V}_{O_2max}$ during cycling or running exercise. Strength training involved combining 3–5 sets of 5–25 RM using free weights and constant resistance machine exercises. Therefore, when individuals with no previous strength-training experience comply with certain minimum training criteria, gains in several components of physical fitness and motor performance tasks may occur.

Specificity in strength training

Specific adaptations as a result of training with explosive and plyometric movements have been reported. For example, sprint and jump training during which fast contraction speeds are emphasised have been reported to effect adaptations in neural activation which increase explosive and plyometric power (Hakkinen *et al.* 1985a and 1985b). On the other hand, heavy weight training loads result in maximal force increases with some muscular hypertrophy (Schmidtbleicher 1992). Emphasis on fast velocity of movement in strength training does not seem to be advantageous to the beginner as maximum force and power gains are similar using both explosive and slow muscular contractions, provided that the resistance is similar. However, for more experienced athletes the velocity of exercise movement may be more important, especially for the development of specific strength and power.

A study by Pipes (1978) also highlights the specificity of method of training. In this study, two groups of subjects trained for 10 weeks using either constant resistance or variable resistance training methods. Subjects who trained on the variable resistance machine were significantly stronger than the constant resistance group when tested on the variable resistance machine; but subjects trained on the constant resistance

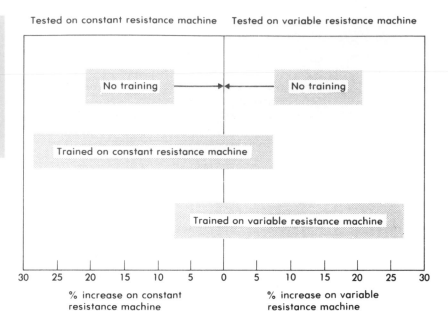

Figure 4.2. Increases in leg-press strength following 10 weeks of weight training, three days per week. At each session three sets of eight repetitions were performed at 75 per cent of the 1 R.M. (Data from Pipes 1978.)

Table 4.4. Features of different methods of strength training.

Method	Feature	Other names commonly used
Isometric	No movement occurs while tension is developed	Static or gross
Free weight-lifting	External resistance is loaded on a barbell or dumbell	Isotonic, dynamic constant resistance
Eccentric Weight training	A weight is slowly lowered under control as muscle lengthens	Negative work
Variable resistance training	The resistance of the weight is applied to the limb by a cam; this is designed to allow the muscle to develop maximum tension throughout the range of movement	Nautilus training
Accommodating resistance training	The resistance to motion is varied in response to the speed of movement	Isokinetic, constant speed training
Circuit training	Any combination of the methods of training and also body weight exercises performed in rotation with limited rest between exercises	
Plyometrics	Rapid eccentric contraction followed by a powerful concentric contraction	Bounding

machine were significantly stronger when tested on the constant resistance machine (see Figure 4.2).

Adaptations are also specific to the joint angles and range of motion employed during training. This implies that specific strength-training exercises are important for the transfer of strength and power to the actual sport. The performance of specific sport exercises agrees well with the observation of many coaches that the closer the speed of movement and movement pattern to the actual sport the greater the carry-over.

Strength training is also of use for athletes involved in endurance activities. Indeed, middle- and long-distance runners frequently include hill training (interval or continuous) in their programmes. This form of strength training is desirable as it is specific to the action of running. Formal strength training using free weights and resistance machines also offer benefits to the endurance athlete. Hickson *et al.* (1988) have shown how well-trained endurance athletes improved short-term endurance performances in both cycling and running following 10 weeks of training using resistances greater than 80 per cent of 1 RM. However, formal strength training for experienced endurance athletes should be carefully implemented so as to avoid training-related injuries (Hickson *et al.* 1988).

Several methods of strength training exist. The features of some of the more common methods are summarised in Table 4.4. Strength training using free weights and isometric exercises are the traditional methods. Other methods have been introduced more recently in an attempt to take account of certain physiological principles discussed in Chapter 2. A review of the methods currently used follows.

Isometrics Isometric contractions can be used to improve strength. The normal training procedure consists of a series of short maximum contractions against the resistance of an immovable object or the opposite limb exercising the same way. The purpose is to develop tension at that particular joint angle. Initial studies suggested that one contraction of two-thirds maximum held for 6 seconds was all that was needed for optimal improvements in strength. It is now clear that this is too little in terms of intensity and duration of contraction for effective strength gains. Maximal contractions appear to be superior to submaximal contractions in promoting strength gains. Optimal gains are the result of either a small number of long contractions (10 seconds or more) or a higher number (30 to 40) of short contractions per session (Fleck and Kraemer 1987). As with other methods of training, there are often variations in the response. Less frequently used muscles tend to respond most rapidly.

Isometric strength gains tend to be specific to the joint angle employed during contraction. However, Knapik *et al.* (1983a) showed how strength increases will have a 'carry-over' effect to 20 degrees on either side of the joint angle exercised. Moreover, it does appear that isometric training carried out using several joint angles may be more effective for general strength improvement. Maximal isometric training has been shown to be effective in increasing both isometric and dynamic strength when several joint angles are stressed (Kanehisa and Miyashita 1983). There is little evidence showing improved motor performance as a result of isometric strength increases and this is a major limitation to its use. Body composition changes as a result of isometric training have been reported. These include increases in body weight and limb circumferences which are usually associated with increased muscle hypertrophy (Kanehisa and Miyashita 1983).

The development of isometric strength is particularly useful for sports where strength is expressed statically. Also, this type of strength is generally developed at the start of a rehabilitation programme for an injured athlete. When an athlete has limited access to resistance-training equipment, isometrics can be employed with good effect provided that several joint angles are used.

Variable resistance training

As a muscle moves through a range of movement the length–tension relationship changes (see Chapter 2). Variable-resistance training-equipment is purposefully designed to alter the resistance throughout the range of movement in an attempt to match the changes in strength of the muscle as it moves throughout the exercise. Because of individual variations in limb dimensions it is difficult to envisage a machine accommodating all individual variations. There is no doubt, however, that strength gains occur as a result of variable resistance training (Manning et al. 1990). Variable resistance training does produce changes in strength and body composition, but, in general, these are no larger than those occurring with constant resistance and isokinetic training. Studies examining the influence of variable resistance training on motor performance are limited. Nevertheless, increases in vertical jump performance have been reported following short-term variable resistance training (Silvester et al. 1984).

Isokinetics

Isokinetic-training devices are designed so that during exercise the resistance varies, or accommodates, allowing the movement to occur at constant speed. Advocates of this method of training argue that the ability to exert maximal force throughout the range of movement leads to optimal strength development. Further, it has been suggested that isokinetic training allows for speeds of contraction close to the speeds encountered during athletic performance. On both counts isokinetic training has limitations. Running, jumping, turning, changing direction and throwing all involve acceleration and deceleration about several joints. Thus pure isokinetic movements do not occur during these athletic movements. Further, the highest velocity that can be tested using an isokinetic dynamometer is much less than the sport-specific velocity that can be achieved during many athletic movements such as sprinting and kicking (Thorstensson et al. 1976b). Nevertheless, improvements have been reported in vertical jump, standing long jump and the short running sprint following fast-speed isokinetic training. This suggests that isokinetic training has much to offer the athlete. Additionally, isokinetic training may be suitable for post-injury rehabilitation.

Isokinetic strength training has been shown to increase isotonic, isometric and isokinetic strength. However, the greatest increases in strength are observed when measurement is made using the same method as was used in training. Additionally, some studies suggest that the greatest increases in isokinetic strength occur about and below the velocity used in training (Kanehisa and Miyashita 1983). These authors reported that an intermediate training velocity caused the greatest carry-over of strength gains both above and below the training velocity. Other authors support the use of an intermediate velocity of training for strength carry over (Fleck and Kraemer 1987). It seems that low-velocity training has little effect upon strength recorded at high velocities (Pipes and Wilmore 1975).

Eccentric training

Eccentric contraction occurs when a muscle develops force in order to resist being lengthened. It is a feature of any activity in which a heavy object is lowered. Eccentric contraction of muscle then resists the force exerted on the object by gravity. This occurs during weight training if the load is lowered back to the starting position.

Heavier loads can be used for eccentric training than are possible with concentric work. If 100 kg is the maximum concentric lift, a lift of 105 kg can normally be controlled during lowering. Johnson *et al.* (1976) found that six eccentric contractions at 120 per cent of the concentric 1 RM produced the same training effect as 10 concentric lifts at 80 per cent of the 1 RM. If more than 120 per cent of the 1 RM is used, the individual has great difficulty controlling the descent of the weight, which falls rapidly. The gains in strength are then minimal.

Eccentric contraction training has been shown to cause significant increases in maximal isometric, dynamic, constant resistance, concentric and eccentric strength. Limited research has been conducted examining the effects of eccentric training on motor performance. From the available evidence it seems that eccentric training can increase vertical jump ability.

Constant resistance training (free and fixed weights)

Weight training can be undertaken either using free weights or using a machine with lever arms and stacked weights. Both methods may be termed 'constant resistance training' as the resistance moved does not change throughout the exercise. The combination of sets and repetitions used in strength training has been the subject of considerable debate. As previously considered, the pre-training status of the individual will influence the magnitude and the time course of gains (Hakkinen 1985). Beginners show a greater rate and magnitude of strength gains as compared to previously strength-trained subjects. Nevertheless, several systems using different combinations of sets and repetitions have been developed. These are outlined in Table 4.5.

Little scientific research has been carried out comparing the effects of these systems. However, Leighton *et al.* (1967) conducted an 8-week study and compared the effects of using 10 different systems of strength training. The authors tested isometric strength using cable tensiometry before and after training and found significant strength gains associated with all systems. This suggests that most methods of strength training will produce gains in isometric strength.

Strength training using a single set of exercises is useful, especially for beginners (Silvester *et al.* 1984). However, the superiority of using a multiple set system has been demonstrated, and this method of training is appropriate for experienced strength-trained athletes. Multiple sets using low repetitions and heavy loads are associated with

	System	Feature	Use
Table 4.5. Different systems of strength training.	Single set	One set of an exercise	Ideal for beginners and during strength maintenance
	Multiple set	At least two or three sets are performed. Any number of sets are possible	Appropriate for intermediate and advanced strength trainers
	DeLorme and Watkins	Three sets using different loads of 10 RM. Set 1 is 10 repetitions at 50% of 10 RM, set 2 is 10 repetitions at 75% 10 RM and set 3 is 100% of 10 RM	Appropriate for beginners
	Pyramid	Repetitions are reduced as the weight is increased over a specified number of sets	Suitable for the intermediate and advanced athlete
	Oxford	The reverse of a pyramid system. Resistance goes from heavy to light while the number of repetitions increases	Both Pyramid and Oxford offer good variation in training for the experienced individual
	DAPRE	The daily adjusted progressive resistance exercise system. This allows the training to be based on recent performance. For example, first two sets use 12 and 8 RM, then the third and fourth sets are adjusted depending on the number of repetitions performed	This is a common system employed by body-builders. The final weight and number of repetitions completed determine the load for the next session
	Circuit	Each exercise is completed in rotation. A second and third circuit is often employed. This system is used for all-round conditioning and strength gains are limited	Ideal for large numbers and all-round fitness
	Super set	This involves completing two exercises without a rest in between. This is popular among body-builders	Appropriate for experienced individuals seeking hypertrophy
	Cheating	This involves the help of a spotter or a body swing to lift a maximal or supra-maximal weight. It can be employed during most systems	An effective system for strength gains, it should be confined to the experienced individual.

increases in maximum isometric and dynamic strength, while light loads using multiple sets of several repetitions are associated with gains in strength endurance (Anderson and Kearney 1982). Figure 4.3 outlines the training effects of different load-repetition combinations.

Constant resistance training has also been shown to produce isometric and isokinetic strength gains. Increases in motor performance tasks such as a short sprint, vertical jump, standing long jump, shot-put and ball-throwing have been reported as a result of constant resistance training (Adams *et al.* 1992; Hennessy and Watson 1994a;

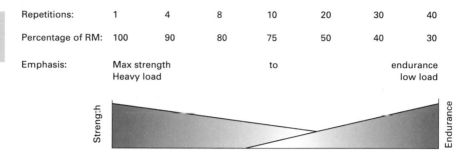

Figure 4.3. The load–repetition continuum for resistance training.

Repetitions:	1	4	8	10	20	30	40
Percentage of RM:	100	90	80	75	50	40	30
Emphasis:	Max strength Heavy load			to			endurance low load

Schultz 1967). Following short-term constant resistance training, increases in muscle hypertrophy and lean body mass, and decreases in percentage of fat, are also commonly found. Many studies report no change in body weight following short-term constant resistance training. This may be explained by the increase in lean body weight and corresponding decrease in body fat associated with strength training.

Comparison of different training methods

In general, all the methods outlined in Table 4.4 are effective in developing strength. Adherence to one method of training – and especially to one system of training – for a prolonged period can, however, result in diminished and insignificant gains. Therefore, varying the method and system of training is important in promoting further strength gains.

For the athlete, free weights have obvious advantages over other methods. Free weight exercises have the potential to mimic the actions, types of muscular contraction, range of movement, joint angles and speed of movement found in many sporting events. Control of the bar's movement in explosive lifts such as the power clean and snatch demands balance and coordination. These are key factors in all sporting movements. Exercising using free weights also demands the utilisation of muscles that stabilise and assist in the execution of the exercise. This is important, especially when the athlete assumes a body position similar to that of the event or sport. Further, with free weights the potential exists to devise exercises that simulate certain actions of the event or sport.

However, it is important to note that most coaches agree that the transfer of developed strength and power is best achieved by practice of event-specific exercises and the event itself.

Beginning a strength-training programme

1   A satisfactory level of health and general fitness is necessary before beginning any intensive training programme. Weight-lifting produces considerable stress on the musculo-skeletal system, and an increase in internal pressure in the abdomen and thorax also occurs. This is reversed as soon as the lift is over but it may cause problems in anyone with an abdominal weakness such as a scar as the result of a recent operation, or a tendency to hernia. It is also undesirable in those with high blood pressure and some types of cardiac disease. For any sedentary individual it is

advisable to have a thorough medical check-up prior to engaging in any resistance-training programme.

2   When the individual has acquired a satisfactory level of general fitness, he or she should select a programme of exercises to develop strength throughout the whole body. Any postural defects should also be taken into account, as should any previous injury. Appropriate exercises should be selected to improve these defects. The athlete should then learn the exercise techniques and how to handle all weights with safety. This step is crucial and a qualified and knowledgeable coach should be consulted before commencing the programme.

3   The programme should begin with high repetitions using reasonably light weights. Two training sessions during the first week or two are sufficient. Following this, the individual can progress to three sessions per week. The emphasis at this early stage is on learning the correct technique of lifting and lowering a resistance. Also, it is important for the beginner to learn the safety rules and regulations pertaining in the training area. Gradually, over a series of weeks, the individual should be able to complete three sets of approximately 15 repetitions of each exercise in the programme. An all-round programme of exercises which alternate upper, mid and lower body parts should be undertaken. The exercises can be completed in circuit fashion and, later, in a set system – completing 2–3 sets of a particular exercise before moving on to the next exercise.

4   If very high levels or a specific type of strength is required, a progressive programme based on the system of periodisation should be employed. This needs to be based on an analysis of the physical and movement demands of the athlete's sport, on the training phase and on the resources and equipment available. The following section discusses periodisation with specific reference to resistance training for sport.

Periodisation of training

In general, periodisation refers to the division of a training and competitive year into different periods or cycles when certain components of fitness are developed. However, while there is only limited scientific evidence showing its superiority over conventional training procedures (Stone *et al.* 1981), periodisation of training has been promoted as an effective procedure for the development of specific strength and power qualities (Matveyev 1992; Fleck and Kraemer 1987). Beginners and experienced strength-trained athletes were studied by Stone *et al.* (1981) during short-term (6 weeks) and moderate duration training periods (5.5 months). For all groups the periodised method resulted in greater strength, power and body composition changes. The authors concluded that the method was superior to other conventional systems. Further, continued increases in lean body mass have been reported as a consequence of periodised resistance training throughout a track and field competitive season (Potteiger *et al.* 1993). Thus, periodisation has much to offer the athlete as it allows for a systematic progression in training, extensive variation and the integration of other fitness components in training. Two periodised models are commonly used: linear and undulating. The linear method was popularised by Stone *et al.* (1981) while the undulating method has also become popular with experienced athletes. Both are outlined in Figure 4.4.

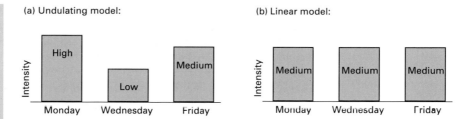

Periodising or cycling different types of strength and power training throughout the training and competitive year involves manipulation of exercises, repetitions, sets, rest periods, velocity of repetition movement, and training loads and volumes. An example of a double periodisation year successfully employed by a thrower is outlined in Table 4.6.

Weeks	Phase	Goal	Training system
1–6	General preparation I	General all-round fitness	High reps/low loads. Steady movement. Learn techniques; 2–3 sets 3 sessions per week
7	Transition and recovery		
8–14	Specific preparation I	Hypertrophy	6–15 reps. 60–90% RM. 3–5 sets, 2–5 mins rest. 4 sessions per week. Varied but controlled speed of movement
15–19	Competition	Maintenance	1–2 sessions per week. ~90% 1 RM. 2–3 sets 4–6 reps.
20	Transition and recovery		
21–26	Specific preparation II	Maximum strength	1–8 reps. 80–150% 1 RM. 3–5 sets, 3–6 mins rest. 4 sessions per week. Steady and explosive movement
27	Transition and recovery		
28–33	Specific preparation III	Specific power (a) Weight training	3–6 reps. 80–100% 1 RM. 3–5 sets. 4–6 mins rest. 3 sessions per week. Explosive movements
		(b) Event specific	Plyometrics. Pulleys and over-weight implements – technique specific
34–35	Tapering		
36–46	Competition	Maintenance of power	Event specific, 2 sessions per week
47–52	Transition	General	Active rest

Periodisation of strength training usually involves the progression from a large volume of exercise with low resistance in the early stages, to more intense, near maximum effort, later. Finally, greater sport-specific training occurs during the latter part of the preparation phase. Limited evidence suggests that the duration of the training period may be critical in effecting gains. Athletes spending 12 weeks on a heavy-resistance slow-movement strength-training programme showed a decreased rate of initial force expression following training (Hakkinen 1989). Short periods of training and greater variety of load and velocity of movement have been shown to promote further strength and power gains (Hakkinen 1989; Schmidtbleicher 1992). As initial gains are attributed to neuromuscular factors it is likely that a relatively short period of training which emphasises neuromuscular efficiency will enhance explosive power, especially following a period of maximum strength training (Bosco 1993). Individual responses to each phase of training should, therefore, be carefully monitored.

Plyometrics

There is some confusion as to the origins of the word 'plyometric'. Some authors consider possible derivations from the Greek word 'pleythyein', which means 'to increase' or 'plio' and 'metric' meaning 'more' and 'measure', respectively (Hennessy 1990). Whatever the origins of the word, for decades plyometrics have been a popular method of training for athletes who seek to run faster, react quicker, jump higher and throw further. Essentially, plyometrics are exercises such as jumps, leaps, hops, rebounds, springs and throws that are carried out with the expressed aim of engaging the stretch-shortening cycle. The stretch-shorten cycle is a reflex and elastic phenomenon involving an immediate shortening of active muscles following a rapid eccentric contraction (Hennessy 1990). The key point to remember in a stretch-shorten cycle is that the force developed in the positive or shortening phase is dramatically increased when the action is preceded by a rapid and short eccentric contraction. The resulting powerful response is due to a contribution from both proprioceptive reflexes and the elastic qualities of the muscle–tendon complex (Bosco 1982). See Figure 2.11.

Plyometric or stretch-shortening cycle actions are common to most sporting events that involve running, jumping, throwing, turning and changing direction in an explosive manner. The stretch-shorten cycle action occurs naturally in a running stride and its contribution to force and power output increases with the speed of running. Further, an inverse relationship has been reported between ground contact time in the long jump take-off and jump performance, emphasising the importance of a rapid transition between eccentric and concentric phases during the take-off (Bosco *et al.* 1976).

Specificity of plyometric training

The principle of specificity supports the use of training exercises that mimic the actions of the sport or event in terms of movement speed, joint angle, body position, range of movement and the types of contraction employed. Thus, athletes who require vertical power should utilise predominantly vertical-jumping exercises. Some sports demand the expression of both linear and vertical power (field games, basketball, long jumping) and plyometric training for these activities should include exercises and drills to replicate both types of movement.

Plyometric actions can be further subdivided into both 'long' and 'short' categories (Schmidtbleicher 1992). A long stretch-shorten cycle occurs in actions such as a block jump in volleyball, a lay-up shot in basketball and in many jumps in ball games. This action is characterised by a relatively large amplitude of flexion about the hip, knee and ankle joints and a relatively long ground contact time. In contrast, a short stretch-shorten cycle involves a shorter ground contact time coupled with a rapid transition from eccentric to concentric contractions with a limited amplitude of flexion about the main joints. This action is seen in a sprinter in full flight and during many high-speed jump take-offs.

Some events or sports will display both types of stretch-shorten cycle actions. For example, during the early stages of a 100 m sprint the athlete exerts force over a relatively long ground contact period on each foot touchdown. Later in the sprint, shorter ground contact periods occur. This implies that in training for speed and power an athlete should seek to develop both types of stretch-shorten cycle actions.

Coaches and athletes seeking to develop short stretch-shorten cycle actions should limit the degree of flexion about the exercising joint, reduce ground contact time and complete the movement as explosively and as rapidly as possible. On the other hand, athletes developing long stretch-shorten cycle actions should seek to express as much force as possible throughout the whole range of movement. Also, each sport has its own specific demands in terms of the joint stressed, the angle and range of movement, contraction type and duration. Therefore, for the greatest carry-over performance, exercises should be sport specific.

Plyometric training studies

Difficulties arise when examining the literature on plyometric training because of the variety of experimental designs and methods employed. Specifically, variations occur between studies in the duration and frequency of training, the level of the subject's fitness and age, the type of plyometric movement employed, the method of execution and the training loads and progressions used. Some studies have found plyometric training to be ineffective in improving explosive performance tasks (Scoles 1978).

These negative results may be partly explained by the experimental design which included limited overload and small numbers of experimental subjects. On the other hand, a large body of experimental evidence has shown plyometric training to be effective in improving explosive athletic qualities. Increases in power, as reflected mainly by vertical jump and maximal dynamic strength, have been reported following plyometric training (Brown et al. 1986; Blattner and Noble 1979; Hennessy 1981). In these studies the frequency of training was two to three sessions per week over a duration of 4–16 weeks.

Depth jumps have been found to be effective in promoting improvements in vertical-jumping ability and are frequently used in plyometric-training studies. However, Bobbert et al. (1987) caution against the use of depth jumps from excessive heights as the effectiveness of the stretch-shorten cycle may be impaired and the

Table 4.7. Guidelines for devising plyometric-training programme.

Equipment
1 Footwear should have good shock-absorbing soles
2 Landing surfaces should be resilient without being too soft
3 Grass is ideal for bounding
4 Durable and firm rubber mat is necessary for depth jumps

Training background
5 Do not attempt depth jumps without good background in strength training and bounding and hopping exercises. The athlete should demonstrate ability to squat at least body weight prior to engaging in intense plyometric exercises
6 Intense plyometrics should not be done by athletes with a history of ankle, knee or lower back injuries

Technique
7 The rate of eccentric contraction is more important than the degree of stretch
8 Identify goal of exercise execution (see Figure 4.7) in terms of ground contact duration and direction of force

Frequency
9 Complete two or three sessions per week during preparation period. During competitive period one session is sufficient for maintenance.

Duration
10 Complete 4–6 week cycles with 1 week recovery between cycles

Selection of exercises
11 Analyse demands of sport and select general and sport specific exercises
12 Limit number of exercises to two or three for beginners

Session organisation
13 Always warm up thoroughly
14 Do not perform plyometrics when fatigued
15 Complete less-demanding exercises before more intense ones
16 Have good rests between exercises
17 Count the number of ground contacts. Base progression on gradual overload of ground contacts
18 Use two-legged take-off exercises for beginners
19 Gradually progress to single-leg exercises
20 Learn proper technique of exercise

possibility for injury exists as a result of the great forces about the ankle, knee and hip joints.

The importance of a background in strength training before engaging in plyometric training has been stressed (Hennessy 1990; Chu 1992). According to Chu (1992) an athlete should be capable of lifting 1.5 times his or her body weight in the free weight squat before engaging in plyometric training. In addition, proper progressions of training and the appropriate selection of exercises or drills will ensure minimal risk of injury. It is possible to include low-impact exercises such as hopping and bounding in general conditioning programmes for both young and mature athletes. Such exercises have also been shown to be effective in improving speed, power and strength qualities

(Steben and Steben 1981). Table 4.7 summarises the recommendations for programmes of plyometric training.

Complex training

Complex training involves a combination of similar methods of training. For example, combining strength and plyometric training during the same period is considered as complex training. Significantly greater increases in explosive performances have been reported following complex training as compared to strength training or plyometric training alone (Adams *et al* 1992). Adams and colleagues used a 6 week progressive strength training programme which combined 60–100 per cent of one repetition maximum efforts in the squat and a plyometric programme of depth jumps (50–114 cm), double-leg hops and split-squats. A gain in the vertical jump of 10 cm occurred in the complex-training group as compared to approximately a 3 cm increase in both the strength and plyometric groups.

While studies in the area are limited, complex training seems to have the potential to produce dramatic increases in explosive strength performances. However, as the intensity of such training is great, this method is appropriate only for experienced athletes.

Maintenance of acquired strength

A complete cessation, or significant reduction, in strength training leads to detraining. Precise guidelines outlining the loads, sets, repetitions, frequency per week and type of training necessary for strength maintenance do not, as yet, exist. However, some tentative recommendations are possible. It has been show that acquired gains in strength can be maintained and even improved by completing one set of maximum effort once per week (Berger 1962). Further, declines in strength tend to occur at a much slower rate than the rate at which strength was gained. Recent research indicates that no measurable detraining effects occur during 7 days of rest following a 5-week, 3 days per week strength programme for well-conditioned athletes (Anderson and Cattanach 1993). Further, substantial retention of power-related tasks (at different types of vertical jump) has been reported by Terry and Nethery (1993) for at least 3 weeks following an 8-week complex-training programme in well-conditioned volleyball players.

Therefore, as a result of strength or power training, acquired gains can be maintained with a reduced frequency of training. Gains may also be maintained in power-related tasks for at least 3 weeks without specific training. It is not clear, however, if strength and power are maintained following this time period.

Strength training and the young athlete

It is well known that young athletes mature at different rates. This maturation process involves variation in rates of bone, muscle, reproductive and emotional development, and also male–female differences. Consideration of these factors is important in planning physical training and exercises for the young athlete. Growth and muscular

Table 4.8. Guidelines for devising resistance-training programme for the young athlete.	1 Always warm up thoroughly 2 Teach good exercise technique 3 Always supervise training session 4 Use proper spotting techniques 5 Use high repetitions – at least 8 repetitions – but never to muscular failure 6 Use sufficient rest intervals so that good technique is maintained throughout all exercise repetitions 7 Complete a balanced programme – upper, lower and mid-drift body exercises

development is directly related to hormonal secretions. For example, in the male, general growth and muscular and sexual development is directly related to testosterone secretion. In the female, oestrogen and growth hormone influence growth but the same development in muscle size and strength does not occur due to the differences in levels of testosterone between the sexes.

Because of the immature skeletal and muscular development of the young athlete intense strength training is not advised. Epiphyseal fractures in young weight-lifters have been documented (Fleck and Kraemer 1987). However, such injuries have generally occurred during unsupervised, near maximum, overhead lifts. Maximum lifts place severe stress and compressive force on the joints involved and as such should not be attempted by the young athlete. The importance of coach education and proper supervision in this area cannot be over-stated. In one study of resistance-training-related injuries in young athletes, a significant number of lumbar, sacral and cervical spine injuries occurred as a result of improper exercise execution (Brady *et al.* 1982). This highlights the need for informed and educated coaches.

Properly planned and supervised resistance training has many benefits to offer the young athlete. Young athletes who engage in proper resistance training have been reported to have greater bone densities than young individuals who do not participate in such training. Participation in general resistance exercise has also been recommended for young females as physical activity may enhance bone density (Loucks 1988). Additionally, other authors have reported the positive influence of strength training on anaerobic and aerobic performances, and flexibility in pre-pubescent males. Young athletes engaging in a properly designed weight-training programme also displayed a reduced risk of injury as compared to athletes who did not engage in weight training (Hejna *et al.* 1982). This study shows the value of weight training for injury prevention in young athletes. Further, properly designed resistance-training programmes may have the potential to improve postural defects in young athletes. Thus, strength training has a positive role to play in preparing the athlete for sports participation provided that proper progressions and guidelines are implemented.

Table 4.8 summarises the guidelines for proper resistance training in young athletes. It is important to realise the potential dangers of such exercise. Consequently, resistance training for young athletes is not recommended without the supervision at all times of a properly qualified adult coach.

Speed (sprinting speed)

The term 'speed' has different meanings in the context of different activities and sports. For example, reaction and the initial rate of force development will determine speed for the combat sport participant. Also, reaction and acceleration and the ability to reproduce these speed qualities are important for participants in court games such as basketball and tennis, and most field games. Reaction, acceleration and full-flight sprinting will be important for the 100 m sprinter. In some activities, such as combat sports, racquet games and throwing activities, limb speed is important. Speed in these activities is related to the skilful execution of the event's technique and is also limited by neuromuscular factors and limb size. Furthermore, some court and field game players demonstrate exceptional anticipatory abilities which give the appearance of a fast response. Several types of speed are summarised in Figure 4.5.

In general, training procedures should seek to improve reaction and acceleration in virtually all explosive sports. For athletes who require sprinting speed (e.g. in running, games, cycling and rowing activities) additional development of maximum speed and the capacity to continue to maintain this is important.

Significant increases in physical fitness components such as endurance, strength, power and flexibility have been repeatedly demonstrated following short-term training periods. In contrast, studies reporting improvements in sprinting performance as a result of short-term training programmes are limited. This is primarily due to the fact that an individual's capacity for speed development is strongly influenced by innate factors and as such its development is difficult and complex. While it is well appreciated that the two factors governing running 'sprinting' speed are stride rate and stride length, the optimal relationship between these two variables has not been determined. Several factors in turn influence stride rate and length. These are outlined in Figure 4.6. Athletic coaches realise that extensive and systematic training carried out over a prolonged period will invariably result in gains in speed. Training several components or cross-component training is common in the training of a sprint athlete. Some evidence exists that strength training on its own produces increases in short sprint performance (Hennessy and Watson 1994; Schultz 1967). As previously outlined in Chapter 2, effecting increases in strength will increase acceleration if the time over which the force is expressed does not change. This in turn will result in a decrease in time for sprint performances over short distances.

In many sports improvements in reaction or acceleration are more appropriate than gains in maximum speed. Moravec et al. (1988) have demonstrated that 100 metre

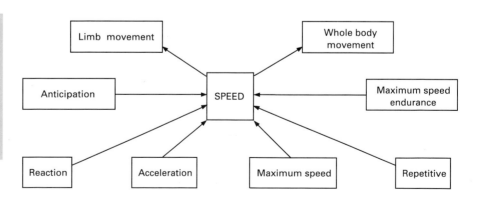

Figure 4.5. Types of speed. Most sports demand the expression of at least one type of speed. Identifying the types of speed required by the athlete is necessary prior to designing a training programme.

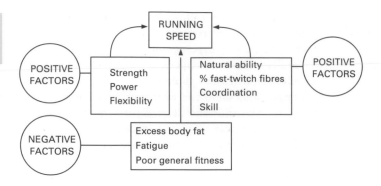

Figure 4.6. Factors influencing running speed.

sprinters do not reach full sprinting speed until they have run 50–60 metres. In sports such as soccer and Australian Rules football distances of up to 20 metres are the most common 'sprint' distances (Douge 1988). Therefore, speed-training programmes for these games should be aimed at increasing reaction and acceleration over short distances.

As reaction is strongly influenced by mental processes and neuromuscular efficiency, it is clear that direct practice of the skill in a non-fatigued state is an effective method of improving reaction time. The ability to respond and move quickly when tired and under pressure, is important especially in team and ball games and combat sports. There is some evidence to show that reaction time improves significantly following intensive game and skill practice in field game players (Mokha *et al.* 1992). The development of this capacity requires practice, ideally under the conditions occuring in the sport.

Methods used to develop speed

For the purposes of this section the methods used to develop running 'sprinting' speed will be considered. In addition to track and field events, this will also be relevant to the majority of field and court games. A wide variety of training methods are used by sprinters. A number of these are summarized below. Caution needs to be exercised when the training routines employed by a successful sprinter are examined. Certainly, particular methods or routines employed by top-class sprinters may be of use to other athletes, but it must be appreciated that it has probably taken several years of progressive development for these athletes to achieve success. The volume and intensity of exercise used in a training programme should be appropriate to the developmental and training status of the individual athlete.

1 *Sprint technique.* This is an essential part of all sprint training. Typically, it involves the practice of drills and exercises that seek to improve the efficiency of different elements of the sprinting action. When technique training is undertaken good recoveries should be used between the repetition of exercises or drills.
2 *Reduction of body fat.* This allows greater acceleration and efficiency of movement (Watson 1988b).

3   *Strength and power training.* Most methods of strength training yield improvements in strength. However, the need to develop different types of strength increases as the athlete progresses. Periodisation of strength and power training has much to offer the athlete in organising progressions. See section on strength training for a more complete discussion.

4   *Flexibility training.* Poor flexibility may mitigate against a good sprinting technique. Thus a certain level of flexibility is beneficial. Both static and dynamic flexibility routines are frequently used by sprinters.

5   *Plyometrics.* Great strength levels are of little use to the sprinter if force cannot be applied explosively in the shortest time possible (Hennessy 1990). The use of hops, bounds, leaps and jumps in an explosive manner are commonly used by all explosive event athletes. Plyometrics seek to bridge the gap between strength and speed. For a more complete discussion of this training method see the previous section on plyometrics.

6   *Specific resistive training.* This involves the use of harnesses, belts, ropes and chutes attached to the athlete. Sprinting drills up slight declines are also used. The aim is to mimic the sprinting action under conditions of increased resistance. This demands more powerful muscular contractions than would normally be experienced during unresistive training. Such overload procedures are commonly used by sprinters to increase specific sprinting strength.

7   *Assistive training.* This aims at getting the athlete to sprint at speeds greater than those normally experienced. Such methods became popular following the disclosure of the training methods employed by the Russian double Olympic-gold medallist, Valery Borzov. Sprinting down a slight decline, releasing a chute at full flight and being towed by a cycle or motor cycle with a harness attached to the athlete, are some assistive methods that have been utilised to develop speed. A major drawback of excessive downhill sprinting is the development of muscle soreness as a result of eccentric muscle contractions. This soreness has been associated with muscle cell damage that may persist for several days following training. However, it is clear that the activity of sprinting, even on level surfaces, involves eccentric muscular work. Therefore, it seems reasonable to include some form of eccentric training in the sprinter's programme. However, for safety reasons, being towed by cycle or motorised cycle is not advised.

8   *Speed ball.* This came into prominence following the disclosure that Alan Wells, Olympic 100 metre gold medallist in 1980, utilised this training method. The objective is to develop upper body power and coordination.

It is important to realise that all training programmes must be sufficiently varied to ensure that both agonist and antagonist muscle groups are trained. For example, quadriceps–hamstring strength imbalance is often associated with injury, in particular of the hamstrings. A thorough training programme for the sprinter will include exercises to develop strength in the hamstring muscle group. Therefore, in order to condition the athlete to meet the demands of the sport, careful planning of training programmes is necessary.

	Month	Weeks	Period emphasis	Method
Table 4.9. Periodisation of preparation and competitive season for a rugby player (see text for details).	March–April	1–4	Recovery Active rest	Tennis, swimming No formal training
	May–June	5–10	(i) Endurance (ii) General conditioning	(i) LSD★, Intervals (ii) Resistance training using high reps, little rest, low loads
	June–July	11–17	(i) Maximum strength (ii) Repetitive running endurance	(i) Near max and max loads with low reps, long rest, vary speed of movement (ii) Short distance repetitions
	July–August	18–22	(i) Explosiveness and specific strength (ii) Speed and power	(i) 50–80% 1 RM with explosive movement. Few reps long rest, sport specific (ii) Reaction, acceleration and speed, plyometrics
	Sept–March	23–52	Maintenance of acquired fitness	Adherence to maintenance criteria†

★ LSD = Long, slow, distance or continuous training
† Note: Playing a competitive game once per week should be recognized as contributing to specific fitness.

Training for major field games

Major differences in training strategies exist between the individual athlete and the team game player. Firstly, whereas an individual athlete may train to peak once or twice a year, the team game player is generally required to produce a number of peak performances throughout a season. Often the season can extent over 9 months. The team game player must also develop several components of physical fitness while an athlete competing in the marathon will concentrate on developing only endurance fitness.

Even though great similarities exist between the various games in terms of the range of the fitness components required, the degree of individual component development will vary between games, and indeed among players from different playing positions within a particular game. This is best illustrated by reference to the great levels of isometric and dynamic strength that are required by the rugby forward. The same high levels of strength and power are not required by players in the back line of the same game. Also goalkeepers in most field games do not require the same levels of aerobic fitness as outfield players. Further, the amount of time available for physical fitness training will be influenced by the demands for skill, tactical and game training. Physical fitness plays an important role in field games in addition to other aspects of preparation. Therefore, effective planning of the time available is essential in achieving an optimal level of development in several areas including physical fitness.

In order to ensure that the various physical fitness components receive sufficient attention, a system of periodised development and maintenance is recommended. Table 4.9 outlines a model of periodisation based on a rugby player's competitive year (September to March) with a 4-week active recovery period and a 5-month preparation period. This is referred to as a macrocycle (Matveyev 1992). The preparation period is further periodised into 4–6 week cycles (mesocycles) and microcycles which are usually one week in duration. Each mesocycle places emphasis on the development of specific physical fitness qualities. Following the development of fitness, maintenance is important during subsequent cycles in the preparation period and throughout the competitive cycle (see Maintenance of strength and endurance on page 105, 127–8).

Detailed plans outlining the content and progression of physical fitness components during each microcycle should be made. As considerable variation may exist between team players in terms of levels of physical fitness, the training session must be sufficiently varied so as to include appropriate training stresses for all players. This demands great attention to planning on the part of coaches. It is also recommended that initial pre-training fitness levels are measured so as to identify training needs. Retesting at a later date will serve to quantify the improvements made and can also be a useful motivator for the player and team. Appropriate testing and correct interpretation of results are essential if the tests are to be of value. For a more complete discussion of this topic, see Chapter 5.

Endurance

In Chapter 2 'Endurance' was defined as the ability to continue to exercise at the highest possible work rate. We saw that it is not possible to exercise at a high rate for particularly long periods because the body has several different mechanisms that provide energy for muscular contraction. The most powerful mechanisms are exhausted quickly and the individual must then rely on others which last much longer but provide energy at a much lower rate. The characteristics of the principal methods of energy production are summarised in Figure 4.7.

In order to improve endurance it is necessary to increase either the total capacity or the maximum output of the appropriate energy sources. A number of factors will influence the sources used. The duration and intensity of exercise are the primary considerations, but the characteristics of the athlete, including his or her state of training, also have an important influence.

Endurance is important when the energy expenditure of an activity is high in relation to its duration. The energy for a very brief activity – e.g. an isolated jump or throw – can be provided from the muscle stores of ATP and creatin phosphate. In a short sprint race the intensity of effort is so great that the energy is derived not only from high-energy phosphates but also from glycolysis. If the activity involves 30 minutes of heavy work, the oxidation of carbohydrates provides the bulk of the energy. In extremely prolonged activities carried out at a low work rate, most of the energy is derived from fats.

During intermittent activities – or multiple sprint sports such as soccer, rugby and Gaelic games – it is more difficult to quantify the contribution of the different energy sources. In these games, however, all energy systems are taxed to varying degrees. The

Figure 4.7. The four principal mechanisms that provide energy for muscular contraction. From: (a) high energy phosphate compounds, (b) production of lactic acid, (c) muscle glycogen, (d) other carbohydrates and fats. The symbols E_1 to E_5 denote different sets of enzymes.

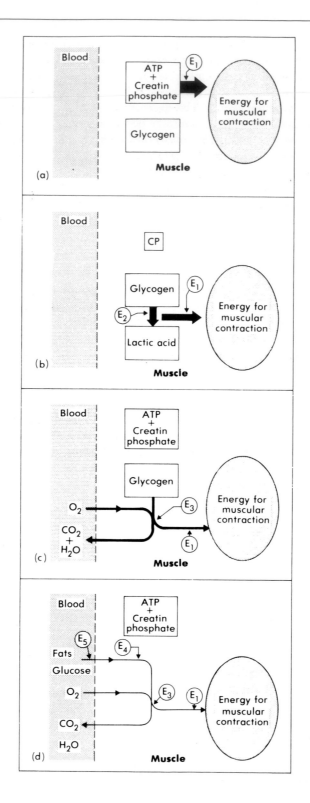

extent of utilisation of a particular energy system will vary between codes and in a particular game between players in different playing positions. Reilly (1990) noted that in soccer the aerobic demands were greater in mid-field players than in either backs or forwards. Additionally, the higher the level of play the greater the work rate.

Match analysis also indicates that the majority of all-out efforts or sprints in multiple sprint sports are over short distances of approximately 20 metres (Douge 1988). This places great demands on short-term energy systems and on the capacity to recover between segments of play. In some sports intense bouts of full body contact are common (e.g. rugby) and this places great demands on the capacity to repeatedly express overall strength. Therefore, it is important to analyse the different demands made on the individual during the performance of the activity. Also it is important to assess the capacity of the individual to meet these demands.

Various types of endurance

When planning a training programme it is useful to distinguish different kinds of endurance. These stem both from the physiological energy sources and the way that they are employed during exercise. The main characteristics of different types of endurance are summarised in Table 4.10.

It is misleading to view endurance solely as a function of energy sources. Other important factors include the type of activity, the efficiency or economy with which it is executed, and the determination of the athlete and his or her general physical condition. It is also a mistake to suppose that each energy source works in isolation from the others. They do not. In almost all kinds of exercise more than one type of endurance is employed and the different mechanisms are interdependent. But training can be made more effective if steps are taken to emphasise the types of endurance that are particularly relevant to the individual. Some of the assessment procedures discussed in Chapter 5 may be useful in this context.

Local anaerobic endurance

This is a feature of intensive activities, usually involving relatively small muscle groups. A prolonged contraction, or short repeated ones, reduces the stores of ATP and creatin phosphate, and lactic acid is also produced. This accumulates and eventually its by-product, the hydrogen ion, prevents the exercise being continued at a high rate. This type of endurance is often known as **local muscular**. It is improved by training using relatively high repetitions during exercise. The increase in muscular endurance is specific to the muscle groups employed. Circuit training is an ideal method of improving local muscular endurance. Additionally, a general training effect such as an increase in maximum oxygen uptake has also been found when local muscular exercise in the form of circuit training is performed with limited rest intervals between sets (Hortobagyi et al. 1991). Details of how to construct circuit-training routines are discussed later in this chapter.

Speed or power endurance

During very brief activities like the shot-put, power output is limited by neuromuscular factors, not by endurance. However, during intense efforts of a longer duration a rise in hydrogen ion concentration occurs in conjunction with an accumulation of lactate. During sprint events this leads to a reduction in power output towards the end of the race. Training leads to an increase in the rate of lactate production so that a greater intensity of effort is possible. The total capacity for lactate production is also increased. In addition, an increase in the buffering capacity of the muscle seems to occur following high-intensity training.

The repetition of near maximum efforts (i.e. greater than 90 per cent) is effective in bringing about improvements in power and speed endurance. Also, repeated intensive bouts of exercise performed against additional resistance have been shown to be effective in increasing high-energy phosphate concentrations (Houston and Thomson 1977). Athletes generally include sprinting uphill and using additional loads in their training programmes in order to improve power endurance. With this type of training the important point to remember is that the intensity of effort must be close to maximum for each repetition.

Prior to the development of speed or power endurance, a period of cardiovascular aerobic endurance training should be undertaken. Hagberg et al. (1980) have reported

	Type	A feature of	Example	Primary energy sources
Table 4.10. Characteristics of different types of endurance.	Local muscular endurance	Intensive activities of short duration involving small muscle groups	Circuit training	ATP–CP and anaerobic glycolysis
	Speed and power	Intensive activities occurring at high speed and lasting for a few seconds	Short sprints	ATP-CP and anaerobic glycolysis
	Lactic endurance	Intensive activities lasting from approximately 30 seconds to a few minutes	800 m running	Conversion of muscle glycogen into lactic acid
	Local aerobic endurance	Strenuous activities which last for several minutes involving small muscle groups	Arm exercise of long duration, e.g. kayaking	Oxidation of muscle glycogen and fatty acids
	Aerobic	Strenuous activities which last for several minutes in which large muscle groups are involved	Running, swimming, cycling	Oxidation of muscle glycogen and fatty acids
	Long-term endurance	Activities which last more than 1 hour	Marathon long-distance cycling, etc.	Oxidation of fats and muscle glycogen
	Repetitive sprint endurance	Intensive bouts of short duration repeated throughout a contest	Field games such as soccer, rugby, Gaelic games	Makes demands on all energy sources

that a greater capacity for anaerobic work exists following endurance training. A strong relationship also exists between maximum oxygen uptake and the maximum, anaerobic work that can be produced after 30 seconds of exercise (Hakkinen *et al.* 1987). This supports the practice of many athletes of devoting the early phase of the training year to aerobic or endurance development.

Local aerobic endurance

Occasionally small muscle groups are required to work hard for an extended period of time. This situation occurs in kayaking and similar sports where most of the work is done with the arms. Energy production seems to be limited by the muscle's ability to extract oxygen from blood, not by the cardiovascular system. Training should thus concentrate on the specific muscle group concerned. This is best done following a period of general cardiovascular training. In addition, strength training has been shown to enhance short-term endurance (Hickson *et al.* 1988). However, its effects on long-term endurance are not as well demonstrated.

Aerobic endurance

Aerobic processes provide the energy for activities of long duration, and aerobic endurance is important for any continuous activity that lasts for more than a minute. It is also necessary in short, intermittent activities where the energy sources are primarily anaerobic. If aerobic endurance is inadequate, the production of lactic acid

Figure 4.8. The threshold of anaerobic metabolism in a trained and an untrained individual. An arbitrary value of 4 mmol lactic acid per litre of blood has been selected as the 'anaerobic threshold'. The untrained subject reaches this value when his oxygen intake is about 60 per cent of his $\dot{V}_{O_2max}$, while in the trained subject the value is 85 per cent. *Inset*: the trained subject also has a greater $\dot{V}_{O_2max}$ so that the anaerobic threshold is not reached until he is consuming over 4 litres of oxygen per minute. In the untrained individual the threshold is reached when the oxygen intake is only half this value.

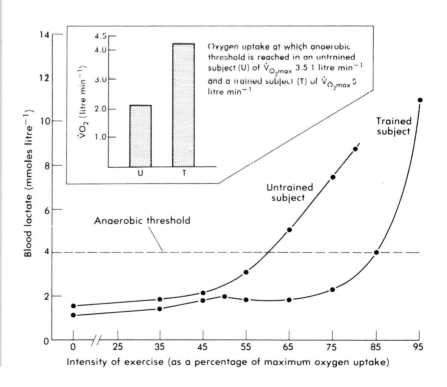

commences at an extremely low level of energy expenditure and causes premature fatigue. This is illustrated in Figure 4.8.

Aerobic fitness is also necessary to enable the athlete to undertake a warm-up which will raise body temperature and allow the athlete to benefit fully from it.

Long-term endurance

A high aerobic capacity and the ability to maintain exercise at a high fraction of this capacity are important factors in determining success in long-term endurance events such as the marathon. Central cardiovascular factors seem to be more important than peripheral ones in determining an individual's aerobic capacity. However, in some well-trained individuals lung function may be a limiting factor to $\dot{V}_{O_2max}$. For a detailed discussion on central and peripheral adaptations to endurance training, see pages 47–56.

Not only do successful marathon runners display high maximum oxygen uptake values (70–$85\,ml\,kg^{-1}\,min^{-1}$) but a good relationship exists between marathon performance and $\dot{V}_{O_2max}$. However, a high $\dot{V}_{O_2max}$ is not a guarantee of success. This is illustrated by the fact that it is possible for a top-class marathon performer to have a $\dot{V}_{O_2max}$ as low as $67\,ml\,kg^{-1}\,min^{-1}$ (Sjodin and Svedenhag 1985). Further, variations in economy of movement during exercise have been shown to influence competitive performance (Hagberg and Coyle 1983). Another factor influencing endurance performance is the level of exercise or level of oxygen consumption at which blood lactate begins to show a systematic increase above a predetermined level. The exercise intensity at the point where blood lactate shows a systematic increase is correlated highly with endurance performance (Sjodin and Svedenhag 1985).

The availability of fuels to muscle is also a major factor in determining prolonged endurance performance. It has been demonstrated that muscle glycogen is the preferential fuel for prolonged distance events (Costill 1986). Also, the longer the duration of exercise, the greater is the contribution of liver glucose as an energy substrate. When muscle glycogen and liver glucose become depleted then the marathon runner experiences fatigue. It is also clear that the contribution of fats to energy metabolism increases as the duration of exercise increases. Additionally, an endurance-trained athlete utilises a greater proportion and quantity of fats during exercise as compared to an untrained individual. Also, it appears that glucose manufactured from amino acids can contribute up to as much as 5–10 per cent of the energy needed to run a marathon (Felig 1977).

Considerable biochemical adaptations are necessary to ensure an adequate supply of fuels during extended periods of exercise. These changes have been observed in trained athletes such as marathon runners. Such effects include a rise in the number of capillaries, and an increase in myoglobin and mitochrondria content of the muscles. Additionally, increases in aerobic enzyme concentration, such as succinate dehydrogenase and citrate synthase, are associated with endurance training (see Table 2.3). As a result of these metabolic adaptations an increased capacity for fatty acid oxidation occurs. This results in a sparing of muscle glycogen stores. During prolonged exercise temperature regulation becomes a problem. Training produces adaptations which increase the contribution of sweating to heat loss. This preserves a greater proportion of the cardiac output for use by the working muscles. Thus, as is the case with most forms of training, the concept of specificity needs to be borne in mind – completing long duration or distance training is a prerequisite for favourable long-term endurance adaptations within the body.

Variables which influence aerobic fitness

Published studies in this area are numerous and a good deal is now known about the variables which affect aerobic fitness. The outcome of endurance training is influenced by several variables including intensity, duration, frequency, placement and recovery, initial level of fitness, age, gender, nutritional status, length and mode of exercise. These terms are also used in other forms of endurance training and are defined in Table 4.11.

Intensity

The training effect is determined by the amount of stress imposed upon the relevant part of the body. For this reason it is usual to quantify the intensity of aerobic training in terms of the percentage of maximum oxygen uptake or the effect upon heart rate. The latter is much easier to measure in a training session. The use of lightweight heart-rate monitors allows highly accurate and convenient heart-rate monitoring

Table 4.11. Terms used in interval training.

Term	Meaning	Example
Work interval	Period during which work is performed	Period during which 400 m is run
Relief interval	A period of rest or light work between bouts	Rest, walking or jogging
Intensive training	Exercise during which high levels of lactate occur	400 m intervals at fast pace
Extensive training	Longer duration and less intense than intensive workouts	800 m repetitions at moderate pace
Training mode	Type of activity undertaken	Running, cycling, swimming, etc.
Training distance	Distance covered in each work interval	400 m
Training time	Time for each work interval	60 seconds for each 400 m
Repetitions	Number of work intervals per set	For work intervals of 400 m running
Set	A specified group of intervals	A set might consist of 4 repetitions of 400 m runs
Session	A group of sets of repetitions	A session might consist of 2 sets of 4 repetitions of a 400 m run
Work : relief ratio	Ratio of duration of work interval to relief interval	1 : 2 means 60 seconds work and 120 seconds relief for each work : relief interval
Frequency of training	Number of training sessions per week	Three sessions per week

117

Figure 4.9. The heart rate reserve and its relationship to resting and maximum heart rates.

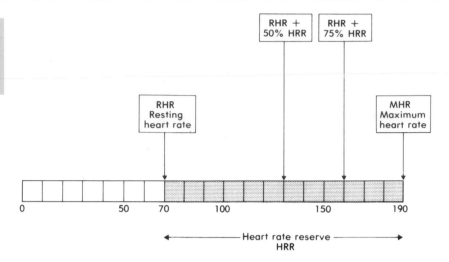

during training. Since there are variations in the resting heart rates of different individuals, the percentage of heart-rate reserve that is used in the exercise gives a better indication of intensity than the absolute heart rate. Heart-rate reserve is the difference between the individual's maximum and resting heart rates, as illustrated in Figure 4.9. Alternatively, a percentage of an individual's maximum heart rate is often used to determine the intensity of effort based on an assumed maximum of 220 minus the subject's age in years. Using this formula an 80 per cent training intensity for a 30-year-old male is 152 beats per minute.

Although it seems that there is a minimum intensity below which no gains in aerobic fitness occur, once this has been achieved other variables are also important. The critical intensity seems to be a level greater than that which the subject normally experiences. Gains in endurance have been reported following exercise at between 120 and 135 beats per minute and using 50 per cent of the heart-rate reserve. However, it does appear that with well-trained subjects higher intensities during both continuous and intermittent exercise are necessary.

Duration

It has been established that the duration of training also affects the increase in aerobic capacity. Greater gains occur during 20–30 minutes periods of work than from 10-minute periods. Several authors have concluded that the intensity of training is a more important influence than duration. However, where subjects exercise at higher intensities, a greater amount of work is generally completed. Where the total amount of work done is held constant then there is no significant difference in the effects of increases in duration or intensity (Olsen *et al.* 1988).

It is clear that if the intensity of exercise is high then the duration must be limited. In contrast, moderate exercise can be continued for a longer period. Manipulation of both intensity and duration of exercise is common, especially as the competitive season approaches. It has been shown that when the training duration of well-trained athletes was dramatically reduced and the intensity of training was increased, a decline in $\dot{V}_{O_2max}$ was observed (Berg *et al.* 1989; Mikesell and Dudley 1984). This shows the importance of the duration of training in maintaining $\dot{V}_{O_2max}$. However, in both the above studies the performances in endurance events (10 000 metres) improved significantly as a result of a reduction in training volume or duration. These studies and others suggest that a large volume of training does not result in further performance gains. It does seem that careful manipulation of both variables (intensity and duration) can be effective in optimising endurance performances. In this regard a reduction in duration, as reflected in training volume, may be beneficial when the athlete nears the competitive season. Further, for experienced athletes it is important that training progressions and responses are carefully monitored so as to avoid over-training.

Frequency

In general, training for only 1 day per week does not yield improvements in aerobic fitness (Shephard 1968). Gains are associated with programmes undertaken for 2 days per week and 3 is usually recommended. It is not clear whether there is an advantage in training for more than 3 days per week. Some studies suggest that greater gains do occur, others come to the opposite conclusion. Training for 5 days per week may increase the risk of injury. However, many experienced endurance athletes train daily and sometimes more often than once per day. In such cases intensity and duration are varied from session to session and it is common to use a low-intensity bout of exercise as a recovery from more intense training.

Placement and recovery

One study has shown that the placement of tri-weekly training sessions is unimportant. Gains were as great when training took place on consecutive days as when training occurred on alternative days (Moffatt et al. 1977). However, Costill (1986) has reported that prolonged duration training on consecutive days can result in an incomplete restoration of muscle glycogen between training sessions. As a result, it is more sensible to ensure a good recovery by alternating intensive training with less intense bouts of exercise. Also, ingesting sufficient amounts of carbohydrates between training sessions is advised in order to ensure a more complete recovery of muscle glycogen. Fatigue may still occur even though muscle fuels have been replenished. Sherman et al. (1984) reported the return of muscle glycogen stores to normal levels 7 days after a marathon run. Work capacity was also normal but muscle strength was significantly reduced. The authors noted that training during the week following the marathon may have affected recovery of muscle strength. Keizer et al. (1987) also examined the effects of working capacity and muscle glycogen 24 hours following intense interval training. While muscle glycogen had returned to normal levels, work capacity had not. These studies indicate that factors other than muscle glycogen replenishment affect the recovery capacity of the muscle. The implication for the athlete and coach is that it may be prudent to allow extended recovery periods so that muscle function can return to normal following intense or prolonged training sessions.

Initial level of fitness   The initial level of fitness has an important influence on the rate of improvement. As with strength, those who begin at a low level tend to improve more rapidly and achieve the greatest gains. An extreme example is a group of post-coronary patients who trained for, and completed, a marathon. Their gains in $\dot{V}_{O_2max}$ averaged 57 per cent (Kavanagh *et al.* 1974). The gains for an average untrained subject would be expected to be between 10 and 20 per cent. In well-trained subjects gains are made at a much slower rate.

Age   In children aerobic capacity is determined primarily by considerations of size. It seems that training results in improvements in the economy or oxygen cost of exercise rather than in improvements in total aerobic capacity. Even though aerobic capacity declines with age, training has been shown to slow down the rate of decline. Training produces a similar percentage increase in individuals up to 80 years of age as it does in younger subjects.

Gender   The majority of training studies have been carried out on males, yet it does appear that women respond to endurance training in the same way as men (Cunningham *et al.* 1979).

Post-puberal females have a lower aerobic capacity than most post-puberal males, but training appears to produce a similar percentage increase in both sexes.

Nutritional status   Manipulation of dietary procedures has been shown to have a direct influence on athletic performance (Karlsson and Saltin 1971). Indeed, the studies of Christensen and Hansen (1939) were the first to establish a link between a high carbohydrate diet and an improvement in endurance exercise performance. Since then the link between muscle glycogen concentration and exercise time to exhaustion has been well established. Fatigue during prolonged submaximal exercise is associated with a depletion of muscle glycogen stores. Karlsson and Saltin (1971) showed how ingesting a high carbohydrate diet several days before prolonged exercise resulted in an improvement of 8 minutes (5.6 per cent) in a 10-kilometre race. However, closer examination of the results of this study showed that the more experienced runners had higher muscle glycogen concentrations prior to the race than the recreational runners. It is not surprising, therefore, that the recreational runners showed the greater improvement in running time (12 minutes for recreational runners versus 5 minutes for experienced runners) as a result of carbohydrate loading. It appears that trained individuals have greater resting muscle glycogen concentrations than untrained individuals. However, Costill (1986) has shown that well-trained athletes who train heavily on a daily basis and consume low carbohydrate diets (40 per cent of total calories) show a decline in resting muscle glycogen stores. Ingesting high carbohydrate diets (70 per cent of total calories) allowed the athletes to achieve near optimum levels of glycogen prior to the next training session. While the practice of carbohydrate loading prior to a major competitive long-distance event is still common, it is important that the athlete consumes sufficient carbohydrates on a regular daily basis.

The problems of muscle glycogen depletion are not solely confined to athletes participating in prolonged continuous events. Jacobs *et al.* (1982) found significant reductions in muscle glycogen following a soccer game. The authors reported an inability in the professional soccer players to maintain normal glycogen stores on the days following a game of soccer. It was considered that the low levels of resting muscle glycogen were probably related to the players' low carbohydrate intake (47 per cent of total calories). Additionally, when normal dietary practices are adjusted it is possible to replenish depleted glycogen stores more rapidly. It has been established that muscle glycogen stores are replenished at a greater rate immediately following prolonged exhaustive exercise if carbohydrates are consumed without delay following exercise (Ivy *et al.* 1988). A carbohydrate intake of between 60 and 70 per cent of total energy intake with protein at 12 per cent and fat less than 30 per cent of energy intake is recommended for individuals involved in sports training. In general, it seems that current nutritional practices among athletes fall short of these requirements (Barry *et al.* 1981). These authors report that international and club athletes consumed approximately 45 per cent of their total energy in the form of carbohydrate, approximately 41 per cent in the form of fat and 14 per cent in the form of protein. It is also possible that an inadequate dietary intake of iron occurs in athletes. Yet Clarkson (1991) reports that women athletes are no more iron depleted than the general population. It has been suggested that plasma expansion as a result of training can dilute serum ferritin values and so imply, falsely, iron anaemia. However, when true iron deficiency anaemia occurs, endurance performance is impaired (Clarkson 1991). Avoiding such a condition in the first place is desirable. Therefore, proper eating habits are essential in maintaining athletic health and achieving optimal endurance performance.

Length of exercise
The majority of studies on endurance training have utilised sedentary or relatively untrained subjects. Significant gains in aerobic capacity are reported following short-term (4–8 weeks) training programmes in these subjects. However, further increases are small when the training load is increased. An example is given in Figure 4.10. Therefore, a training period of about 6–8 weeks seems to be effective in promoting a significant increase in aerobic capacity for non-endurance sport specialists. Longer periods of training are necessary for endurance athletes but further gains in aerobic capacity do not usually occur unless the work load is progressively increased over several months.

Mode of exercise
The mode of exercise employed in endurance training has an important effect upon the result. This is because a considerable proportion of the physiological changes that occur take place in the muscles that are exercised. These changes were discussed in some detail in Chapter 2 and the point is illustrated in Figure 4.11. Swim training was

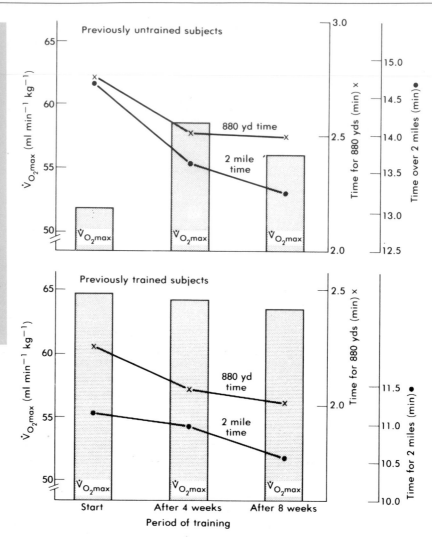

Figure 4.10. Changes in $\dot{V}_{O_2max}$, and time over 880 yd and 2 miles following training. *Above:* for previously untrained individuals. *Below:* for previously trained subjects. In both groups running speed increased as the training proceeded. These changes did not parallel those occurring in $\dot{V}_{O_2max}$. In the previously trained group no change in $\dot{V}_{O_2max}$ occurred and in the previously untrained group it rose only during the fist four weeks of training. (Data from Daniels *et al.* 1978b.)

found to have no effect upon the maximum oxygen uptake measured while running, and running had only a small effect on the maximum oxygen uptake during swimming (Magel *et al.* 1975; McArdle *et al.* 1978). The authors of these studies speculate as to whether running has a more general effect upon aerobic fitness than swimming. They consider that it may have, but do not rule out the possibility that the increase in swimming $\dot{V}_{O_2max}$ after run training was due to a local training effect upon the leg muscles. Many studies have since reported increases in mitochondrial content, capillary density and oxidative capacity of the trained muscles following endurance training. These peripheral adaptations are specific to the muscles exercised and enable the athlete to exercise more efficiently at the exercise mode used during training. Bouchard *et al.* (1979) measured the $\dot{V}_{O_2max}$ of moderately active subjects while performing five different tasks. They found that the overall common variance between $\dot{V}_{O_2max}$ scores measured during different tasks was only about 50 per cent of the total variance. These studies indicate that the effects of aerobic training are highly

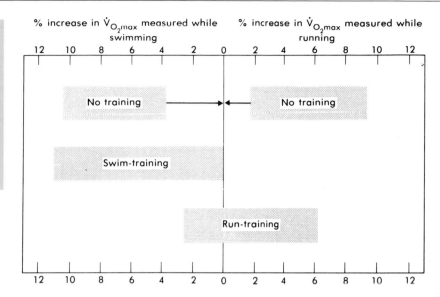

Figure 4.11. Increases in maximum oxygen uptake following swim training and run training. The values on the left were measured while the subjects were swimming; those on the right during running. (Data from Magel *et al.* 1975 and McArdle *et al.* 1978.)

specific to the activities undertaken. Local adaptations contribute to the improvements in endurance capacity. If the aim of the training is merely a non-specific improvement in general physical condition, perhaps for health reasons, then almost any form of continuous exercise is capable of improving the cardiovascular function. But if the objective is to improve endurance in a particular activity, the training should be specific to the activity or the results will be disappointing.

Aerobic capacity is so specific that changes in the maximum oxygen uptake of the whole body may not be a good guide to increases in endurance in relation to a particular activity. Figure 4.10 shows changes in running speed and $\dot{V}_{O_2max}$ of two groups who trained for 8 weeks. In the previously untrained group the change in $\dot{V}_{O_2max}$ during the first 4 weeks (+9 per cent) closely paralleled that in running speed (+8 per cent). But after 4 weeks, and in a previously trained group, running speed increased despite the fact that $\dot{V}_{O_2max}$ remained approximately constant. The authors suggest that this may be due to local adaptations in the muscles concerned in running. Similarly, other studies report significant improvements in endurance performances without any corresponding increase in $\dot{V}_{O_2max}$ and even with a reduction in $\dot{V}_{O_2max}$ (Olsen *et al.* 1988; Berg *et al.* 1989).

Types of training

Inverval training

Essentially, interval training involves raising the heart rate to maximum or near maximum values during an exercise bout and using a recovery period – the relief interval – to allow the heart rate to return to 120 beats per minute. This method of training was popularised by the German coach Gerschler in the 1930s and has since become a universally accepted method of training for all athletes involved in short- and long-term endurance events.

Nowadays, interval training has developed to include a wider range of exercise effort and duration. The terms **intensive** (i.e. high intensity of exertion) and **extensive** (long duration) are frequently used when prescribing interval-training programmes. A description of these and other terms used in interval training is given in Table 4.11.

A large number of variables can be manipulated in order to produce different types of programme. The combination of intensity and duration of exercise will determine the extent of lactate accumulation and thus exercise tolerance. When attempting to improve aerobic capacity both variables should be manipulated to minimise lactate accumulation and optimise oxygen uptake. Intervals carried out for periods of about 3 minutes and longer, and which result in an exercise intensity greater than 90 per cent of $\dot{V}_{O_2max}$, have been reported to effect increases in both beginners and trained subjects (Moffatt *et al.* 1977; Olsen *et al.* 1988).

With the use of lightweight heart-rate monitors it is convenient to measure heart rate during training. However, in order to utilise heart rate as an effective monitor of physiological and metabolic responses to exercise, certain points need to be made. Heart rate and oxygen uptake are, up to a point, linearly related. Also, it is well known that the heart rate reached during maximal exercise decreases with age. The submaximal heart-rate response at a fixed work rate also decreases with training. Consequently, the use of heart rate as a reflection of intensity of effort and recovery during training needs to be done on an individual basis and varied as the athlete progresses. The heart-rate response to exercise is frequently used as a guide to lactate accumulation. Greater inter-individual variations exist in the lactate response to exercise. Several factors influence this response, including ambient temperature, nutritional status, state of training and anxiety level of the athlete. Ideally, lactate and oxygen uptake responses to different intensities and durations of exercises should be individually assessed prior to training. From this, training programmes can then be individually tailored to suit the current fitness level of the individual.

Continuous training   As previously described, the adaptations occurring as a result of continuous or prolonged training include both **central** and **peripheral** adaptations. A well-developed oxygen transport system and a high rate of fat oxidation in the working muscles ensure that optimal effort can be maintained without a significant rise in lactate concentration. While there are some common adaptations from both interval and continuous types of training, continuous-training programmes have invariably resulted in a greater degree of development of the muscle's oxidative capacity (Gorostiaga *et al.* 1991). While there is debate as to the existence of an anaerobic threshold, it does appear that continuous training at a certain lactate level (e.g. $4 \, mmol.l^{-1}$) will result in a favourable shift of the lactate curve (Sjodin and Svedenhag 1985). Several categories or intensities of continuous training, based on different lactate levels, are frequently used by athletes. The underlying assumption is that by training at these intensities for a prolonged period optimal adaptations occur that shift the lactate curve to the right at a particular intensity (see Figure 4.8). Additionally, the heart-rate response during exercise, even though limited by several factors as previously discussed, is frequently used to reflect the physiological and metabolic stress imposed on the athlete. Such an approach to endurance training provides a method of monitoring training based on the individual athlete.

Designing the training programme

Both continuous and interval forms of training are used by most endurance athletes. Continuous training is likely to be the best type of training for very long events. The terms used to quantify endurance-training programmes are outlined in Table 4.12. Precise combinations of the two methods are, however, dependent on several factors, including the fitness level and training background of the athlete, the sport or event being trained for and the period of training available. For beginners who wish to

Table 4.12. Terms used to quantify programmes of endurance training.

Term	Meaning	Example
Intensity	The severity of degree of overload produced. Usually measured in terms of the effect upon cardiorespiratory variables	The heart rate produced by the exercise or the % of $\dot{V}_{O_2max}$ used
Duration	The length of each training session	
Frequency	The number of training sessions per week	Three per week
Placement	The distribution of training sessions in the week	Monday, Tuesday and Wednesday or Monday, Wednesday and Friday
Length	The number of weeks of training	
Type	Whether continuous or interval	
Mode	The type of exercise	Swimming, running or cycling

Table 4.13. A progressive programme of jogging.

Stage	Activity	Distance (miles)	Target time (min)
1	Walk	1	20
2	Walk	$1\frac{1}{2}$	30
3	Alternate: walk 660 yd, fast walk 220 yd	$1\frac{1}{2}$	$28\frac{1}{2}$
4	Alternate: walk 440 yd, fast walk 440 yd	$1\frac{1}{2}$	27
5	Alternate: walk 220 yd, fast walk 440 yd	$1\frac{1}{2}$	$25\frac{1}{2}$
6	Fast walk	$1\frac{1}{2}$	24
7	Alternate: fast walk $\frac{3}{8}$ mile, slow jog $\frac{1}{8}$ mile	$1\frac{1}{2}$	22
8	Alternate: fast walk $\frac{1}{4}$ mile, slow jog $\frac{1}{4}$ mile	$1\frac{1}{2}$	20
9	Alternate: fast walk $\frac{1}{8}$ mile, slow jog $\frac{3}{8}$ mile	$1\frac{1}{2}$	18
10	Slow jog	$1\frac{1}{2}$	16
11	Slow jog	2	22
12	Slow jog	2	20
13	Alternate: slow jog $\frac{3}{8}$ mile, jog $\frac{1}{8}$ miles	2	19
14	Alternate: slow jog $\frac{1}{4}$ mile, jog $\frac{1}{4}$ miles	2	18
15	Alternate: slow jog $\frac{1}{8}$ mile, jog $\frac{3}{8}$ miles	2	17
16	Jog	2	16
17	Jog	$2\frac{1}{2}$	23
18	Jog	$2\frac{1}{2}$	20
19	Jog	3	27
20	Jog	3	24

improve cardiovascular endurance, continuous training at low to moderate intensity has been shown to promote significant gains in aerobic capacity even following short-term training programmes (see page 121).

Table 4.13 outlines a sample of a progressive endurance-training programme for a previously inactive individual. Interval training may also be incorporated into the programme but only at an intensity and duration appropriate to the fitness level of the individual. Further, the principles of overload and progression, as determined for each individual, should be borne in mind when planning any training programme.

Both continuous and interval methods can be usefully employed at the start of a training season for a games player. As the games player may have a greater initial level of endurance fitness, as compared to the sedentary individual, a greater volume of training can be prescribed. For example, this can be done beginning at stage 19 of the programme in Table 4.13 and omitting the odd-numbered training sessions. A progression can then be made to short-distance interval work or Fartlek training.

For the experienced athlete a combination of methods is frequently prescribed. In the early stages of training the athlete should seek to develop a large volume of training progressively. This will mainly include continuous training at a low to moderate intensity. The aim of this is to promote favourable central and peripheral adaptations which will allow the athlete to maintain an optimal pace of exercise for a specific duration. More intensive training is then completed using a variety of both continuous- and interval-training methods. As competition approaches the athlete should seek to reduce training volume so as to ensure sufficient recovery and competition readiness.

Continuous vs interval training

There is much debate as to the relative merits of interval vs continuous training. However, there is general agreement that both methods produce similar gains in $\dot{V}_{O_2max}$ when the total work done is equal. It would be expected, however, that high-intensity interval training would be a more effective method of increasing power endurance than continuous running; but the evidence is unequivocal. Gorostiaga *et al.* (1991) reported that interval training at 100 per cent of $\dot{V}_{O_2max}$ resulted in a greater peak power output following 8 weeks of training as compared to a continuous programme exercising at 50 per cent of work rate. Other studies did not report an increase in anaerobic power output following interval training (Houston and Thompson 1977). However, in the latter study the anaerobic test used involved less than a second of intense activity. It is possible that a longer work period might have produced a different effect. On the other hand, Gorostiaga *et al.* (1991) have reported increases in glycolytic enzymes associated with rapid utilisation and re-synthesis of ATP following interval but not continuous training. In contrast, continuous training produced an increase in the activity of the aerobic enzyme, citrate synthase, which was not observed in the interval-trained group. Also a reduction in the respiratory exchange ratio was observed – indicating that a greater utilisation of fats occurred following continuous training.

Therefore, while both methods produce comparable gains in $\dot{V}_{O_2max}$, limited evidence suggests that different local adaptations may occur within muscle during interval and continuous training. Additionally, most athletes realise that a greater amount of intense training is possible with interval methods. For example, this method of training allows the middle-distance runner to complete a large volume of event-specific work. Exercising at or close to the pace used during competition can be expected to improve running economy (Snell 1990). In addition, higher blood lactate levels can occur during interval training.

Such high levels of lactate undoubtedly occur during middle-distance running events and so training using high-intensity intervals seems to be appropriate for this event. It has been suggested that high-intensity training promotes an increased buffering capacity in the working muscles (Parkhouse and McKensie 1984). Such an adaptation would be of benefit to the middle-distance athlete.

However, there is some evidence to suggest that high-intensity training may interfere with or impair aerobic capacity (Ibara et al. 1981; Berg et al. 1989). Following a period of anaerobic training a decrease in the oxidative enzyme, succinate dehydrogenase, was found by Ibara and colleagues. Also Berg et al. reported a decrease in $\dot{V}_{O_2max}$ following the introduction of intense interval training even though endurance-running performance improved.

In order to prepare effectively for athletic events where both speed and endurance are required, it is advisable to include varying combinations of both interval and continuous training. However, care is demanded in the manipulation of both interval and continuous methods so as to optimise performance.

Maintenance of cardiovascular endurance

Following a period of endurance training an athlete may have to devote time to the development of other aspects of fitness and the skills of the particular sport. In this case it is possible to maintain previously acquired gains in endurance with a reduction in the amount of endurance training. However, if training is stopped completely for any length of time, adaptations are reversed. Cullinane et al. (1986) found that endurance-related gains in $\dot{V}_{O_2max}$, cardiac dimensions and body fat percentage were unaffected following 10 days of detraining. After 2–4 weeks of detraining, however, Coyle et al. (1986) reported decreases in $\dot{V}_{O_2max}$, oxygen pulse, oxygen recovery debt and increases in body fat percentage. Other studies have reported decreases in the rate of fat metabolism during exercise following 3 weeks of detraining. Likewise, Bangsbo and Mizuno (1988) reported decreases in oxidative enzyme concentration during the first week of detraining in well-trained soccer players but no changes in $\dot{V}_{O_2max}$ following 3 weeks of detraining. These studies suggest that while detraining has a rapid effect on cellular adaptations, functional adaptations, such as $\dot{V}_{O_2max}$ may not be as dramatically affected following a lay-off period of about 2 weeks.

Maintenance of training-induced adaptations were reported by Hickson and Rosenkoetter (1981) when training frequency was reduced from 6 to 2 days per week. Following 15 weeks of reduced training frequency, $\dot{V}_{O_2max}$ and performance on a maximum exercise test were unaltered. Also it has been reported that a reduction in training duration from 40 minutes to 26 or 13 minutes per session did not alter $\dot{V}_{O_2max}$, cardiac dimensions, short-term endurance performance or blood lactate after maximum exercise. Long-term endurance was, however, affected when training was reduced to 13 minutes but not to 26 minutes (Hickson et al. 1982). Thus, if maintenance of long-term endurance is a priority, a dramatic reduction in training duration is not advised.

The importance of maintaining a high exercise intensity has been illustrated by Hickson *et al.* (1985). Subjects who reduced exercise intensity during a maintenance programme to less than 70 per cent of maximum heart rate had reductions in $\dot{V}_{O_2max}$ and long-term endurance performance. Therefore, it appears that all gains associated with endurance training are reversed following complete cessation of training for any extended length of time. A short absence from training (up to 2 weeks) does not, however, seem to adversely affect endurance performance even though cellular adaptations may be adversely affected. Nevertheless, it is possible to maintain endurance fitness with a reduced number of work-outs. Completing two training sessions per week for at least 15 minutes is suggested for maintenance of $\dot{V}_{O_2max}$ and maximal short-term endurance fitness provided that the training intensity is high. If maintenance of long-term endurance fitness is the goal then a longer training duration is suggested while keeping the intensity of exercise high.

Circuit training

Circuit training was originally popularised by Morgan and Adamson (1962). Typically, it consists of a series of exercises carried out in rotation. When one set of each has been completed the series is performed again, with the number of sets depending on the fitness level and training background of the individual. Exercises using body weight as the resistance, medicine balls, benches, ropes, pulleys, free weights and machine weights are frequently employed in the construction of a circuit.

It is possible to construct circuits which emphasise different aspects of fitness such as strength, muscular endurance, speed, flexibility or even skill. It is usual to perform the exercises in rotation and against the clock. This will overload the cardiovascular system and result in an increase in aerobic capacity if the initial level of aerobic fitness is low. Circuit training is thus a way of developing all-round fitness. Decreases in body fat and increases in strength, as assessed by the one repetition maximum effort, and maximum oxygen uptake have been reported as a result of circuit training (Hortobagyi *et al.* 1991; Haennel *et al.* 1989). Gains in strength and maximum oxygen uptake are not, however, of the same magnitude as those reported for strength- or endurance-training programmes alone. Nevertheless, circuit training is extremely adaptable and with efficient organisation large numbers of individuals can be accommodated with the minimum of space and equipment.

Body-building

Successful body-builders display exceptional muscular mass and development throughout the whole body. Therefore, it is not surprising that body-builders are characterised by greater body weight and lean body mass as compared to untrained individuals, and indeed, most other athletes. While not all athletes require the same degree of muscular development as the body-builder, many individuals seek an increase in lean body weight so as to enhance anaerobic power and strength. Extra muscle also helps to absorb the momentum of opponents, especially in contact sports. Extra muscle also helps protect a joint against injury and aids joint stability.

	Monday	Tuesday	Wednesday	Thursday	Friday	Saturday	Sunday
	Upper body Abdominals	Lower body	Upper body Abdominals	Rest	Lower body	Upper body Abdominals	Rest

Table 4.14. Seven-day cycle of training for body-builder. This cycle is frequently used by body-builders at an intermediate stage (i.e. over 2 years consistent training). Training occurs on 5 days with 2 days off. The cycle is a split routine, with upper body trained on Monday, Wednesday and Saturday and lower body on alternate days.

Several strategies are employed by the body-builder to promote greater muscle mass. Some of these are outlined in Table 4.5. Increased muscle mass has been associated with hypertrophy of the existing muscle fibres. While evidence is limited, It does appear that using heavy resistances in an explosive manner promotes selective enlargement of fast-twitch fibres (Tesch *et al.* 1984), while individuals, such as body-builders, who train using a high volume of exercise but with less resistance, achieve hypertrophy predominantly of the slow-twitch fibres. Body-builders also tend to use short rest periods (1–2 minutes) between sets. Where hypertrophy of fast-twitch fibres is sought, then longer rest intervals using heavy loads (greater than 80 per cent 1 RM) may be required.

In general, weights in the range 6–12 repetition maximum are utilised to promote muscle hypertrophy but there is little scientific evidence available to demonstrate that this is the most effective range. Nevertheless, several sets (3–5) and 6–12 RM are frequently employed by body-builders and increases in muscle mass do occur as a result. There is some evidence to suggest that the progression of resistance used is of equal or greater importance than the total volume of exercise. Training frequency depends on whether an all-round programme or a body part programme is employed. It is usual for a body-builder to employ a training cycle such as that outlined in Table 4.14. A cycle in this instance comprises a number of training and rest days. Following the completion of a cycle the process is repeated. A 5-day cycle involves training for 4 days and then resting on the fifth. The process is then repeated for another 5 days. This may not be a practical programme for athletes who have to incorporate other fitness components or skill practice into their programme. In such cases an all-round body programme where three training sessions per week are completed may be more suitable.

Losing body fat

A negative relationship exists between body fat and aerobic- and anaerobic-related physical performances (Watson 1988b). Heat dissipation is also affected by excess subcutaneous fat. Consequently, it is desirable for athletes to possess only a limited amount of fat for efficient physical performance. Yet, it must be recognised that precise body fat levels have not been determined for optimum physical performance in sport even though certain levels and ranges of body fat are common to specific sporting groups.

Exercise programmes involving walking, jogging, cycling and resistance training have been effective in reducing body fat levels (Zuti and Golding 1976). Increases in lean body mass have been shown to occur following both endurance- and strength-training programmes.

Where increases in lean body tissue are desirable, engaging in resistance training on 2–4 days per week over 7–10 weeks is effective and also produces gains in strength and power. Zuti and Golding (1976) showed how weight and body fat could be controlled by combining exercise with energy intake restriction or manipulation rather than restricting energy intake on its own. In this study subjects who combined an exercise programme with food intake restriction lost an the same amount of body weight as the group that restricted food intake alone. Interestingly, the diet and exercise group showed an increase in lean body mass and reduced body fat while the diet-only group reduced body fat but also lost lean tissue. Where the maintenance of lean body tissue is important, in addition to a reduction in body fat, a combination of exercise and modification of food intake is effective.

Training for flexibility

The factors that limit flexibility were discussed in Chapter 2. The one that can most easily be altered by training is the extensibility of the connective tissue that occurs inside muscle and in ligaments and tendons. Flexibility-training programmes therefore need to be designed to achieve the greatest and most long-lasting changes in the length of these tissues.

It has been shown experimentally that both the contractile part of muscle and connective tissue increase in length in response to stretch (Warren *et al.* 1971, 1976). There are two types of change in length: **elastic**, where the changes are quickly reversed, as in a warm-up; and **plastic**, where the changes in length are more permanent. The research shows that high-force, short-duration stretches favour elastic changes that are soon reversed. More permanent, plastic, changes are likely to be produced by lower forces applied over a longer period. Temperature also has an effect. Permanent changes in length are more likely at elevated body temperatures. Thus this basic research suggests that gentle stretches of long duration, carried out when the body is fully warmed up, are the best way of increasing the length of connective tissue and improving flexibility.

Types of flexibility training

There are a number of different ways of carrying out flexibility exercises. The main variations are summarised below.

Ballistic stretches consist of dynamic movements like arm and leg swings, or bounding movements. The method is widely condemned by most authors on physical training as it is said to be dangerous. There is no research on this issue but it is easy to anticipate that ballistic exercises could cause injury, particularly in people who are poorly conditioned. Ballistic stretches mimic the movements that occur in many sporting situations and could be useful in phase 4 of a warm-up, or in specialised training situations (see page 82).

In **static** stretches the muscles remain stationary while the stretching force is applied. This force can be supplied either from other muscle groups in the athlete's own body when the stretch is known as an **active stretch**, or from a partner or training device when it is called a **passive stretch**. In theory, passive stretches are superior to active ones for two reasons. Firstly, the degree and range of the stretch is not limited by the force that can be developed by the subject's antagonist muscles so that the amount and range of stretch can be greater. This fact has been confirmed experimentally by Iashvili (1983) who also suggests that passive stretches are more highly related to athletic performance. Secondly, there is a better chance that the subject's body is more relaxed during a passive stretch. This would result in a greater range of movement.

PNF is shorthand for 'Proprioceptive Neuromuscular Facilitation'. This is a technique involving a prior contraction of a muscle before it is stretched. PNF is actually not a single technique. In a review on flexibility Alter (1988) describes nine variants of the method, some of considerable complexity. The theoretical basis of PNF is that the initial contraction of muscle sets off a chain of reactions in the nervous system that ultimately results in greater relaxation. This, in turn, allows a greater degree of stretch in the muscle. However, the human nervous system is so complex that theoretical predictions carry considerable hazards and some authors have questioned the theoretical basis of PNF (Eldred *et al.* 1976; Suzuki and Hutton 1976). A number of authors suggest that PNF stretches produce greater increases in flexibility than other methods, but this is not a universal finding and PNF has been criticised for being uncomfortable and carrying a greater risk of injury.

Scientific studies on flexibility

In contrast to the large number of studies on aerobic and strength training there is a dearth of information on flexibility. It has been established that ballistic, static and PNF stretching methods are all effective in increasing flexibility (Corbin and Noble 1980; Logan and Egstrom 1961; Sady *et al.* 1982) but there is little definitive information on the effects of such variables as length of stretch, number of repetitions or duration and frequency of training. A number of studies point to longer stretches of 30 to 60 seconds duration being more effective than shorter ones but there is, as yet, no definitive information.

Warm-up and flexibility training

Warm-up produces a transient increase in flexibility that is reversed after exercise when the body cools down. These changes should not be confused with the long-term changes in flexibility that occur following a properly designed stretching programme.

Individual stretching exercises

Controversial exercises   Exercises that place excessive amounts of stress on any part of the body should be avoided unless they are a necessary part of preparation for a particular sport. For example, the hurdle stretch was once widely used as a flexibility exercise but is now generally avoided because it places excessive stress on the medial ligaments of the knee. A large number of exercises have been identified as 'controversial' by some authors – often in the context of aerobics classes. When evaluating the potential risk of an exercise a number of factors need to be taken into account. These include:

- age, physical and medical condition of the subject
- benefits of undertaking the exercise
- feasibility of alternative exercises
- quality of supervision of training.

Complex or multi-muscle group exercises   Flexibility exercises are effective only if the degree of stretch on a muscle is carefully controlled. This is difficult to achieve in exercises which stretch more than one muscle group at a time. Such exercises are not an efficient way of improving flexibility and should be avoided.

Principles of flexibility training

A great deal remains to be discovered about the most effective way of improving flexibility. The suggestions below are based on an analysis of the research that is presently available.

1   A special programme of stretching exercises is necessary in order to achieve high levels of flexibility. Stretching only during warm-up is not sufficient.
2   A flexibility programme must take into account the specific requirements of the individual undertaking the programme. His or her:
- sport, level of participation and previous experience
- level of flexibility at the start of the programme
- age, previous injuries, medical factors.
3   Avoid potentially hazardous exercises.
4   Avoid complex exercises which stretch more than one muscle group at a time.
5   Stretches carried out while lying on the floor are generally more effective than those undertaken in a standing position. This is because less muscles are contracting and the body is more relaxed. In addition, there is less risk of injury.
6   Ensure that the athlete carries out each exercise with the correct technique. In the author's experience a lot of time is wasted on incorrectly executed flexibility exercises.
7   Carry out exercise indoors in a room that is quiet, warm and comfortable. It should not be simultaneously used for other forms of training. Provide a carpet or mats for the athlete to lie on. A full length mirror is also useful.
8   Correct breathing is important.
9   The athlete should wear kit that allows freedom of movement and makes it possible to see that the exercise is being carried out correctly. Kit that is not used for other forms of training has psychological advantages in helping the athlete to focus on the principles of stretching.
10   The athlete should warm up fully before stretching. Alternatively, flexibility training can be carried out after other forms of training.
11   In the initial stages of training the stretch should be held for 10 seconds.
12   This should be increased to 30 or 60 seconds over a period of 1 to 2 weeks.
13   Repeat each exercise five times.
14   If possible the athlete should undertake flexibility training every day.

15 Education of the athlete on flexibility and the principles of training promotes compliance with the programme and improves results.

16 Experiment with PNF stretching by having the athlete hold a 6-second maximal stretch before stretching the muscle.

17 Stretch statically; do not bounce or jerk. Avoid ballistic stretches except during phase 4 of warm-up (see page 82).

5 EVALUATION OF FITNESS LEVELS

Introduction to fitness testing

Ten years ago physiological testing was almost exclusively confined to laboratories in universities and other specialist institutions. It has now become much more widespread and various forms of fitness testing are currently available in such places as sports centres, health studios and sports clubs. Assessment techniques have improved and become more automated. It is now possible to provide better information to the athlete, more easily and more quickly.

At the same time the limitations of fitness testing have become much more apparent. Laboratory measures of such basic variables as strength and endurance seldom replicate the demands placed on the athletes during their sport. This is especially true of those involved in multiple sprint activities like the majority of team games. When it *is* possible for the athletes to undertake their normal mode of exercise in the laboratory, the interpretation of the test results is a further difficulty. Performance in the most straightforward endurance sport is now known to be dependent upon the interaction of several different factors. The analysis of such data is difficult and requires an up-to-date knowedge of physiological principles, and considerable skill. The expert physiologist will now give more useful information to the athlete than would have been possible 10 years ago. However, the adoption of fitness testing by individuals who lack such a background is a different matter and a source of concern. While the quality of the best fitness assessments is superior to anything available in the past, there is an unwelcome increase in the volume of inexpert and inappropriate testing.

There are numerous pitfalls to the assessment of fitness. It is easy to mislead – and even frighten – subjects if the testers lack basic knowledge and skills. Requirements include the ability to ensure that the measurements taken are appropriate to the subject, are of a high level of accuracy and are correctly interpreted: it is also necessary to know what information to feed back to the subject and how this should be done. For example, it may be very distressing and harmful to inform an individual that he or she has abnormal blood pressure or serum cholesterol – especially if the measurements are inexpertly carried out and are of doubtful accuracy.

Advantages of physiological testing

1 May identify weakness in the athlete that can be corrected by means of modifications to training.
2 May act as a form of motivation to train – particularly in individuals not involved in competitive sport.
3 May act as a monitor of training effectiveness and progress.

Disadvantages of physiological testing

1   Can easily mislead the athlete if the tests are not:
    (a) accurately carried out
    (b) relevant to the athlete's sport
    (c) correctly interpreted.
2   May unnecessarily alarm the subject if the measurements are of a clinical nature.

Requirements for valid fitness testing

In order to provide useful information from a fitness assessment it is necessary for the tester to be clear about all of the following:

1   The nature of the measurement being taken, including its theoretical basis and the treatment and minimisation of errors.
2   The amount of error involved in the tests as they are carried out by the tester.
3   The factors responsible for variations in particular aspects of fitness; for example, the effects of age, gender, physique and training on strength measurements.
4   Normal values for each measurement taken, with which those from the subject can be compared.
5   The background and aspirations of the subject. Is he or she an inactive individual who wishes to become a little less unfit? Or is the individual a champion swimmer competing in the Olympics in two days' time?
6   The appropriateness of the test to the needs of the subject. Very demanding tests are unsuitable for most individuals. They may be necessary to detect the small increases that occur with training in athletes who are already well conditioned; but there is no guarantee that the results will be of any benefit.
7   The purpose of the test. Tests are justified as a means of motivation for the subject, for the formulation of a training programme, and for genuine research. For all three purposes the informed consent of the subject is necessary. If none of the above justifications applies, the test should not be carried out.
8   Feed-back of the results to the subject. The tester must be prepared to give advice that can be used to overcome any problems or deficiencies that are detected. For example, non-medical personnel are not in a position to treat high blood pressure or elevated serum cholesterol and should avoid alarming subjects with the results of such clinical tests.

    The psychological state of the subject also influences the type of feedback that it is appropriate to give. Fitness tests should be carried out early in the season when there is time for the athlete to improve. They should not be carried out close to important competitions when a poor result may have a devastating effect.
9   The confidential nature of test results. Personal information should not be divulged to *any* third party without the written permission of the subject. The provisions of the Data Protection Act should also be observed.
10 The action to take if a mishap occurs.

Levels of measurement

There is a hierarchy of types of observation that can be made on athletes. The simplest level is known as **nominal** and is where individuals are placed in categories that are different but not ordered. 'Male and female', 'swimmer, runner, footballer and hockey player' and 'injured and uninjured' are examples of nominal scales of measurement.

The second level of observation, **ordinal**, is where individuals are placed in categories that fall into a logical order. For example, an athlete's flexibility or posture might be evaluated by placing him or her into one of the following five categories: POOR, BELOW AVERAGE, AVERAGE, ABOVE AVERAGE, EXCEPTIONAL. This is an example of an ordinal scale of measurement. With the two highest levels of measurement, **interval** and **ratio**, observations are expressed numerically. For example, body weights expressed in kg:

50 kg, 60 kg, 70 kg, 80 kg, 90 kg

or flexibility measurements in degrees:

50deg, 60deg, 70deg, 80deg, 90deg

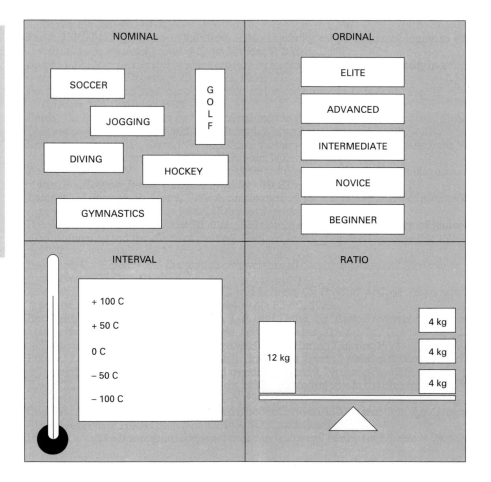

Figures 5.1. Examples of the four levels of measurement as applied to observations made on athletes. *Nominal*: describe categories, not ordered. *Ordinal*: categories that fall into a logical order. *Interval*: measurements with equal intervals. *Ratio*: ratios are also equal, e.g. one 12 kg measure is exactly the same as three measures of 4 kg.

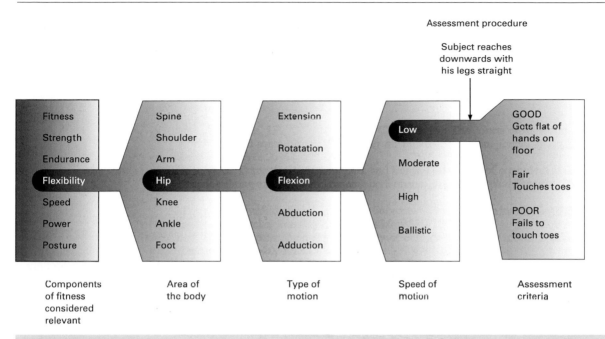

Figure 5.2. Steps in the construction of an ordinal scale for the measurement of fitness variables in an athlete. *Step 1*: Identify aspects of fitness that are relevant to the athlete's sport. *Steps 2 to 4*: Be precise about what is to be evaluated. With flexibility assessment the joint involved, type of motion and speed of movement. *Step 5*: Finally, three levels of achievement are precisely specified. In this example they are arbitrarily labelled as 'GOOD', 'FAIR' and 'POOR'.

With ordinal level measurements the intervals between the various categories are not necessarily equal. 'AVERAGE', 'EXCELLENT', etc., are merely categories — no exact measurements are involved. With interval and ratio measurements the intervals *are* exact. The difference between 80 kg and 90 kg is exactly the same as the difference between 50 kg and 60 kg, i.e. 10 kg. Hence body weights are interval level measurements.

Or they should be. Scores that are expressed as interval level measurements are *truly* interval only if they are absolutely accurate. When there is a significant amount of error it is misleading to express a fitness score as a number. The error involved in flexibility measurements can easily be ±30 per cent. In such a circumstance it is more realistic to express flexibility scores as a small number of ordinal level categories such as:

UNSATISFACTORY   SATISFACTORY

It may also be more helpful. If the purpose of the fitness assessment is to identify athletes who need to undertake special flexibility training, two categories are enough: athletes who require extra training and those who do not.

Tests that employ ordinal scales of measurement are extremely appropriate for fitness assessments because evaluation can be built into the measuring scale. The steps necessary for the construction of such a scale are summarised in Figure 5.2.

The accuracy of tests of physical fitness: validity, relevance, reliability

Anyone attempting to measure physical fitness variables needs to be aware of the accuracy of the procedures that are used. This will involve the acquisition of an understanding of the concept of accuracy as it relates to fitness assessment.

Validity

The **validity** of a test indicates the extent to which a test measures what it sets out to measure. In theory, the validity of a test is determined by comparing it with the results of another test that is known to be a valid measure of the item being investigated – the so-called **criterion measure**. For tests of physical fitness, validity is often a very academic concept for two reasons. In some cases it is not possible to know what the criterion measure ought to be. In others it is simply not possible to measure it. Assessments of endurance are an example of the first kind of difficulty. Endurance is influenced by many different factors: the operation of several different energy sources, the economy of the subject's movement, and psychological factors, to mention only a few. No laboratory test takes all of these into account. Thus, there is no criterion measure with which tests of endurance can be compared.

Estimates of body fat are an example of the second type of difficulty. In theory, estimates that are made from skinfold thicknesses ought to be compared with the actual amount of fat that can be extracted from an athlete's body. But it is not possible to undertake such a procedure in a living person. Thus the validity of an estimate of body fat can never be known.

Relevance

Because of the above difficulties a concept that is often of greater importance in relation to fitness testing is one of **relevance**. Will the athlete benefit from having the test carried out? In order to be of value the test will need to identify a problem that the athlete is able to correct, or suggest ways in which the athlete can improve his or her training. Tests that relate to the needs of a particular sport are likely to be more relevant than general tests. It is by no means clear how relevant an isolated $\dot{V}_{O_2max}$ test is to a soccer player since aerobic capacity is only one component of the demands of this particular sport. A test that quantified the kind of endurance required in a soccer game *would* be relevant if one were developed that was based on the specific demands of the game. At the moment few sports-specific tests of endurance are available.

Reliability

The reliability of a test is a measure of how *reproducible* it is. Figure 5.3 illustrates a typical study of the reliability of a fitness test. PWC_{170} was measured on two occasions, separated by 24 hours, on a group of 29 individuals: 19 were students who had undertaken the test before and 10 were school children, new to the test. The percentage change in score when the measurement was repeated is shown for each subject. When the results for the students are examined it is clear that for most individuals there is a slight variation between the two scores. This varied between a gain of 7.5 per cent and a loss of 6.5 per cent. The mean change was 0 per cent and

Figure 5.3. Changes in
PWC$_{170}$ scores when
19 experienced and 10
novice subjects were
tested and then retested
24 hours later. (Data
from Watson and
O'Donovan 1976.)

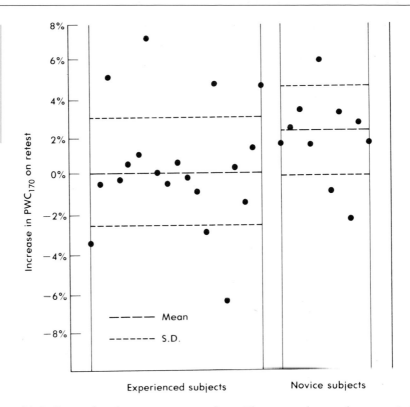

Figure 5.3. Changes in PWC$_{170}$ scores when 19 experienced and 10 novice subjects were tested and then retested 24 hours later. (Data from Watson and O'Donovan 1976.)

this indicates that the errors were random. They were due to chance variations in the measuring instruments, or the way that they were read by the observer, or in the physiology of the subjects. The standard deviation of the changes was ±3 per cent. Statistical tables indicate that 95 per cent of all scores would be expected to lie within +2 standard deviation of the mean. Thus, in the case of this particular test 95 per cent of repeat measurements would be expected to be accurate to within ±6 per cent. This is the reliability of this test as carried out in one particular set of circumstances. If the equipment had been in a slightly worse condition, or if the observer had been less skilled or less careful, the error would have been greater. In this case we can be 95 per cent certain that a subject who obtained a score of 1000 units had an actual value somewhere between 940 and 1,060. If he or she took the test again after a period of training and obtained a score of 1050 it would not be justified to conclude that the individual had increased his or her fitness.

The right-hand side of the graph shows the change in score of the school children. The random variations are similar to those for the students but in these subjects there is also a systematic error because the mean change in score is greater than zero. Systematic errors move all scores in the same direction. They can be due to a variety of causes, including changes in the subjects, the equipment, or the administration of the test.

A second method of quantifying testing error, and one that is easier to compute, is by calculating the Standard Error (SE):

$$SE = SD_y . \sqrt{1 - r^2}$$

where SD_y is the standard deviation of the retest measurements and r is the test–retest correlation coefficient.

In the example in Figure 5.10 the standard error of the Margaria power test is $0.074\,\text{kp}\,\text{m}\,\text{s}^{-1}\,\text{kg}^{-1}$. Sixty-eight per cent of repeat measurements are within ± 1 standard error and 95 per cent are within ± 2 standard errors. Thus the 95 per cent confidence limit for this test is $\pm 0.148\,\text{kp}\,\text{m}\,\text{s}^{-1}\,\text{kg}^{-1}$. This is the absolute error of the measurement; it is expressed in the same units as the measurement itself. The percentage error of the test is

$$\text{Percentage error} = \frac{\text{Absolute error}}{\text{Mean score}} \times 100$$

which in the example is 7.12 per cent.

Figure 5.4. *Upper graph*: Test–retest correlation of 0.241 and a standard error of 3.68. *Lower graph*: The addition of just two more points to the graph raises the correlation coefficient to 0.952 while the standard error remains almost unchanged at 4.83. This is because the test–retest correlation is influenced by the range of scores in addition to their reliability. For this reason it is not a satisfactory measure of reliability and its use for this purpose should be discontinued.

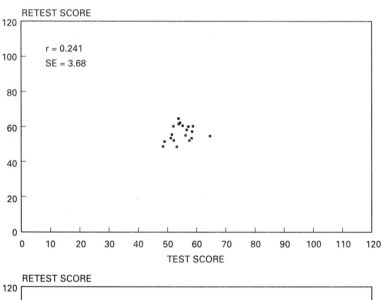

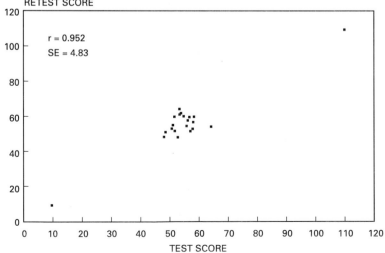

Reliability is often expressed as the test–retest correlation but this is not a satisfactory way of stating experimental error for two reasons:

1 The test–retest correlation is as much influenced by the spread of scores as by their reliability. This is illustrated in the two graphs in Figure 5.4.
2 No indication of the absolute or percentage errors is provided so that correlation coefficients are difficult to interpret.

An appreciation of the concept of measurement error is essential for anyone attempting to measure or interpret fitness variables. Testers should determine the reliability of any measurements they take by carrying out a test–retest on a group of at least 20 subjects. The standard error, 95 per cent confidence limits and percentage error should then be computed.

The following points will help to maximise the reliability of fitness tests:

1 Calibrate all instruments before each testing session.
2 Rigorously standardise the measuring techniques used.
3 Record all observations immediately.
4 Standardise the testing location and the kit and footwear worn by the subjects. For some tests the laboratory should provide standardised kit for the subjects to wear.
5 Take repeat measurements at the same time of day.
6 Standardise the temperature and humidity of the testing environment.
7 Do not carry out tests on subjects who have just eaten or taken previous exercise.
8 Follow a consistent organisational procedure in terms of the number of subjects tested at a time, the presence or absence of observers, etc., otherwise the level of motivation may vary.
9 Standardise the amount of warm-up and practice allowed.
10 Record precise details of the test protocol and measuring techniques for future use. A photograph is a useful way of doing this.

Figure 5.5. Example of a calibration curve. The gas flow rate obtained from a flow head is plotted on the vertical axis against the actual flow rate on the horizontal axis. Once a calibration curve has been plotted it can be used to convert the output from a measuring instrument to a true reading. In this example flow-head outputs of 102 and $200\,l\,min^{-1}$ correspond to true flow rates of 92 and $240\,l\,min^{-1}$ respectively.

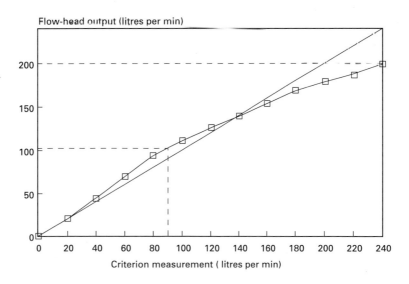

Figure 5.6. Calibration of (a) an electronic spirometer using a 1 litre syringe, and (b) a beam balance using known weights. The weights used for weight training are not always of the mass specified on them and must themselves be calibrated using a known standard.

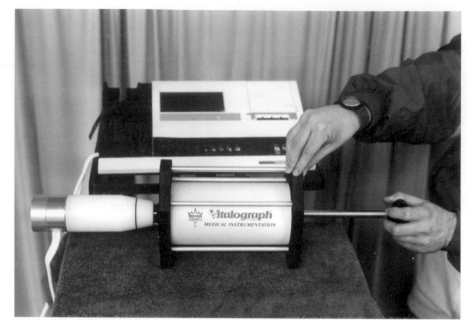

(a)

(b)

The calibration of the instruments used for fitness tests is of great importance as many exhibit systematic errors. The effects of such errors can be removed by the use of a calibration curve, as shown in Figure 5.5 (see also Figure 5.6).

Training programmes for individuals undertaking fitness testing

The acquisition of an acceptable level of skill in fitness evaluation is a long process. A detailed and sound knowledge of human physiology is a prerequisite. Specific training should then begin with the theory of measurement and the statistical treatment of results and errors. This must be followed by instruction on the procedure for specific fitness tests and their theoretical basis. At least six months of supervised experience in a recognised testing centre is then required. This experience should include the determination of reliability coefficients for all tests likely to be undertaken, and practice in the interpretation of test results. Regular 'refresher' courses are essential. Medical and para-medical courses do not on their own provide skills in fitness assessment: special training is essential. Athletes and coaches are advised to ask detailed questions concerning the qualifications and experience of testers before making use of their services.

Assessment of specific aspects of fitness

Health status of the athlete

Most forms of sport and training are physically demanding and require that participants are free from conditions that place them at risk, or that increase the chances of injury. All coaches, trainers and exercise teachers have a responsibility to ensure that every one under their care will come to no harm through pre-existing medical conditions. It is beyond the scope of this book to enter into a discussion about the implications of various types of clinical problems, and coaches and trainers are advised to consult with the medical officer of their Governing Body of Sport about what is considered to be safe practice.

Some information can be obtained about the health status of an individual from a simple questionnaire, provided that it is answered accurately and honestly. Such a device is often used for intending participants in exercise classes and is the minimum precaution that should be taken prior to the start of a fresh programme of exercise or training. A questionnaire that has been validated, is given below.

PARQ QUESTIONNAIRE

1 Has your doctor ever told you that you have heart trouble?
2 Do you frequently have pains in your chest?
3 Do you often feel faint or suffer from spells of severe dizziness?
4 Has a doctor ever told you that your blood pressure is too high?
5 Has a doctor ever told you that you have a bone or joint problem such as arthritis that has been aggravated by exercise?
6 Is there a good physical reason why you should not follow an exercise programme?
7 Are you over 65 and not accustomed to vigorous exercise?

Subjects who make a positive response to any of the above questions should obtain medical advice before taking up an exercise programme.

A more comprehensive questionnaire that may be suitable for those taking up more demanding activities is given below.

HEALTH QUESTIONNAIRE

1   Are you suffering from any chronic disease?
2   Do you frequently suffer from pains in your chest?
3   Do you have high blood pressure?
4   Do you often have headaches, feel faint or have spells of severe dizziness?
5   Have you had an operation or a serious illness in the last 6 months?
6   Are you presently suffering from, or recovering from, an illness or injury?
7   Are you presently on any form of medication?
8   Are you presently being treated by a doctor?
9   Have you ever been unconscious as a result of an accident or from unknown causes?
10   Do you suffer from joint or bone pains?
11   Do you have serious difficulty with coordination or balance?
12   Have you suffered from the same sports injury (such as a sprained ankle) several times in the last 3 years?
13   Has your body weight changed by more than 5 kg in the last 12 months?
14   Do you lack one of the following organs: eye, kidney, oviduct, testicle?
15   Are you over 35 and unaccustomed to vigorous exercise?

Subjects making a positive response to one or more of the above questions are advised to consult a physician before beginning any demanding programme of physical activity.

For participants in top-level sport the medical requirements are more stringent. This grade of competition and training places greater demands on the body of the athlete so that it is important to detect and correct any deficiencies or latent problems. Even minor clinical abnormalities are capable of disturbing the finely balanced equilibrium of the athlete. This will result in a significant degradation of performance. The stresses of travel to competition and any changes in climate and diet will tend to exacerbate minor medical problems. It is thus essential that the athlete be in an optimum state of health before embarking upon top-level sport. He or she should be assessed on a regular basis by a specialist in the health care of athletes.

Measurement of strength

As discussed on page 23, most sports involve a complex interaction of different types of muscular contraction that often take place at high speed. In most cases the forces developed, and thus the strength of the athlete, can be estimated only by means of a complex biomechanical analysis of the action. Such procedures are available in only a few research laboratories and have been applied to only a handful of specific movements.

Presently available measures of strength quantify the forces developed in movements that are important components of the activities undertaken by athletes. Such measures may be of isometric, isotonic, or isokinetic aspects of strength. All three are capable of supplying useful information provided that the measurements selected are of relevance to the athlete's sport. This must be determined by the tester in consultation with the athlete and his or her coach. There are at present no universally agreed strength tests that are applicable to different sports. Some of the various types of strength assessment available are discussed below.

The cable tensiometer

This (Figure 5.7) is a universal dynamometer that can be used to measure almost any aspect of isometric strength. One end of the cable is securely fixed to the floor or a wall while the other end is attached to the subject via a harness. The forces developed in either single- or multi-joint actions can be measured. In single-joint measurements a rigid bench, or other support for the subject, is required and it is also necessary to standardise the joint angle at which each measurement is taken.

In comparison with some other strength-measuring devices the cable tensiometer is inexpensive and well within the budget of even the humblest laboratory or club. It is capable of reproducible measurements of isometric strength. The instrument has two disadvantages: (1) the dial is small and difficult to read with accuracy, and (2) isometric strength is not a good predictor of performance at very high speeds of movement. Both these problems can be overcome in electronic versions of the instrument

Figure 5.7. The cable tensiometer. (A) secure hook in wall, (B) cable, (C) tensiometer, (D) harness.

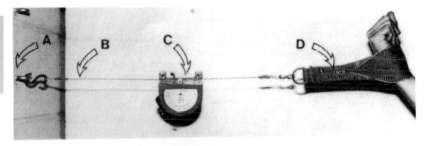

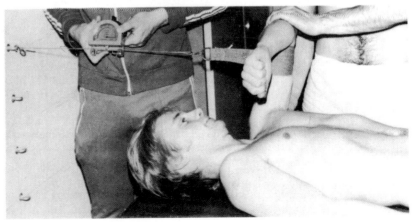

Figure 5.8. Battery of basic cable tensiometer tests.

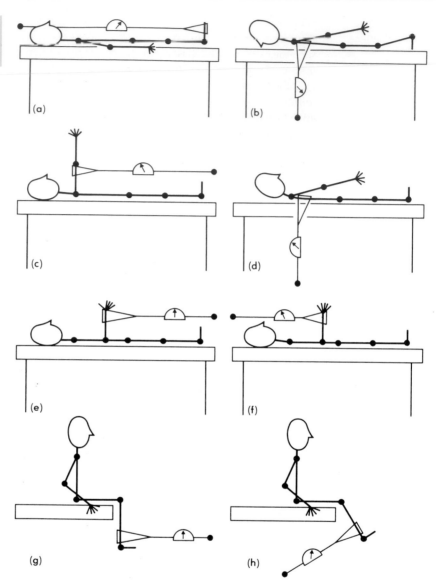

where it is possible to measure the rate of force production (Alen *et al.* 1984). See Figure 5.8.

Isokinetic testing devices

Isokinetic testing devices are able to measure strength at one or more selected speeds of movement. A dozen or more such machines are now available and they differ from other strength-measuring instruments by constituting almost a self-contained strength-testing laboratory. Most come complete with a high-speed force transducer, seats and benches to secure the subject, fittings that allow almost any single-joint action – and some multi-joint actions – to be examined, and a computer with dedicated software that is capable of recording and analysing power and acceleration as well as force and strength. They are extremely convenient to use but only one aspect of strength is measured at a time and the administration of a battery of several tests can be very time consuming.

Isokinetic machines are very expensive and their use is confined to specialist testing centres and clinical units where much of the pioneering work was carried out on injury rehabilitation. The tests that are available to the athlete are only those that such centres are willing to carry out: in many the range offered is extremely limited. There are also other disadvantages. Only one or two of the most modern machines allow strength to be tested at speeds as high as those occurring in most land-based sports. And at the higher speeds of movement the measurement is truly isokinetic only over a fraction of the range of movement. None of the machines presently available replicates the high speed and complex interaction of different types of contraction of different muscle groups that occur in most sports.

Isokinetic strength-testing machines are contributing to our knowledge of the development of strength and power. Such machines provide useful information in the hands of skilled interpreters. But the data presently available is not yet sufficient to provide any generalised advice on strength assessment and training in the majority of sports (Klausen 1990; Sale 1992b).

Lifting weights

One repetition maximum (1 RM) tests are a very useful measure of strength. They can be carried out either with free weights or on a weights machine – equipment that is freely available to most athletes and coaches. Lifts should be selected that have relevance to the athlete's sport; data obtained then provides useful information about the training needs of the subject. 1 RM tests are a very sensitive way of following the effects of strength training that is carried out using weights.

Muscular endurance tests

The number of repetitions of exercises such as chins, dips and sit-ups that can be performed in a given period – usually 30 or 60 seconds – is sometimes used as an indication of strength. Strictly, these are tests of muscular endurance rather than strength but the two are closely related. Such tests are a very inexact way of quantifying strength, but they are easy to carry out and cost the athlete nothing. Their validity is greatest in individuals who have not recently undertaken strength training. In such a situation their precision is often sufficient to place individuals into categories such as 'satisfactory' and 'unsatisfactory'.

Jumps, vertical jump, etc.

Performance on the vertical jump provides a useful indication of leg strength and power. There are many variations on this simple test – chiefly concerning the use of the arms. There are also a number of devices to assist in measuring the subject's score – head boards, photo cells and tapes that are extended during the jump. Apart from the reflection on leg power, jumping ability is important in many sports and the test is useful for this reason alone.

A number of other types of jump have also been used as a measure of leg power. These include jumping while holding a barbell on the shoulders (weights as high as 180 kg have been used; Hakkinen *et al.* 1987) and *depth jumps*. In this test the subject jumps up as high as possible after first jumping down from a height of between 200 mm and 1 metre (Komi 1984). This type of jump is influenced by the energy stored in the series and parallel elastic components of muscle, due to the initial depth jump. Such tests are a logical way of examining the stretch-shortening cycle that occurs in most activities, but particularly in jumping and throwing. However such jumps can be extremely hazardous and should not be attempted without taking the precautions observed by the originators of these tests.

Other methods: Clinical and anthropometric

Strength is a complex phenomenon. Even the simplest movement involves the cooperation of so many different muscles that it is usually impossible to test each one quantitatively. A clinical examination of the athlete's joints and muscles – observation, palpatation and measurement against a resistance – often provides valuable information about muscle development and balance that is impossible to obtain in any other way.

Power

Power is the rate at which work is done; or force multiplied by speed. It is a crucial determinant of athletic performance: of considerably more significance than strength. The power that the human can develop declines with the duration of the effort. This is due to the involvement of different energy sources. Power tests are available that last from a fraction of a second up to several minutes (Figure 5.9). When selecting one for an athlete it is important to match its duration to that of the period of maximum effort during competition. For example, the maximum effort for throwers, footballers and rowers varies between a fraction of a second and several minutes.

Power is also specific to combinations of muscle groups and to their mode of action in particular activities. A sports-specific ice-skating power test has been developed, and others have been proposed for cycling, boxing, football, skiing, baseball, softball and basketball power. This is an area ripe for further research and there is an urgent need for the development and evaluation of further power tests that are specific to particular sports. In such tests power can either be measured directly or be estimated from such variables as the distance covered, speed attained, or the length of time that a particular intensity of work can be maintained. The characteristics of some more general power tests are described below.

Margaria power test The subject runs up a flight of about 12 steps. Photocells or switch mats are placed on the third and ninth steps and the subject is timed through a vertical distance of about

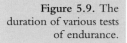

Figure 5.9. The duration of various tests of endurance.

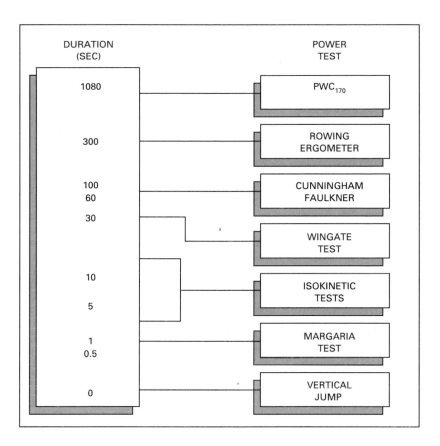

1 metre. The test works best if the run-up is confined to a horizontal distance of 2 to 3 metres.

A certain amount of skill is required to bound up a flight of steps two or three at a time and this causes difficulties for some subjects. On the other hand, highly coordinated individuals are able to devise a strategy for 'cheating' the timing device, and this can inflate their scores by 10 per cent or more. The reliability of the test (see Figure 5.10) is optimised if each subject is allowed 10 attempts at the test and power output is then computed from the fastest 5 attempts. Power is computed as follows:

$$\text{Power} = \frac{\text{Body weight} \times \text{Vertical distance between timing devices}}{\text{Time}}$$

$$\text{Power per kg} = \frac{\text{Body weight} \times \text{Vertical distance between timing devices}}{\text{Time} \times \text{Body weight}}$$

$$= \frac{\text{Vertical distance between timing devices}}{\text{Time}}$$

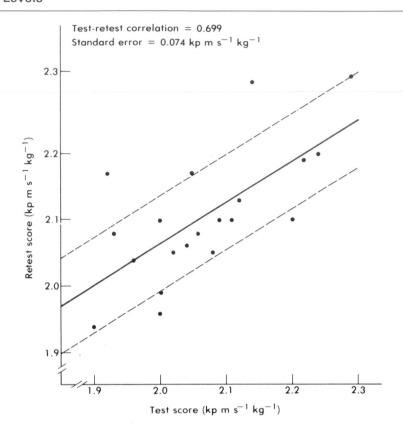

Test-retest correlation = 0.699
Standard error = 0.074 kp m s^{-1} kg^{-1}

Retest score (kp m s^{-1} kg^{-1})

Test score (kp m s^{-1} kg^{-1})

Figure 5.10. Reliability of the Margaria power test. Retest scores are plotted on the vertical axis against the test scores on the horizontal axis. The test–retest correlation is only 0.699 but this is due to the narrow range of scores in this group of subjects. The 95 per cent confidence limits of the test is within ±7 per cent.

30-second Wingate test This is one of the most widely used tests of anaerobic power and can be performed with either the arms or the legs. The subject pedals or cranks an ergometer as fast as possible and after a few seconds an appropriate resistance is added. Revolutions of the ergometer flywheel are electronically recorded and from this, and the magnitude of the resistance, instantaneous power output is computed. Results are normally reported as

1 *Mean power* The average power over the 30 seconds of the test.
2 *Peak power* The maximum power generated over a period of 5 seconds.
3 *Fatigue index* $100(P_p - P_{min}) . P_p^{-1}$, where P_p is the peak power and P_{min} is the lowest power output recorded over 5 seconds of the test.

Jump tests Various forms of vertical jump can be used either as a direct measure or as an estimation of anaerobic power. These include

1 Standard vertical jump. The height of the jump is used as an estimation of power, or power is computed from jump height and body weight.
2 Vertical jump, in which 'flight time' is measured by means of a photo cell or a switch mat. Power is then computed from flight time and body mass.

3   60 second vertical jump test (Bosco *et al.* 1983). Consecutive maximal vertical jumps are performed for a period of 60 seconds. Power is computed from the total flight time during this period.

$$\text{Power} = \frac{g^2 \cdot T_f \cdot 60}{4n(60 - T_f)}$$

where g is the acceleration due to gravity, n is the number of jumps in 60 seconds and T_f is the total flight time.

4   Depth jumps.

5   Jumps with weights.

Aerobic capacity

There are two types of adaptation to aerobic training: **central**, involving mainly changes in blood volume and control of the circulation, and **peripheral**, which take place in and around individual skeletal muscle fibres. Central adaptations to aerobic training occur earlier than those of peripheral origin and are also easier to detect. They do not depend upon the mode of exercise used for training and are apparent regardless of whether the subject is tested during the course of running on a treadmill, cycling or swimming. In contrast, peripheral changes are extremely sensitive to the mode of exercise. For example, they may be detectable in a cyclist only if that individual exercises at racing pace on his or her own machine: they may not be obvious if the subject is tested on the standard laboratory bicycle ergometer or using any other mode of exercise.

The consequence of the above is that it is relatively easy to measure aerobic fitness, and changes that occur with training, in unconditioned individuals. Tests that do not actually measure oxygen uptake, but that estimate it from heart rate or other variables, may be quite satisfactory However, in athletes who use one particular mode of exercise for training, changes in aerobic capacity are detectable only when the athlete is tested using that form of exercise. Over the last 10 years greater efforts have been made to simulate various forms of exercise in the laboratory. Special ergometers that mimic the action of kyaking, rowing, and various forms of skiing have been developed. Swimming flumes and tethered swimming are also used more widely.

Maximum oxygen uptake

Determinations of maximum oxygen uptake are undertaken while the subject exercises on an ergometer at a gradually increasing rate while his or her oxygen consumption is measured. This increases with work load and gradually reaches a plateau, as is illustrated in Figure 5.11. The maximum value is recorded as the subject's maximum oxygen uptake.

In theory, $\dot{V}_{O_2max}$ should reach a plateau and then remain steady. In practice, fluctuations occur and it is then necessary to make an arbitrary decision as to the maximum value. Several different criteria for establishing this have been proposed by different groups of workers, and Glassford *et al.* (1965) found only 50 per cent of common variance between three standard protocols for the measurement of $\dot{V}_{O_2max}$.

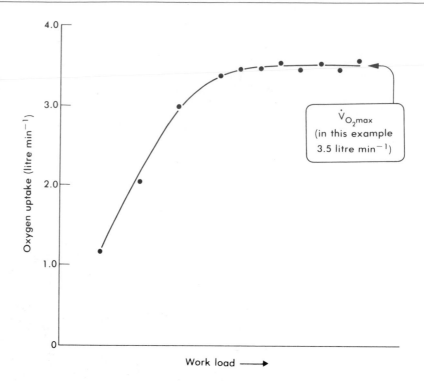

Figure 5.11 The oxygen intake of a subject at increasing work loads. The value eventually reaches a plateau known as the 'maximum oxygen uptake' or $\dot{V}_{O_2max}$.

There are two technical difficulties with the measurement of maximum oxygen uptake. The accurate measurement of gas volumes at high flow rates, and the measurement of the oxygen concentration of the air that is expired by the subject. During maximum exercise the oxygen extracted amounts to only 2–5 per cent of the total volume of air. This means that the effect of any error in gas analysis is multiplied 20–50 times when the oxygen uptake is computed. The collection of gases also presents difficulties. It is not easy to avoid leaks and the design and construction of mouthpieces and valve units can have an important influence on the measured uptake of the subject (Figure 5.12).

Oxygen uptake measurements and other forms of gas analysis are now frequently carried out using integrated analysers, which are currently produced by a number of different manufacturers. The measurement of gas volumes and flow rates, oxygen and carbon dioxide analysis and the computation and storage of results are all carried out automatically by such devices. They have, however, advantages and disadvantages. Plus points are that automatic analysers are compact, and are quicker and easier to use than the older methods. They are also capable of breath-by-breath analyses and the study of short-term responses to changes in exercise intensity. On the other hand, gas flow measurements made during maximum exercise may be suspect. This is a serious problem as this is precisely the situation in which greatest accuracy is required. The 'black box' approach to gas analysis of these instruments masks potential problems which would identify themselves with the older methods. It also encourages operation by individuals who lack experience of classical gas analysis and this is a serious constraint on the accuracy of the test.

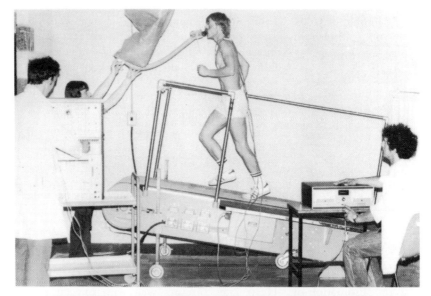

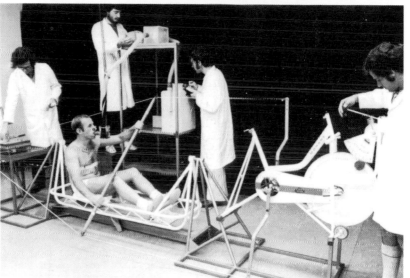

Figure 5.12. Determination of maximum oxygen uptake: (*top*) during running on a treadmill; (*bottom*) during simulated kyaking. (Photograph by kind permission of Dr F.S. Pike.)

Under ideal conditions the reliability of determinations of maximum oxygen uptake is of the order of ±6 per cent. But it is unlikely that this accuracy is often achieved. In an attempt to investigate systematic errors in oxygen analysis Cotes and Woolmer (1962) had a cylinder of gas analysed for oxygen content by six laboratories that specialised in this type of work. The differences found would have resulted in variations of $\dot{V}_{O_2max}$ of 25 per cent. Bonjer (1966) found similar errors in Dutch laboratories. When the effects of differences in gas collection equipment and experimental procedures are added to these errors of gas analysis the variations in $\dot{V}_{O_2max}$ may be very large indeed.

Anaerobic or lactic threshold

In already well-trained athletes changes in oxygen uptake as a result of further training are very small and difficult to detect. Shifts in the lactate threshold (anaerobic threshold) are usually a more sensitive guide to the effects of aerobic training in such individuals. Since there is a lack of agreement over many issues concerning the concept of anaerobic threshold, it is not surprising that there are many different views about how this variable should be measured. At the simplest level the anaerobic threshold is the intensity of exercise at which lactate begins to accumulate in blood. It therefore represents a point of inflexion in the curve obtained when lactate concentration is plotted against work load. In order to determine the anaerobic threshold it is necessary to measure the concentration of lactate at a number of different work loads. At least six readings are required – three before the point of inflexion and three after – but a larger number is preferable. Time is required for lactate to diffuse from muscle into blood and from 3 to 5 minutes of steady-state exercise is necessary at each work load.

Estimation of maximum oxygen uptake

Heart rate correlates well with oxygen uptake during progressive exercise and maximum heart rate occurs at about the same work load as maximum oxygen uptake (Astrand and Rodahl 1986). These facts form the basis of a number of tests used for *estimating* $\dot{V}_{O_2max}$ or for assessing aerobic fitness from submaximal exercise tests. The original test is due to Astrand and Rhyming (1954) and still works well. The subject exercises on a bicycle ergometer, as described for the PWC_{170} test, except that only one work load is used. This should be selected so as to produce a final heart rate of between 125 and 170 beats per minute. Maximum oxygen uptake is then estimated from the heart rate during the final 60 seconds of exercise using the nomogram in Figure 5.13.

PWC_{170}

PWC_{170} is the work capacity of the individual when his or her heart rate is 170 beats per minute. As described below, the test has greater validity and reliability than others that employ only one heart-rate measurement and is recommended as a submaximal test of aerobic capacity. It is highly correlated to maximum oxygen uptake (Cumming and Danziger 1963; Knutten 1967) and is more sensitive to changes in the aerobic capacity of children than $\dot{V}_{O_2max}$ (Daniels *et al.* 1978).

PWC_{170} is measured by having the subject exercise at three different work loads on a bicycle ergometer (Figure 5.14). The steady-state heart rate is measured at each work load and then plotted against work load, as shown in Figure 5.15. The best straight line is then drawn through the three points and the work load that corresponds to a heart rate of 170 beats per minute is read off.

Several precautions are necessary:

1   The ergometer must be maintained in good mechanical condition and the force scale zeroed at the start of each test.
2   The pedalling rate of the subject and the force setting must be checked once each minute throughout the test.

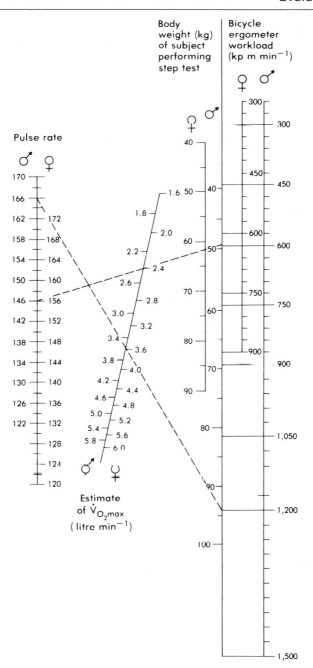

Figure 5.13. Nomogram for estimating maximum oxygen uptake from pulse rate during exercise on the bicycle ergometer, or during a step test. The subject's exercise heart rate is joined to the workload (bicycle ergometer test) or to body weight (step test) and the estimate of maximum oxygen uptake read off from the centre scale. In the examples, a female of body weight 61 kg has a heart rate of 156 on the step test; her estimated $\dot{V}_{O_2max}$ is 2.4 litre min^{-1}. A male working with a heart rate of 166 at a work load of 1,200 kp m min^{-1} has an estimated $\dot{V}_{O_2max}$ of 3.6 litre min^{-1}. (From Astrand, I. *Acta Physiol. Scand.* 1960, 49 suppl. 169, by kind permission.)

3 The test should not be carried out following a meal or after a period of heavy exercise.
4 The subject should work for 6 minutes at each work load or until his or her heart rate becomes steady.
5 The subject should wear a minimum of light clothing and be cooled by a fan. The testing environment must be cool and the relative humidity low.

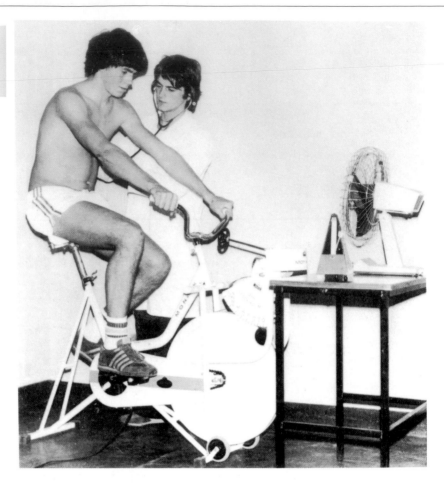

Figure 5.14.
Measuring PBC_170
during work on a
bicycle ergometer.

6   Steps should be taken to put the subject at ease and to reduce apprehension, otherwise the heart rate may be artificially elevated.

Failure to observe precautions 3, 5 and 6 may lead to low results. Under ideal conditions the PWC_{170} test is reproducible to within ± 6 per cent (see Figure 5.3). It is possible to shorten the test by the use of shorter exercise periods or fewer work loads but the reliability is then reduced (Watson and O'Donovan 1976).

Run tests   A number of ways of assessing aerobic capacity using running tests have been described. When used with sedentary subjects, or the untrained, all produce reasonable correlations with laboratory measures of aerobic fitness. All are well capable of placing such subjects into different categories of aerobic fitness. However, none is suitable for following the progress of long-term aerobic training in such non-running activities as cycling, swimming or rowing.

In the 6-minute run–walk test and the 12-minute run–walk test the distance covered is used as an estimation of aerobic capacity. The former test has been used

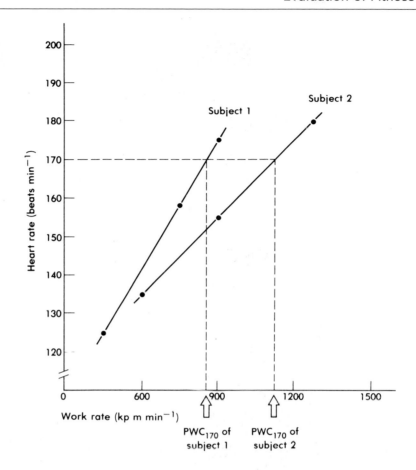

Figure 5.15. Graphical determination of PWC_170. The best straight line is drawn through the three points and the work load that corresponds to a heart rate of 170 beats per minute is the subject's PWC_170.

with children of primary school age: the 12-minute test is more suitable for older subjects. Runs of 1, 1.5 and 3 miles have also been used. With these tests the subject's running time is used as the score. More recently, a 'bleep' test, in which the subjects run at increasingly higher speeds in time with taped 'bleeps', has become very popular. The novelty of the procedure is its chief advantage.

Economy Economy is quantified by measuring the oxygen uptake during work at some submaximal work load that can be maintained by all the subjects. It should be as close as possible to racing pace as economy varies with intensity of effort. For accurate assessments subjects should be measured under field conditions using portable oxygen analysers.

Lung function

During an asthma attack the smooth muscle in the bronchioles contracts, reducing the diameter of the airways. This results in a considerable increase in the resistance to air flow and increases the work of breathing. The condition is common (it affects 10–12

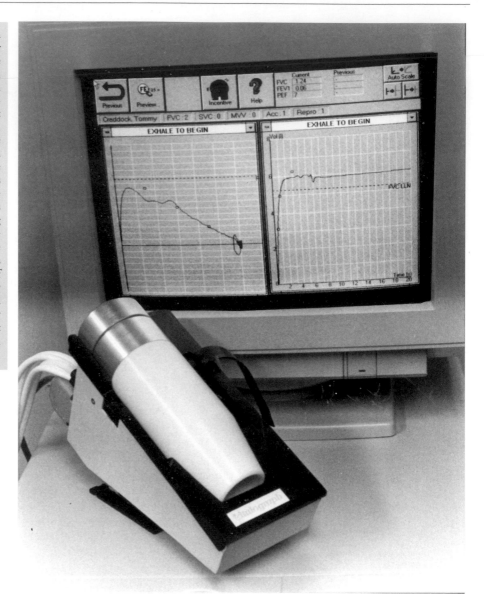

Figure 5.16. A modern electronic spirometer operating on the Fleisch pneumotachograph principle. The flow-head, seen at the front of the photograph, measures pressure changes against a constant resistance when the subject blows into it. These are converted into volumes and flow rates using hardware and software that is located inside the computer. This instrument is capable of responding accurately to the high volume and flow rates generated by athletes. Instrument courtesy of Vitalograph Ltd, Ennis, Ireland.

per cent of the population) and its incidence is rising. At the start of exercise the release of catacholamines normally has the opposite effect – relaxing branchial smooth muscle and dilating the air passages. However, in some individuals it instead produces a degree of asthma which seriously degrades athletic performance. The condition can be detected by measuring inspiratory and expiratory flow rates before and after exercise.

In another 10–15 per cent of athletes lung function is defective due to a number of other factors: weak or badly coordinated respiratory muscles, tightness of the thorax due to lack of flexibility or the presence of posture defects, and other clinical causes. Lung function assessments are capable of identifying such problems but in order for treatment to be prescribed they must be carried out in combination with a number of other assessments that include: (1) the subject's medical history, (2) analysis of respiratory mechanics, (3) evaluation of upper body flexibility and posture, (4) percussion of the chest, and (5) auscultation of the lungs and air passages.

Many lung function tests are available, but for screening athletes the four most useful are: forced vital capacity, peak inspiratory flow rate, peak expiratory flow rate and MVV_{15}. Age-, gender- and size-corrected norms are available for these variables for the general population. For athletes involved in endurance activities, 120 per cent of the norms for non-athletes is a satisfactory score.

Modern spirometers measure volumes and flow rates electronically (Figure 5.16). They are capable of accurate results but require careful calibration prior to the assessment of each individual subject. Many instruments are able to compare test results with built-in age-, gender- and size-corrected norms. Some lung function tests are complex and physically demanding on the subject. It is essential that clear instructions be given and that up to six attempts are allowed at each procedure.

As with other fitness tests, lung function assessments should be carried out only if facilities are available for the correction of any deficiencies that are detected. This may involve the treatment of clinical defects, the modification of training programmes or the provision of special corrective breathing exercises.

Flexibility

There have been few significant developments in the assessment of flexibility over the last two or three decades. While almost all sports involve active movements – which often take place at extremely high speeds – the only readily available procedures for assessing flexibility consist of measuring the extent of static stretches. This fact probably goes some way towards explaining the lack of agreement on the relationship of flexibility to such factors as athletic performance and the incidence of injury in sport. The development of new types of tests is needed. However, tests of static flexibility are all that is available at present.

Static flexibility can be measured either as the distance travelled by a part of the body – as in the sit-and-reach test – or as an angle of movement. The latter is preferable because body segments vary in length. Angles can be measured either with a protractor-like device – often with extensions and then known as **goniometers** – or with variations on the Leighton **flexiometer**. This instrument consists of a counter-weighted pointer that is free to move with respect to a circular scale graduated in degrees. In use the flexiometer is strapped to a limb or segment of the subject's body so that the angle of rotation can be measured. Both instruments have advantages and disadvantages, but with careful use either is capable of satisfactory results.

Flexibility measurements need to reflect the movements that are important in particular athletic activities. Since there are few established procedures, athletes and coaches have an important part to play in selecting measurements that are relevant and in developing new ones that are specific to particular sports. Measuring devices are inexpensive and flexibility assessments need not be confined to specialist laboratories.

When measuring flexibility with devices that are based on protractors the following points should be borne in mind.

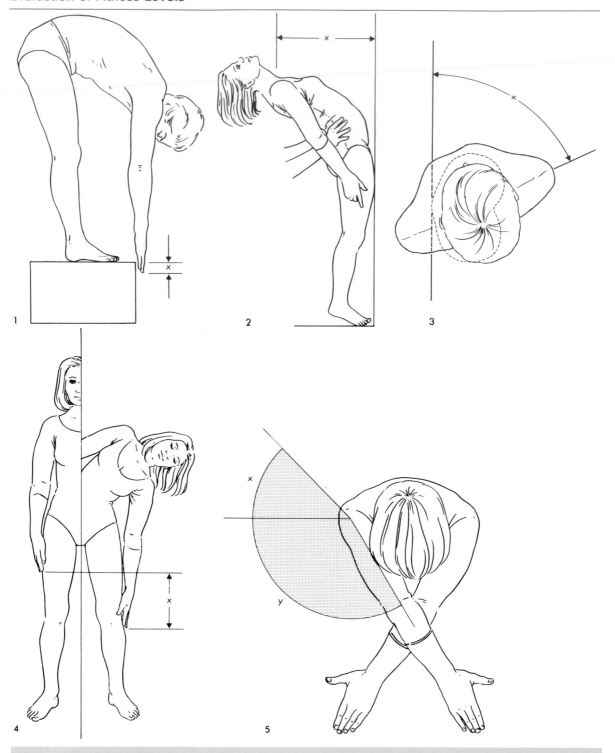

Figure 5.17. A battery of nine basic flexibility tests.

Figure 5.17. Continued.

1 Select measurements relevant to the athlete's sport.

2 Where possible confine measurements to the movement of a single joint.

3 Identify the axis of rotation (which remains stationary), and the point of maximum movement. This can be either a bony prominence or a flesh mark made on the body with a felt tip pen.

4 Ensure that all other parts of the body remain stationary and in a position that is carefully standardised for all subjects and for each test. It is often necessary to support the subject in this position using belts or assistants. Movement of parts of the body not being tested is one of the major errors in flexibility tests. For really accurate work it is necessary to use a specially designed test rig that is equipped with micro-switches to detect extraneous movement.

5 During the test the subject must wear kit that allows observation of (a) the axis of rotation (b) the point of maximum movement (c) all other parts of the body where movement might influence the outcome of the test. For accurate measurements of flexibility it is necessary for subjects to wear swim-wear or leotards.

6 Record the best of two attempts at each test.

7 Flexibility measurements should be taken without a warm-up and before undertaking any other physical activity that might result in an indeterminate amount of muscle stretch.

Measurements of flexibility are less reproducible than many other fitness tests and with even the best assessments the 95 per cent confidence limits may be ±9 to 12 per cent. This is because of the difficulty of preventing movement in other parts of the body and because it is always possible for a subject to stretch 'just a little bit further' if he or she really makes the effort. With inexperienced testers flexibility measurements are often *extremely* inaccurate.

A basic battery of flexibility tests is illustrated in Figure 5.17. These may be supplemented by others that are specific to particular sports.

Accurate measures of flexibility are useful for monitoring the progress of training but they are not always essential. When devising a training programme for an athlete it is often sufficient to identify the areas in which he or she is weak. This can be done subjectively if the tester is clear about what constitutes 'satisfactory' and 'unsatisfactory' flexibility in different areas of the body. Such an assessment can be carried out as part of a clinical examination of the athlete.

Posture and body mechanics

Specialisation in one, or a small number of, activities can produce excessive development and or tightness of some muscle groups which cause posture defects. The risk of certain injuries is then increased. In children and sedentary individuals poor posture is more likely to be due to weak muscles, particularly those of the chest, upper back, shoulders and abdomen.

The more obvious posture defects that are likely to cause problems in sport can be identified using the chart illustrated in Figure 5.18.

Great care must be taken with assessments of posture or the subject will be misled or even alarmed. The subject should stand on a level floor that is at right angles to a wall on which vertical and horizontal lines are marked. The observer requires

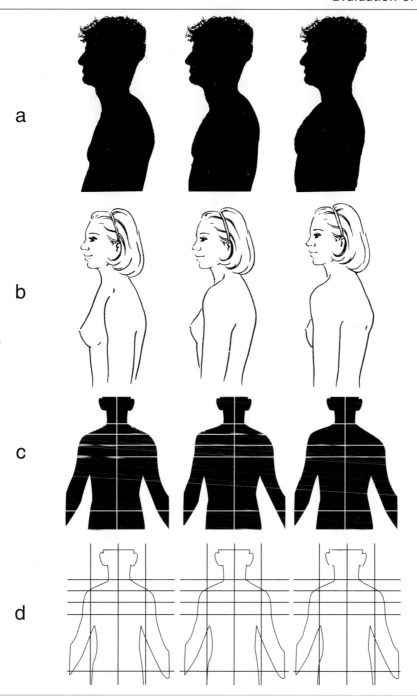

Figure 5.18. Diagrams for the evaluation of posture in athletes. With the exception of (g) the left-hand diagram illustrates ideal posture (a score of 5), the middle diagram a moderate deviation (a score of 3) and the right hand diagram a major deviation (a score of 1). In (g) going from left to right the diagrams correspond to the following scores: – male = 3, female = 1; male = 5, female = 3; male = 3, female = 5; male = 1, female = 3. Diagram (h) illustrates outward deviations of the foot. Inward deviations are also possible and are scored on the same scale.

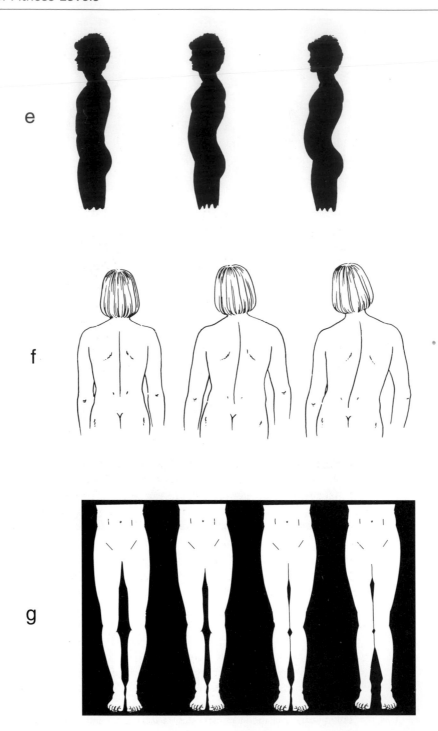

Figure 5.18. continued.

h

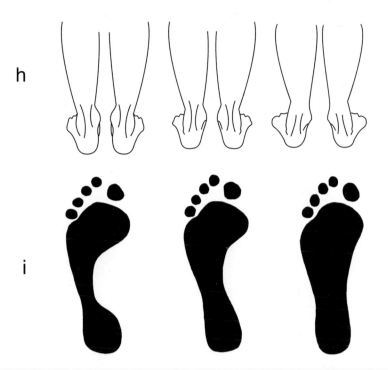

i

Figure 5.18. continued

considerable experience and a good knowledge of human anatomy. When carefully carried out such evaluations can be very reliable. Using the chart illustrated in Figure 5.18, 78 per cent of measurements were reproducible within ±1 unit and 53 per cent were within ±0.5 unit. Assessments made from a photographic print, as described below, had greater accuracy: 95 per cent of measurements were reproducible within ±1 unit and 71 per cent were within ±0.5 unit.

More subtle imbalances may cause problems in individuals who are involved at a high level in particular activities. Their effects have been documented in rowing, running, soccer, football, hurling, diving and basketball. They can be most easily quantified from accurate photographic prints on which a metric grid has been super imposed. An example of this technique is illustrated in Figure 5.19.

The quadriceps or 'Q' angle is the acute angle that is formed by the intersection of two straight lines: (1) from the superior anterior iliac spine to the centre of the patella and (2) from the tibial tubercule to the centre of the patella. It is difficult to measure this angle directly and it can be more easily assessed from a high-quality photographic print.

The overall muscle development and balance of a subject can be assessed at the same time that posture is examined. Again, different areas can be rated on a five-point scale. In the absence of published standards such assessments are hardly quantitative, but they are quick to carry out and do not involve the use of expensive equipment.

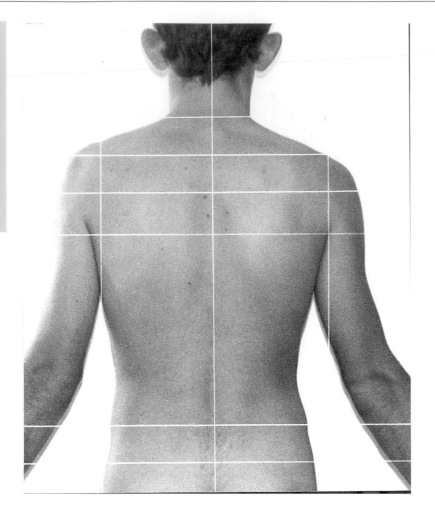

Figure 5.19. Posture photograph on which a metric grid has been superimposed. This technique is useful for quantifying asymmetric development of the muscles that frequently lead to overuse injuries. In the illustration the left shoulder is higher than the right and lateral back muscles are better developed on the right hand side.

They can provide information that is not presently available from even the most sophisticated strength tests. Such assessments are of particular value to athletes involved in field games and other team sports.

Body composition
Body mass index

Body mass index has been widely used in epidemiological studies on mortality and morbidity. It is computed as follows:

$$\text{Body mass index} = \frac{\text{Weight}}{\text{Height}^2}$$

where height is measured in metres and weight in kg.

The World Health Organisation classifies the body mass index for adult males and females as follows:

	Males	*Females*
Underweight	<20.1	<18.7
Acceptable	20.1–25.0	18.7–23.8
Overweight	25.1–29.9	23.9–28.5
Obese	>30.0	>28.6

Body mass index provides a crude indication of body fatness in untrained adults where excesses of body weight are likely to be due to reserves of fat. It is quite unsuitable for use with athletes because it does not differentiate between fat and lean tissue. Many power event athletes and field games players record body mass indexes as high as 27 or more, despite having less than 10 per cent of fat.

Estimation of body fat content

It is not possible to measure the amount of fat in the body of a living human. As a result, a number of different procedures have been devised for its estimation. These include: measurement of body density by weighing the individual in air and under water, body density from weight and body volume, estimation of muscle mass by counting radiation from whole body potassium, measurement of whole body water from the dilution of tracer drugs or radioactive isotopes, measurement of the electrical conductance of the body, anthropometric measurements, X-rays, ultrasonics and skinfold thicknesses. The great proliferation of methods suggest that none is wholly satisfactory, and this is indeed the case. While it is possible to measure the thickness of subcutaneous fat layers reliably, the problem arises in the conversion of such data into an estimate of overall fatness.

Estimation of body density by underwater weighing used to be the method of choice for quantifying body fat. The procedure does not measure fat directly and is based on a number of assumptions first formulated by Keys and Brozek (1953) and Siri (1961). They include the following presumptions:

1   The human body can be divided into two compartments: fat and non-fat tissue.
2   The density of the fat and non-fat tissue remains constant at about 0.9 and 1.1 g ml^{-1} respectively, both in different individuals and in the same individual before and after a programme of training.

More recent investigations show that the second assumption is wildly optimistic, especially in the context of the adaptations that occur in those involved in sport. Reports of investigations carried out on human cadavers show wide variations in density due to differences in the amount of muscle tissue, and also the amount and density of bone (Clarys *et al.* 1984; Martin *et al.* 1986; Mazess *et al.* 1984). Since exercise is likely to change both the amount of muscle and the amount and mineralization of bone, the assumption of a constant density for the fat-free component of the body is not tenable (Figure 5.20). Thus estimates of fatness made from body density should not be given undue credence and simpler procedures may give results that are just as good.

Figure 5.20. Changes in body weight, fat content and fat–free weight: (a) body weight remained constant due to the gain in fat-free weight being equal to the loss in fat content; (b) the rise in fat content was the same as the loss in fat-free weight and body weight again remained constant; (c) a loss in weight due to a reduction in fat content; (d) loss of fat but a greater increase in fat–free weight – the outcome of a successful training programme.

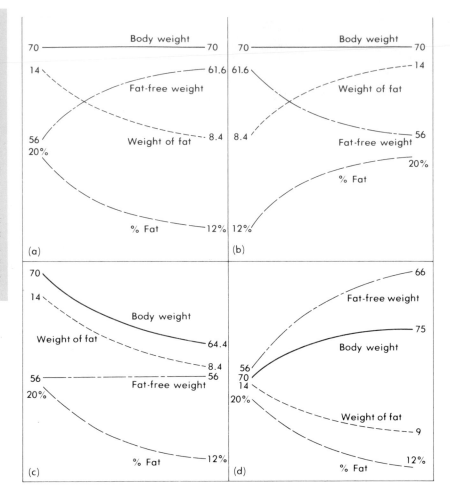

Estimates from skinfold thicknesses have been most widely studied. They work best when the prediction equations have been developed on a population that is similar to the subjects being measured; and when skinfolds are measured on at least six different sites. Attempts have also been made to develop 'generalised equations' that give reasonable results on a range of different subjects. An example is given below (from Jackson and Pollock 1978).

For males:

$$\% \text{ Fat} = 0.29288 \left(\sum \text{SF} \right) - 0.0005 \left(\sum \text{SF} \right)^2 + 0.15845 (\text{AGE}) - 5.7637$$

For females:

$$\% \text{ Fat} = 0.29669 \left(\sum \text{SF} \right) - 0.00043 \left(\sum \text{SF} \right)^2 + 0.02963 (\text{AGE}) - 1.4072$$

where $\sum \text{SF}$ is the sum of the following four skinfolds: abdominal, supra–iliac, triceps, front thigh.

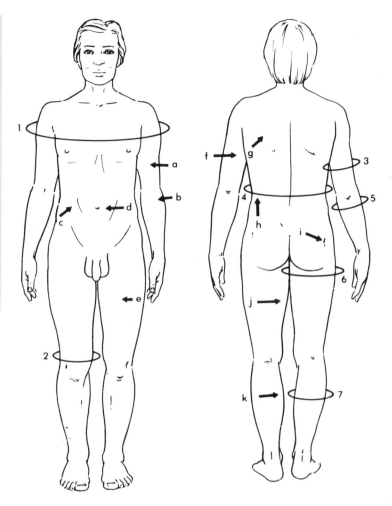

Figure 5.21. Body circumferences and skinfolds. Circumferences: (1) bideltoid; (2) lower thigh; (3) arm; (4) waist; (5) forearm; (6) thigh; (7) calf. Skinfolds: (a) biceps; (b) forearm; (c) supra-iliac; (d) abdominal; (e) front thigh; (f) triceps; (g) subscapular; (h) lower back; (i) gluteal; (j) rear thigh; (k) calf. The skinfolds should be raised at right angles to the direction of the arrow in the diagram, e.g. the abdominal skinfold is vertical.

The following equation was developed on British and Irish males who were actively involved in sport and training. It works very well and is recommended for use with this type of subject.

$$\text{percentage fat} = 29.481 \, \log_{10}(\textstyle\sum \text{six skinfolds}) - 40.101$$

where the six skinfolds are taken on the following sites: triceps, biceps, abdomen, front thigh, lower back, gluteal.

Physique

Physique is a very important determinant of athletic performance, as was discussed in Chapter 1. It provides an indication of potential for different types of sports activity, the potential for muscle development and the tendency to lose or gain body fat. Changes in physique can be used to follow the progress of certain aspects of strength training that are otherwise impossible to measure.

Unfortunately physique is extremely difficult to quantify. This is because the human body is made up of such a large number of different segments that it is impossible to quantify it using only a small number of measurements. The concept of somatype, as developed by Sheldon in the 1940s and 1950s, has proved to be a useful way of classifying physique that has been successfully used in studies on athletes and physical performance variables. The technique has some limitations but it is the most satisfactory, non-statistical, way of quantifying physique. Unfortunately few laboratories now use the method and it is a difficult technique for an investigator to learn.

Readers should not confuse the Sheldon somatype with the so-called **anthropometric somatype**, which is based on the analysis of a small number of anthropometric measurements, rather than the overall shape of the body. Although widely used in studies on athletes, the measurements selected are unfortunate and do not constitute a satisfactory measure of physique. For example, the first component is computed from only three skinfold thicknesses, and the second component (bone-muscle) completely ignores the subject's trunk. The method has been criticised by this and other authors (Malina and Bouchard 1991).

Anthropometric measurements are measures of the lengths and diameters of bones and other segments of the body, the circumferences of muscles and other body segments and of the thickness of skinfolds (Figure 5.21). A large number of such measurements are possible and complex mathematical procedures are necessary in order to analyse the data that result. A detailed description of anthropometric procedures is beyond the scope of this book and readers requiring more information are referred to the following sources: Sheldon (1940, 1954), Weiner and Lourie (1969), Tanner (1964a, 1964b), Malina and Bouchard (1991).

Other issues relating to fitness testing

Management of the feedback of information and advice to athletes

Many different individuals may be concerned with assisting and advising the athlete. In high-level sports squads this may include: team manager, skills coach, fitness coach, one or more sports scientists, physician, one or more medical specialists, physiotherapist, dietician, sports psychologist. Any or all of these individuals may feel qualified to give advice on such matters as diet, flexibility and strength training. In addition, each may have their own agenda concerning the purpose of the tests.

Before any testing programme is undertaken it is important that a procedure be developed for the management of information and advice to the athlete (Figure 5.22), and that each member of the team then adheres to his or her agreed role. Small teams work better than larger ones and, where possible, procedures such as fitness, medical, posture and dietary assessments should be combined. Conflicting advice is worse than no advice at all and must be avoided at all costs. Poorly managed fitness tests remind me of being taught to drive by two uncles who never met. One advised me not to drive so near the centre of the road, while the other felt that my only fault was that I tended to hug the pavement.

Field tests of physical fitness

Field tests are not simply scaled down versions of laboratory tests that are performed *in situ* under conditions that are less than ideal. The best of such procedures are valid attempts to measure aspects of physical fitness as they are manifest during competition in a particular sport.

Laboratory fitness tests seek to measure variables that are known, or assumed, to be relevant to athletic performance. They do so under favourable conditions so that the reliability of such measurements is usually high. During certain tests, such as those of

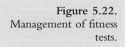

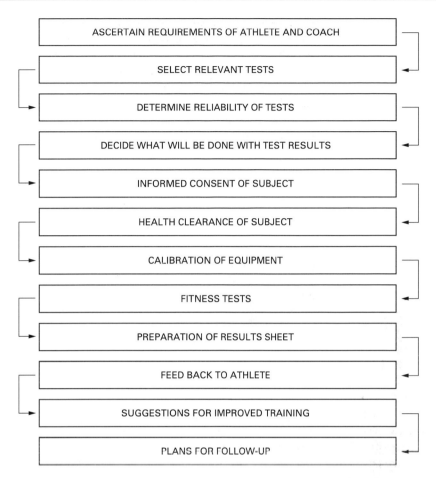

Figure 5.22. Management of fitness tests.

aerobic capacity and power, an attempt is often made to simulate the athletes movement during competition by the use of such devices as swimming flumes and special ergometers. The success of such attempts is very variable. With other aspects of fitness, such as strength and flexibility, laboratory assessments are usually far removed from the actions that occur in practical sporting situations. Thus, although the reliability of laboratory assessments may be high, their validity is often very questionable.

In field tests, measurements are taken during the athlete's normal activity. For example, using portable equipment, oxygen uptake can be measured while rowing outdoors under actual race conditions. The validity of such tests is much greater than with a laboratory assessment. Reliability may sometimes be more problematic due to variations in such external factors as weather conditions, and the lower precision of some portable testing equipment. But advances in electronics are bringing constant improvements and portable equipment is now more accurate than laboratory versions of a few years ago. The fitting of force and movement transducers onto sports equipment offers great potential for the measurement of force, speed and power during training and competition. Output from such devices can be transmitted, recorded and analysed electronically.

Field tests offer particular potential for the study of the fitness exhibited in many team games. These activities involve complex interactions of different varieties of strength, endurance, speed and power – in addition to skill – and laboratory attempts to analyse fitness in such activities has met with very limited success.

The use of portable equipment for the analysis of fitness during field tests offers great potential and is an area of research likely to develop considerably in the future.

Developing your own fitness tests

The limitations of existing tests of flexibility, strength and power have been discussed elsewhere. There is immense scope for the development of fitness tests that measure these variables, and their various combinations, in situations that occur in specific sports. Coaches and athletes with a knowledge of testing are ideally placed to undertake such work as they have an unrivalled knowledge of the demands of particular activities.

When developing a new test the first step is to identify a fitness variable of unique importance in a particular sport. This may be an unusual movement, peculiar to a specific sport, or an expression of strength that involves an unusual combination of muscle groups or types of contraction. It may even be a burst of power that uses a unique combination of energy sources. Whatever is selected as the basis of the test, to be of value it must be diagnostic and of practical value to the athlete in suggesting a way that training can be improved. If the test is either too general or too sports specific it will provide no new information at all. Measuring speed over 100 metres is unlikely to assist a sprinter; however, a 20 metre speed test might be of value to a field game player.

The next step is to develop a test that measures the new fitness variable. Precise instruction for the conduct of the test need to be drawn up so that the procedure is reproducible. Finally, the reliability of the new test needs to be established by carrying out repeat measurements on a typical group of at least 20 subjects.

If the test is reliable and its results are predictive of performance in the sport for which it was devised, it is a valuable fitness test suitable for use with other groups who are involved in the same activity.

Assessment of fitness: Summary

1 Many athletes and coaches have had unsatisfactory experiences regarding fitness assessments and, as a result, have little confidence in such evaluations.

2 The proliferation of testing centres staffed by individuals who lack satisfactory qualifications means that the above situation is unlikely to improve in the short term.

3 Many variables that are measured in fitness assessments have no direct relationship to performance in individual sports.

4 Athletic performance is mediated by a complex interaction of different physiological parameters so that the interpretation of test results is difficult and requires great skill.

5 There is a need to develop sports–specific field tests of physical fitness for individual sports.

6 Despite the above comments, physiological testing can be a valuable aid to the athlete when properly carried out and the results are correctly interpreted.

6 SPORTS INJURIES AND THEIR PREVENTION

Introduction

It is vital that everyone involved in sport be aware of the serious problem of athletic injuries. The incidence of these conditions is rising at such an alarming rate that international bodies like the Council of Europe and the World Health Organisation have expressed the need for effective intervention measures to be implemented. At least part of the reason for this state of affairs is the increasing demands of present-day training programmes and competition schedules. Both competition and training are capable of producing changes in the athlete's body which, if not corrected, substantially increase the risk of injury. The possible consequences of this range from an inability to complete the competition schedule successfully, up to serious and permanent damage to the athlete. The incidence of sports injuries is now so high that training programmes need to be formulated in such a way that injury prevention is a primary objective. The first step in this process involves the development of an awareness of the extent of the problem of sports injuries.

The time-loss caused by sports injuries is considerable. It is underestimated in many published studies because of the way in which the data was collected. The results of a recent investigation into the consequences of sports injuries in Irish sportsmen and women who were engaged in a cross-section of different sports is summarised in Figure 6.1. The data is typical of the situation in most countries.

Figure 6.1. Percentage of the year injured and not injured in 324 sportspeople involved in a cross-section of 10 different sports who were studied over a 12-month period. These subjects suffered from the effects of injuries for 14 per cent of the year; 53 per cent of the time loss was due to over-use injuries and 47 per cent was due to acute injuries. (Data adapted from Watson 1993.)

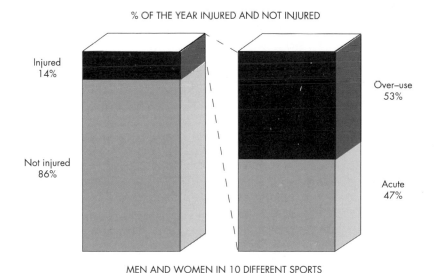

% OF THE YEAR INJURED AND NOT INJURED

Injured 14%

Not injured 86%

Over–use 53%

Acute 47%

MEN AND WOMEN IN 10 DIFFERENT SPORTS

Quantification of sports injuries
Definition of a sports injury

It is surprisingly difficult to define what constitutes a sports injury. There is no universally agreed definition and this makes it extremely difficult to compare data collected in different investigations. Many of the studies are published in medical journals and, in consequence, definitions are often formulated from the point of view of the doctor who carries out treatment rather than the athlete who is the victim of the trauma. In some research only conditions that receive medical attention are counted as 'injuries' (for example, Schafle *et al.* 1990). In other studies medical treatment or a one-week time-loss is demanded (see studies by Ekstrand and Gillquist 1983a, b, c). Other investigators require some time-loss from sport (Albert 1983; Lorentzon *et al.* 1988; Sullivan *et al.* 1980).

All the above definitions are too clinically oriented and too *exclusive* to be adequate descriptions of 'injury' from the standpoint of the athlete or coach. For example, none of them would count, as injured, a marathon runner with shin splints who was forced to cut training to a mile per day at half pace – provided he or she did not go to see a doctor.

At the other end of the spectrum there are definitions such as 'physical damage caused by a sports related incident', that have been used by researchers such as Backx *et al.* (1989), McMaster and Walter (1978) and many others. These are very *inclusive* definitions and have the disadvantages of producing too many injuries that are of little consequence – a gnat bite occurring during a fishing tournament is an extreme example.

From the point of view of the athlete it is the effect upon competition and training that is the crucial consequence of most injuries. A chronic knee or shoulder affliction that restricts performance for months is far more serious to the sports person than a wound that requires a couple of stitches but heals quickly; or a contusion which results in a few days of time-loss but has resolved completely within a week. The definition which comes closest to accommodating this is one used by McLennan and McLennan (1990) and Watson (1993):

Sports injury: *A mishap occurring during sporting activity which results in the inability to train or compete normally.*

Seriousness of injury

The seriousness of an injury is usually quantified in terms of its effects upon the athlete. Death is the most serious possible consequence, followed by some form of permanent disability. The seriousness of other injuries is rated in terms of one the following:

- Amount and nature of the disability sustained
- Implications for the long-term health of the athlete
- Complexity of the treatment necessary
- Cost of treatment and after-care.

Sports injuries without long-term consequences are the most common type, and these are quantified in terms of the number of:

- days in hospital
- days during which training and competition are impossible
- days during which physical activity is restricted.

Risk of injury Studies on sports injuries often seek to make comparisons of the risk of sustaining an injury in different circumstances; for example, the chances of injury in different sports or the risk of injury to athletes of different ages. In some studies statistics are adjusted for different exposure times – usually the number of hours of training and competition. This allows a fairer comparison of the risk of injury in different sports. But it does not take into account differences in the seriousness of injuries occurring in the different activities. One recent study from our own laboratory has attempted to allow for this by quantifying injuries in terms of days of incapacity per 1000 hours of participation (Watson 1993). The characteristics of some commonly used methods of quantifying sports injuries are summarised below.

Number of injuries

The total number of injuries is recorded.
No indication of risk or seriousness is provided.

Risk of injury

1. Number of injuries per month, season or year.
   This method of quantifying risk does not allow for different participation levels between individuals or sports.
2. Number of injuries per 10,000 hours of participation.
   Allows for different participation levels but not for differences in the seriousness of different injuries, or for the fact that some sports require far higher levels of participation than others.

Incapacity

Number of days of incapacity per month, season, year.
No account taken of differences in levels of participation.

Risk of incapacity

Number of days of incapacity per 1000 hours of participation.
Allows for differences in seriousness of injury and activity levels.

Type of injury The more important ways of classifying sports injuries are summarised in Figure 6.2. Most commonly, injuries are classified by describing both type and site, e.g. 'fracture of the wrist' or 'dislocation of the shoulder'. A more precise anatomical description is better, in order to distinguish between closely related injuries, e.g. 'fracture of the styloid process of the radius', 'sprain of the glenohumeral joint', or 'dislocation of the acromioclavicular joint'.

Classification of injuries according to cause is useful as it is one step on the way to thinking about prevention. Williams (1980) has proposed the following definitions:

Extrinsic: due to external violence, e.g. a kick or fall.
Intrinsic: due to stress developed within the victim.

Figure 6.2. Summary of different methods of classifying sports injuries. The different methods of classification are shown to the left of the diagram going from top to bottom. Subdivisions of the various classifications, and examples are illustrated to the right of the diagram.

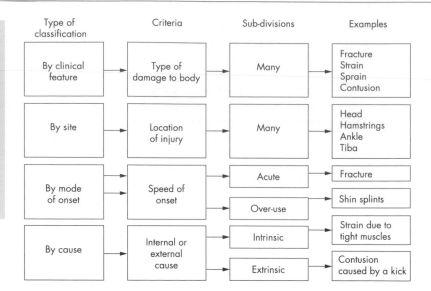

Type of classification	Criteria	Sub-divisions	Examples
By clinical feature	Type of damage to body	Many	Fracture Strain Sprain Contusion
By site	Location of injury	Many	Head Hamstrings Ankle Tiba
By mode of onset	Speed of onset	Acute	Fracture
		Over-use	Shin splints
By cause	Internal or external cause	Intrinsic	Strain due to tight muscles
		Extrinsic	Contusion caused by a kick

A strain, or pulled muscle, is an example of an intrinsic injury as it is usually caused by forces developed by the victim's own muscles. Most over-use injuries are also intrinsic in origin. The term intrinsic is now more commonly used to describe any injury that is caused by the personal characteristics of the athlete. Thus, for example, injuries attributed to the athlete's physique, lack of fitness, or even his or her psychological state, are normally classified as intrinsic. This meaning of 'intrinsic' will be used in the remainder of this chapter.

A third method of classification lists injuries as **acute** or **over-use**. An acute injury is the result of one single, sudden, episode of trauma such as occurs in a kick, a fall, or when a muscle is suddenly pulled. In contrast, over-use injuries develop gradually, over an extended period of use of the effected body part. Shin splints, runner's knee and tennis elbow are all examples of over-use injuries. It could be argued that 'instantaneous' would be a better name for the so-called acute injuries and that 'repetitive' would provide a more accurate description of over-use injuries. The latter term is used in the name 'Repetitive Strain Injury' – an over-use injury suffered by keyboard operators and other industrial workers. However, in the case of sports injuries the terms *acute* and *over-use* are now so well established that their use is likely to continue.

Specific types of sports injuries and their prevention
Common acute injuries

Concussion

Concussion is a reduction in, or loss of, consciousness usually resulting from a blow to the head. It is a potentially serious injury for three reasons. Firstly, there is a risk of obstruction to the subject's airways due to loss of nervous control. If this is not corrected, it could lead to suffocation. Secondly, any blow to the head is capable of causing bleeding inside the skull, whether or not there was unconsciousness initially. This is likely to cause compression of the brain and requires urgent surgical intervention in order to avert irreversible brain damage. Thirdly, repeated episodes may result in damage to the nervous system. Professional boxing is capable of producing chronic neurological damage (Ross *et al.* 1987) but there is no conclusive evidence that it occurs in amateur boxing (Haglund and Eriksson 1993).

A variety of factors can contribute to situations where concussion arises, including fatigue of the victim, environmental factors and disorderly conduct. The most effective preventative measure is the wearing of properly designed protective helmets. These items are now commonly used in many sports where there is a risk of head injury – including motorised sports, equestrian activities, cycling, canoeing, American football, cricket, hockey and hurling. Such helmets must be scientifically designed in order to dissipate the forces encountered in each particular activity. In some cases they must also be capable of protecting the subject's eyes and nose. Not all the available helmets meet these criteria and the author is aware of a number of athletes who have suffered permanent damage to eyes, ears or brain while wearing poorly designed helmets that failed to offer the protection claimed by their manufacturers.

Contusion

A contusion is an injury that occurs when soft tissue is crushed between two hard surfaces, such as when an individual's quadriceps are crushed between his or her thigh bone and an opponent's knee. Inflammation and internal bleeding occur. Swelling and the development of a bruise are the usual result of a contusion.

Contusions are a very common injury in body contact sports and in others, like hockey and cricket, where a hard projectile is used. Intrinsic factors offer no protection from contusions. The only solution is effective padding, which ought to be much more widely used than is the current practice.

Epiphyseal injury

Growth in long bones occurs at rings of cartilage known as **epiphyseal plates** (Figure 6.3). During adolescence the epiphyseal plates 'fuse' or turn into bone and growth is no longer possible. Epiphyseal plates are particularly vulnerable to sports injury, being the weakest part of a growing bone. In serious cases of epiphyseal injury the plate may be permanently damaged, preventing further growth.

Epiphyseal damage can occur either as a result of an acute injury, or from repeated trauma.

Fracture

A fracture is an injury to bone which results in a discontinuity; either a break or a crack. A complete break is the most common type of fracture. Fractures are subdivided into the following types: **simple**, where a single break is the only problem; **compound**, where there is more than one break in a single bone; **multiple**, when more than one bone is fractured; **open**, where the fractured bone protrudes through the skin; and **complicated**, where other tissues, such as nerves or blood vessels, are also involved in the injury.

Figure 6.3. (a) bones of children contain rings of cartilage known as *epiphyseal plates*. This is where growth in the length of the bone occurs. In the epiphyseal plate cartilage cells divide to produce new cells. These become larger and then calcify. Finally, the cells degenerate leaving new bones. (b) The epiphyseal plate is the weakest part of a growing bone. Damage to its blood supply may compromise further growth. (c) All the force developed by the quadriceps muscle is transmitted to the tibial tubercule via the patella and the patella tendon. In children, excessive use of the quadriceps may pull the tibial tubercule away from the underlying epiphyseal plate, resulting in Osgood Schlatter's disease.

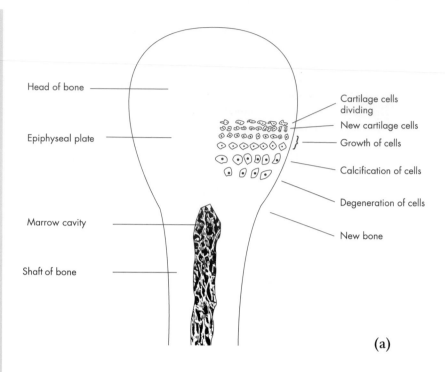

Head of bone

Epiphyseal plate

Cartilage cells dividing

New cartilage cells

Growth of cells

Calcification of cells

Degeneration of cells

Marrow cavity

New bone

Shaft of bone

(a)

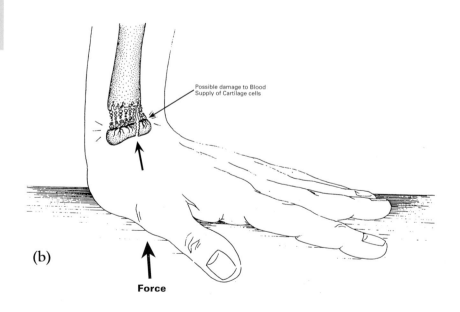

Possible damage to Blood Supply of Cartilage cells

(b)

Force

Figure 6.3. Continued.

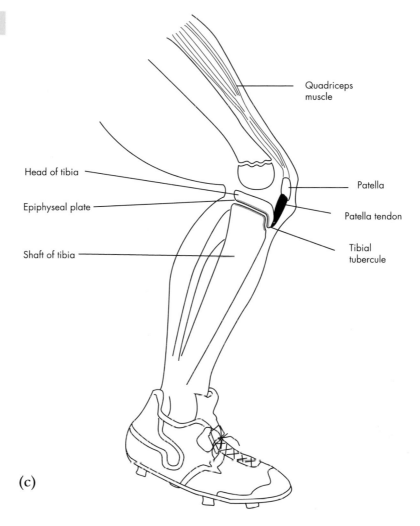

Quadriceps muscle

Head of tibia

Epiphyseal plate

Shaft of tibia

Patella

Patella tendon

Tibial tubercule

(c)

An **avulsion fracture** occurs when a violent muscular contraction 'avulses', or pulls away, a fragment of bone where the muscle attaches to it. In children such injuries frequently occur in the region of an epiphyseal plate. The most common avulsion fractures arise in the elbow (triceps insertion), the hip (origin of sartorius, rectus femoris or hamstrings) and the groin (origin of the adductors muscles).

A **stress** fracture occurs where there is a break in a bone without displacement of the fragments. Such injuries are usually due to over-use. Common stress fractures in athletes include those of the tibia or fibula (one of many causes of shin splint-like symptoms), and of the bones of the feet (March and Dance fractures are examples). A number of factors increase the risk of stress fractures, including:

1   Over-training
2   Training on hard, non-resilient, surfaces
3   Use of poorly designed, or worn-out, footwear

Table 6.1. Common sites of epiphyseal injury	Site of injury	Common name of condition	Activity or predisposing factors
	Olecranon process of ulna (elbow)	Little league elbow	Baseball pitcher, throwing events tennis
	Distal radius (wrist)	—	Fall onto hand, gymnastics
	Iliac crest (hip)	—	Violent twisting, shot, javelin
	Anterior hip (origin of rectus femoris, sartorius, hamstrings)	—	Jumping, kicking, intensive training, obesity; more common in females
	Proximal tibia (just below knee cap)	Osgood Schlatter's disease	Football, kicking
	Attachment of Achilles tendon to calcanei	Still's disease, Apophysitis calcanei	Jumping, running

4   Sudden increases in training duration or intensity (usually greater than 10 per cent per week)

5   Posture defects which place increased stress on the shin, and other, bones.

Sprain

A sprain is a partial or complete tear of a ligament. A sprain is one of the most common sports injuries and as such ought to be targeted in injury prevention programmes. The most specific measure that can be taken is to increase the stability of joints – usually by strengthening the muscles that surround them. Some athletes have very lax joints that require special strengthening programmes before participation in any body contact sport can be considered safe. Posture defects can increase the likelihood of certain sprains and such deficiencies should be corrected before competition is undertaken.

Ankle sprain is one of the most common sports injuries – especially in females, and ankle instability is a predisposing factor (Tropp *et al.* 1984). The injury tends to recur unless special exercises are undertaken to strengthen the joint and to improve proprioception in the tissues that surround it. Recovery from a sprain is a slow process and may take as long as a year. The healed ligament reaches only 50–70 per cent of its initial strength, and 20–50 per cent of individuals who have suffered ankle sprains have some form of subsequent weakness (Clayton *et al.* 1968; Smith and Reischl 1986). Achilles stretching, proprioceptive training, peroneal muscle strengthening, taping and ankle braces have all been reported to reduce the incidence of ankle sprains (Garrick and Requa 1973; Kuland 1988; Rovere *et al.* 1988; Smith and Reischl 1986).

Strain

A strain is an injury that results in a partial or complete tear of a muscle or the tendon that attaches it to bone. A partial rupture is often known as a 'pulled muscle'. A complete tear is a serious injury that requires prompt surgical repair.

Strains are the most common of all sports injuries and should be specially targeted in all prevention programmes. Effective preventative measures include:

1   Improving flexibility in the muscle groups at risk
2   Elimination of posture defects which place extra stress on vulnerable muscles groups
3   Elimination of imbalance in strength between opposing muscle groups
4   Improvements in warm-up procedures.

Wound

This injury consists of mechanical damage to the surface of the body. There are a number of different types of wound including: **abbrasions**, **lacerations** and **puncture wounds**.

Common over-use injuries

Bursitis

A bursa is a sac containing fluid that separates two tissues such as a tendon and an underlying joint (Figure 6.4). Its purpose is to reduce friction when the tendon moves with respect to the tissue underneath it. There are a large number of bursae in and around the knee and shoulder joints and in other parts of the body.

Impact or over-use can result in damage to a bursa. This causes pain, inflammation and swelling. In sports such as American football, volleyball and roller-skating prepatella bursitis is common, due to falling on the knee cap. This can be prevented by the use of padded knee protectors. Infrapatella and suprapatella bursitis are common injuries due to over-use in a variety of different sports, including running and field games (Table 6.2).

Tenosynovitis

Tenosynovitis is inflammation of a tendon. It is a very common condition in a large number of activities: a particular injury is often named after the sport in which it was first described (Table 6.3).

Tenosynovitis is almost always due to over-use but defects of equipment or body mechanics may also contribute in certain circumstances. For example, tenosynovitis of the doriflexors of the foot may be caused by wearing tight footwear. The misalignment that occurs as a result of posture defects often results in tenosynovitis. For example, tenosynovitis of the tibialis muscle (at the inside of the ankle) is more common in athletes with flat feet.

Epicondylitis

This over-use injury is an inflammation of the point on a bone where tendons insert – the **epicondyle**. Tennis and golfer's elbow are the most well-known examples. **Tennis elbow** is epicondylitis of the lateral radius. This is the point where the tendons

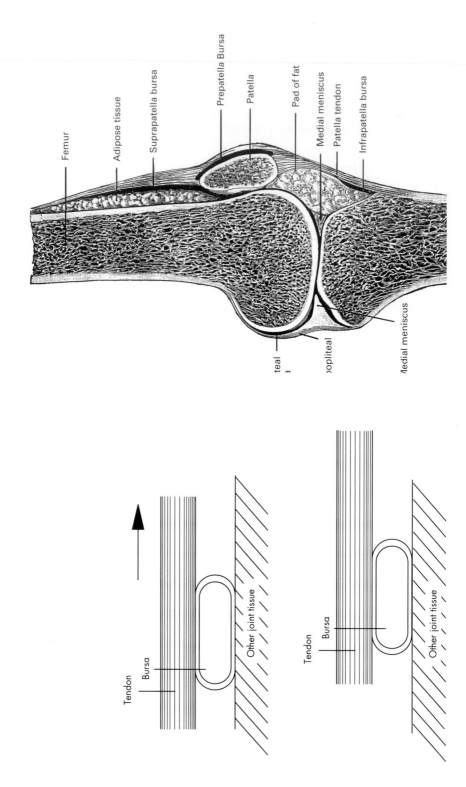

Figure 6.4. *Left:* Bursae reduce friction where tendons or muscles move with respect to other tissues. *Right:* Diagram showing some of the bursae associated with the knee joint.

Table 6.2. Common sites of bursitis.	Site of injury	Common name of condition	Activity or predisposing factors
	Shoulder (subacromial bursitis)	—	Swimming, Racquet sports
	Elbow (olecranon bursa)	Student's elbow	Direct blow, Repeated pressure
	Hip (trochanteric bursitis)	Runner's hip	Running
	Knee (infrapatella bursa)	Parson's knee	Running
	Knee (prepatella bursa)	Housemaid's knee	Falling on knee, Volleyball, American football
	Knee (suprapatella bursa)	—	Running, Field games
	Ankle (Achilles or calcanela bursa)	Pump bump	Running, Tight heel protector

Table 6.3. Common sites of tenosynovitis.	Site of injury	Common name of condition	Sport or activity
	Shoulder (tendon of supraspinatus)	Frozen shoulder	Swimming Throwing
	Biceps tendon (bicipital tenosynovitis)	Golfer's shoulder Baseball shoulder Tennis shoulder Swimmer's shoulder	Golf, Baseball, Canoeing, Swimming, Weight-lifting
	Flexor tendon of wrist	—	Tennis, Racquet sports, Rowing
	Toe dorsiflexors	—	Soccer, Kicking activities
	Achilles tendon	—	Use of shoes with protector

of the extensor muscles of the wrist insert near the elbow. They are used in back-hand shots in tennis, badminton and squash, and in activities that involve a similar action.

Epicondylitis is a typical over-use injury and any factor that increases the work of the extensor muscles of the wrist predisposes to it. The following factors have been suggested: a heavy racquet, incorrect size of grip, fast court or balls, faulty technique in which the wrist is flexed during the back-hand shot instead a being maintained rigid so that the force is developed by the arm, shoulder and trunk. However, few of these suggestions have been confirmed experimentally. An Australian study found the use of over-sized aluminium racquets to be the only predisposing factor to tennis elbow, which was the sixth most common injury to tennis players (Kamien 1989).

Golfer's, thrower's or **javelin elbow.** This is epicondylitis of the flexor muscles of the wrist which insert at the medial side of the elbow (Figure 6.5). It can occur in any activity in which wrist flexion is forceful, including baseball pitching, bowling at cricket and serving in tennis. Preventative measures for epicondylitis include elimination of the causative factors listed above and a *gradual* development of strength in the muscle-tendon-bone units likely to be affected in particular sports.

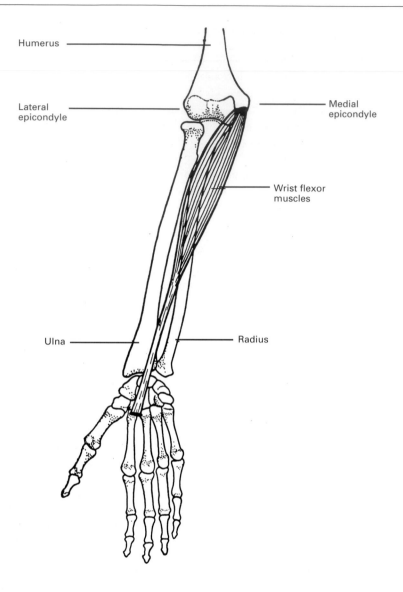

Figure 6.5. The muscles that flex the wrist have their origin on the medial epicondyle of the humerus. Pain in this region is known as medial epicondylitis – also known as golfer's or thrower's elbow. The origin of the extensor muscles of the wrist is on the lateral epicondyle. Over-use results in lateral epicondylitis – tennis elbow.

Groin pain

Groin pain is a common condition that can be due to a number of different causes. These include acute or over-use strain of the adductor muscles, the rectus femoris, sartorius or iliopsoas muscles; an avulsion fracture at the origin of one of the adductors; hernia; inflammation of the pubic bone. Groin pain is common in athletes involved in soccer and other field games and in sprinters, hurdlers, swimmers and jumpers. It is especially prevalent in individuals with lumbar lordosis and those with poor hip adduction and quad flexibility. It is an injury which can easily become chronic so its prevention is particularly important. Appropriate measures include:

1   Elimination of excessive lumbar lordosis
2   Development of good hip abduction and hyper-extension
3   Strengthening of the abdominal muscles.

Rotator cuff syndrome

This is an injury to small muscles in the shoulder. It can be the result of throwing, racquet sports or handball, or damage following a fall or dislocation. Preventative measures include improving shoulder flexibility and strengthening the muscles of the rotator cuff.

Shin splints

Soreness on the front of the leg (the shin) is a very common condition and is described as **shin splints**. It may be due to inflammation of the muscles of the leg at the point where they attach to the tibia (true shin splints), a stress fracture of the tibia, or excessive pressure in the anterior compartment of the leg. It is common in many activities which involve the legs. Although traditionally associated with running, recent research has shown that it is just as common in field games, such as soccer, when participation levels are equated.

The occurrence of shin splints is associated with a number of factors, including: hard surfaces, the use of poor footwear, flat feet, other defects of body mechanics which result in excessive or uneven forces on the foot.

Chondromalatia patellae

This is an over-use injury that is due to inflammation of the cartilage on the underside of the patella or knee cap. A chronic pain is experienced behind the patella that is worse when walking up or down stairs. It is one of the conditions known as **runner's knee**. Chondromalatia patellae is more likely when the knee cap is not properly aligned with the groove in the femur in which it moves (Figure 6.6). This is often due to weakness of the vastus lateralis muscle which allows the patella to move laterally. Athletes with a high 'Q' angle are very vulnerable to chondromalatia patellae, even if the vastus lateralis is of adequate strength.

An assessment of 'Q' angle and quadriceps muscle balance, followed by corrective exercises, is effective in minimising the incidence of this common condition.

Runner's knee

Two separate conditions are commonly known as runner's knee: **chondromalatia patellae** (see above) and **iliotibial band friction syndrome** (see below).

Jumper's knee

This is strain or tendonitis of the patellar tendon, which is situated just below the knee cap. It most commonly presents as an over-use injury in sports where a high level of force is developed by the quadriceps muscle: high-, long- and triple-jumping,

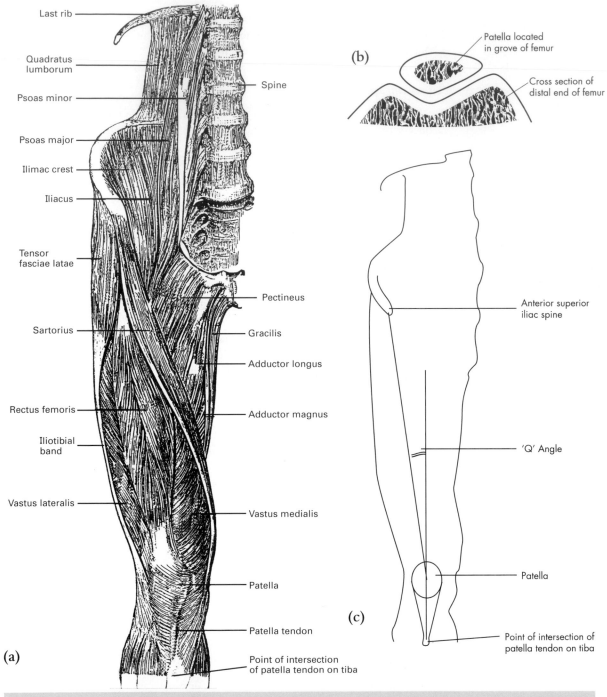

Figure 6.6. (a) Flexor and adductor muscles of the hip joint. The psoas, iliacus and adductor muscles insert directly onto the femur. In contrast, the three quadriceps muscles – rectus femoris, vastus medialis and vastus lateralis – insert onto the patella. This means that the forces they produce are directed to the tibia via the patella and the patella tendon. (b) The patella moves up and down in a groove in the femur that is illustrated in this diagram. (c) The 'Q' or 'quadriceps' angle. This is the angle between the direction of the quadriceps muscle and the direction of the patella tendon. It is the angle formed by intersection of a line draw from the origin of the quadriceps to the middle of the knee cap with a second line drawn from the tibia tubercule to the middle of the knee cap.

Figure 6.7. Iliotibial band friction syndrome, or runner's knee. The iliotibial band is tensioned by the tensor faciae latae muscle and is important for stability of the knee. It passes over the knee joint. Over-use and tightness of the iliotibial band may result in friction and inflammation at the point where it comes into contact with the lateral epicondyle of the femur.

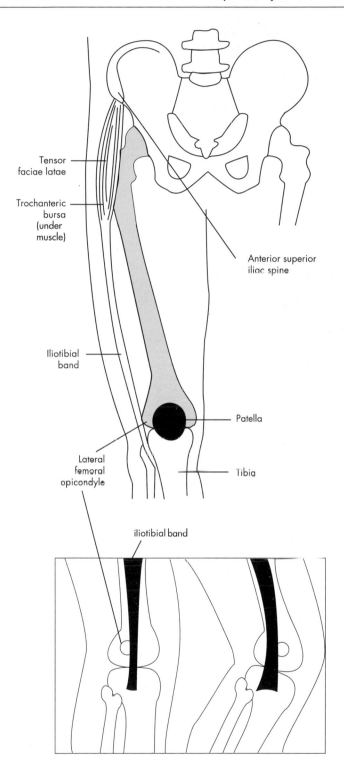

sprinting, weight-lifting, rowing, volleyball and basketball. It also occurs in racquet sports: tennis, squash and badminton.

Osgood Schlatter's disease

This is damage to the epiphyseal plate that is situated at the top of the tibia, resulting in a slight separation of the tibial tubercule from the rest of the bone. This produces a bony lump on the tibia, just below the knee cap. Osgood Schlatter's disease can occur only in children and adolescents, prior to the fusion of the epiphyseal plates. It is caused by excessive use of the quadriceps muscle, usually in kicking or jumping activities, occasionally in running. Prevention consists of the avoidance of over-training in pre-puberal children.

Iliotibial band friction syndrome

The iliotibial band is a tendon that runs from muscles in the lateral part of the upper thigh and which inserts onto the fibula, just below the knee (Figure 6.7). It has an important role in stabilising the knee joint. As the knee bends and straightens the iliotibial band moves backwards and forwards across the lateral epicondyle of the femur. Under certain conditions friction occurs, causing pain on the lateral side of the knee. The problem is common in running and many other sports. It is more likely to occur if the iliotibial band is tight, in the presence of body mechanics defects which result in misalignment of the legs and feet, and as a result of running on roads with a pronounced camber.

Capsulitis of shoulder

In this condition the capsule which lines the shoulder joint becomes inflamed and painful. Over a period of weeks or months the pain is replaced by stiffness. This condition may follow a strain or knock or can occur spontaneously, particularly in older athletes. Good shoulder flexibility offers some protection.

Other types of injury

Cartilage injury

See meniscal injury.

Meniscal injury

The articulating (touching) ends of the bones in all movable joints are lined with **hyaline cartilage** which reduces friction and promotes freedom of movement. The knee joint contains two extra pieces of cartilage known as **meniscii**. They are located on top of the tibia and are shaped like disks with holes in their centres. They are thicker at their outside edges than in their centres and thus produce two slight cavities into which the two condyles of the femur fit. This arrangement (Figure 6.8) enhances the stability of the knee joint.

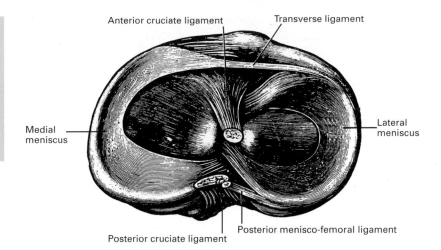

Figure 6.8. The knee joint viewed from above with the femur removed. Part of the anterior and posterior cruciate ligaments are shown. The medial and lateral meniscii are located on top of the tibia.

The meniscus on the inside of the joint is known as the **medial meniscus** and the one on the outside as the **lateral meniscus**. The medial meniscus is attached to the medial collateral ligament in addition to a number of other structures in the knee.

The meniscii can be damaged by being torn, or by being ground between the femur and the tibia, such as in a twisting strain of the knee. Since the medial meniscus is attached to the medial ligament it is likely to be torn during a medial sprain of the knee. Thus the medial meniscus is more likely to suffer damage than the lateral meniscus.

Increasing the stability of the knee joint is the only effective means of protection from meniscus damage. If the joint is weak, increased stability may be achieved by strengthening the muscles that surround it and those which tension the iliotibial band. Such exercises are normally carried out as part of a rehabilitation programme following meniscus surgery or the reconstruction of the ligaments of the knee. However, it is much more sensible to strengthen the knee as part of an injury prevention programme, rather than wait for it to be injured. Serious knee injuries are extremely disabling and surgery is of only limited success. Athletes involved in body contact field games should ensure that they develop adequate levels of strength in the muscles around the knee. (See also Knee and Ankle Supports, p. 208.)

Cruciate ligament injury

The anterior and posterior cruciate ligaments are located inside the knee and are a major source of stability of the joint. Rupture of one or both of these ligaments is a very serious injury that requires specialised surgical repair.

Internal derangement of the knee

This is a collective term for serious internal injuries of the knee joint – most commonly meniscal or cruciate ligament injury.

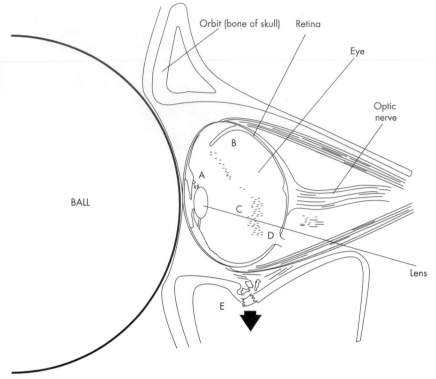

Eye injuries

Due to the nature of the task it is required to undertake, the eye is a very delicate organ which has to be located in an exposed position at the front of the skull. The bony **orbits** of the skull offer some protection from large, blunt objects, but sharp or small projectiles are liable to cause very serious damage to the eye. Cricket and hockey balls are very dangerous; squash and golf balls are even more lethal, despite their softer texture (Figure 6.9). In a serious injury the internal structures of the eye are disrupted and internal bleeding occurs. The eye ball may be ruptured, in which case vision will almost certainly be lost. The consequences of eye injuries are potentially so serious that effective protection is vital. Specialist assessment of all eye injuries should be obtained at once as many can be successfully treated if seen in time.

Nose injuries

These occur following a fall, collision, or blow from an implement or opponent. The nasal bone may be fractured or the cartilage of the nasal septum displaced. The latter is particularly troublesome and may require surgical treatment. An effective face guard should be worn for all activities where the risk of nasal injury is significant.

Dental injuries

Dental injuries are painful, disfiguring and not self-correcting. Repair tends to be expensive. They are common in contact sports and in such games as hockey and cricket where hard implements or projectiles are used. These injuries can largely be prevented with customised mouth guards that are fashioned and fitted by a dental surgeon. Cheaper mouth guards are available but are not nearly as effective.

Back injuries

Back injuries are common in sport and are often very troublesome. A large number of different conditions are possible including: fractures, degenerative changes in the vertebrae, disk lesions which result in pressure on a spinal nerve and radiation of pain to other parts of the back or to a limb, ligament sprains and muscle strains. The nature of a back injury is often difficult to determine and specialist advice should be sought for all persistent problems. The risk of back injury is increased when strength, flexibility and body mechanics are poor, and when the individual is overweight.

Stitch

This is a symptom rather than an injury but can cause a good deal of trouble. It consists of pain under the rib cage at the start of exercise. A number of causes have been suggested including air trapped in the intestines after eating or drinking, and a temporary lack of oxygen reaching the diaphragm muscle at the start of exercise. Sportsmen or women who suffer from stitches should try the following preventative measures.

1 Eat and drink slowly, avoiding the ingestion of air.
2 Avoid eating for 2 or 3 hours before exercise.
3 Avoid gassy or gas-producing foods.
4 Avoid fizzy drinks.
5 Take special care over warm-up.
6 Undertake a series of exercises to strengthen the respiratory muscles.

Metatarsal pain

This is pain on the underside of the foot. It is very common, especially in older athletes. There are a variety of different causes, including stress fractures and ligament strain. Flat feet, hard surfaces, poorly cushioned shoes, excessive mileage and being overweight are contributory factors.

Plantar fasciitis

Sometimes known as policeman's heel. This is a sprain of a ligament-like structure on the underside of the foot which runs from the sole to the ball.

Myositis ossificans

This is a complication of blood-clot formation, following a fracture, dislocation or contusion. The most common sites are the thigh, elbow, shoulder and ankle. Its cause is not known but it is more likely to occur following inappropriate first aid treatment,

Table 6.4. Named injuries.	Common name	Anatomical description
	Dance fracture	Stress fracture of 5th metatarsal
	Footballer's ankle	Bone formation in capsule of ankle joint
	Golfer's elbow	Medial epicondylitis of elbow
	Housemaid's knee	Bursitis of prepatella bursa
	Javelin elbow	Medial epicondylitis of elbow
	Jumper's knee	Strain or tendonitis of patella tendon
	Little league elbow	Epiphyseal fracture of distal humerus
	March fracture	Stress fracture of 3rd metatarsal
	Parson's knee	Bursitis of infrapatella bursa
	Pitcher's arm	Epiphyseal fracture of distal humerus
	Policeman's heel	Plantar fasciitis
	Runner's hip	Bursitis of trochanteric (hip) bursa
	Runner's knee	Iliotibial band friction syndrome
	Student's elbow	Bursitis of olecranon bursa
	Tennis elbow	Lateral epicondylitis of elbow
	Tennis leg	Calf strain
	Thrower's elbow	Medial epicondylitis of elbow

such as massage, during the acute stage of an injury. Expert first aid is the best preventative measure.

Named injuries

Many injuries are named after the activities in which they are most common or in which they were first described. Some examples are given in Table 6.4, and see also Figure 6.10.

Studies on the incidence and causes of sports injuries

Older studies on sports injuries were largely based on information obtained from clinics, hospital casualty departments or insurance company claims. Such data tended to include only the more serious injuries. In consequence, such research underestimated the total number of injuries and provided misleading information on those conditions that were the most common.

More recent research has employed other techniques, including: longitudinal surveys of children at school and adults at work; studies of athletes during both training and competition; whole population surveys carried out by post, telephone or personal interview.

Total number of injuries

A number of countries have carried out studies which allow the total number of sports injuries to be estimated. In Finland (population 4.9 million) there are at least 90,000 per year, or 1.84 injuries per 100 people (Vuori 1988). A Belgian study found that 1.2 per cent of the population had a sports injury treated by their doctor over a one-year period (Lijsens 1987). These constituted half the medically treated injuries. In Holland

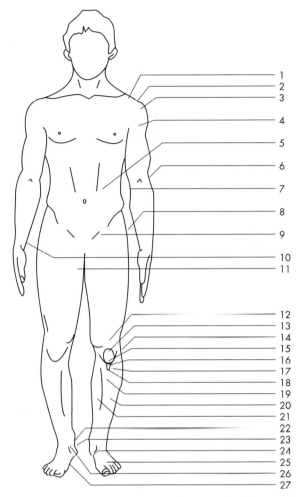

Figure 6.10. Site of some common sports injuries: 1 supraspinatus tendonitis, 2 capsulitis of shoulder, 3 rotator cuff syndrome, 4 biceps tendonitis, 5 stitch, 6 lateral epicondylitis of humerus (tennis elbow), 7 medial epicondylitis of humerus (golfer's elbow, thrower's elbow), 8 trochanteric bursitis (runner's hip), 9 groin pain, 10 wrist flexor tendonitis, 11 adductor strain, 12 suprapatella bursitis, 13 chondromalatia patellae (runner's knee), 14 iliotibial band friction syndrome (runner's knee), 15 prepatella bursitis (housemaid's knee, volleyball knee), 16 patella tendonitis (jumper's knee), 17 infrapatella bursitis (parson's knee), 18 Osgood Schlatter's disease, 19 stress fracture or shin splints, 20 anterior compartment syndrome, 21 shin splints, 22 Achilles bursitis (pump bump), 23 Achilles tendonitis, 24 plantar faciitis, 25 tendonitis of toe dorsiflexors, 26 tendonitis of tibialis posterior tendon, 27 metatarsal pain, stress fracture (dance and march fractures).

2.9 per cent of the population had medically treated injuries in one year (Inklaar 1986). When non-medically treated injuries are included, the percentages are likely to be much higher. A telephone survey of 90,000 households in western Germany found an incidence of sports injury of 37 per cent (Pfundt 1985). A similar Dutch study of 24,141 households reported an injury rate of 58 per cent of the population per year, with just under half the injuries being medically treated. In the UK, 45 per cent of the population aged 16–45 reported taking part in sport over the previous 28 days and 19 per cent of these sustained an injury. This suggests an annual injury rate of 2.5 per year. Only about 30 per cent of these were medically treated. About half the UK injuries were intrinsic and half occurred to the lower limb (Nicholl *et al.* 1992).

Sports injuries in relation to other accidents

Of all injuries in Finland, 13–14 per cent are sports injuries. In the 10–14 age group over 30 per cent of the medically treated injuries are due to sport. In a major industrial enterprise 40.0 days were lost per 100 workers per year due to sports injuries, compared with 103.5 days due to industrial accidents.

In children under 15 years of age sports injuries account for 11 per cent of accidents in France and 16.7 per cent in Sweden (Tursz and Crost 1986). Unintentional injuries are the major cause of death in adolescents. An American study on teenagers found that 1 in 14 were treated in hospital each year with a sports injury, compared with 1 in 50 as a result of road traffic accidents (Gallagher *et al.* 1984). In the same study it was found that 17 per cent of the injuries that resulted in hospital admissions were sustained in sport compared with 14 per cent from motor accidents.

The financial cost of sports injuries

The economic cost of sports injuries includes the financial costs of: using health services for the treatment of the injury, costs resulting from lost production of individuals who are unable to work, and 'welfare' costs resulting from the reduced quality of life of the injured and their carers. Nicholls *et al.* (1992) have estimated that the total cost of sports injuries in the 15–45 age group in the UK exceeds half a billion pounds per year.

Sports injuries in children

Age and the rate of injury

The incidence of sports injuries in children has been well documented. Such conditions are rare below the age of 6 or 7. If the two sexes are combined, the incidence then rises with age until the end of childhood (Sullivan *et al.* 1980; Tursz and Crost 1986; Watson 1984a; Watson 1986; Zaricznyj *et al.* 1980). The injury rate for girls drops in the teenage years due to a decline in participation levels (Figure 6.11).

The injury rate of boys in the final years at school is high – especially in those individuals who are involved in competitive sport. The rate is of the order of 20–30 injuries per 100 pupils per year.

Figure 6.11. Injuries per 100 pupils per year for boys and girls between the ages of 10 and 18. In girls the injury rate peaks at age 15; in boys it continues to rise with age. (Data adapted from Watson 1984a and 1986.)

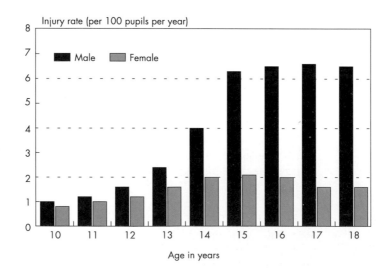

One of the more serious types of injury to young children is epiphyseal fracture which has the potential to disrupt growth. There is a dearth of information on the incidence of this injury but one French study found that 10 per cent of sports-induced fractures were epiphyseal and that 12 per cent of children admitted to hospital suffered angulation or shortening of a limb due to this type of trauma (Tursz and Crost 1986).

Type of injury   The majority of sports injuries to younger children arise from falls and very few are due to contact with opponents, equipment or projectiles (Tursz and Crost 1986; Backx 1991). This is in marked contrast to the situation in adolescents where contact injuries are very common (Watson 1986; van Galen 1988; Hoy *et al.* 1992). Another difference is the type of injury sustained. Acute injuries are the norm in children and over-use injuries are rare. When a particular sport such as soccer is considered, the incidence of fractures, dislocations and contusions declines with age, and older players are more likely to suffer from over-use injuries such as tenosynovitis (Albert 1983; Backous *et al.* 1988; McMaster and Walter 1978; Sullivan *et al* 1980).

Injury in adults   *Age and injury*

Population studies from several different countries agree on the distribution of sports injuries with age (Lijsens 1987; Inklaar 1986; Pfundt 1985; DeHaven and Lintner 1986; van Galen 1988). Approximately 40 per cent of all injuries occur in individuals between the ages of 10 and 19, with just over 30 per cent in the 20–29 age group. Only 3–4 per cent of injuries arise in children under 10.

The type of injury sustained also varies with age. Fractures, dislocations and wounds tend to occur in younger sportsmen and women while muscle strains, internal derangements of the knee and over-use injuries such as tenosynovitis, patellofemoral pain and other inflammatory injuries are more common in older individuals (DeHaven and Lintner 1986; Keller *et al.* 1987).

Gender and injury

All of the many population surveys carried out indicate a higher incidence of sports injury in males than in females. The ratio varies from about 3:2 in a few studies up to 5:1 (DeHaven and Lintner 1986); 3:1 is about average. When the statistics are corrected for the greater exposure time of males the difference between the sexes narrows, but men still have a higher risk of injury per 1000 hours of participation than women.

There have been few, if any, studies of differences in the types of injuries sustained by males and females. In children, Watson (1986) found that girls suffered from more sprains of the ankle, while in boys knee injuries were more common.

Training and competition   In all sports the chances of injury are considerably greater during competition than during training (Watson 1986; van Vulpen 1989). Preventative measures should, therefore, be directed particularly towards competitive situations.

	Sport	Activity	Reported rate	Corrected rate
Table 6.5. Rates of injury per 10 000 hours of exposure.	Mixed activities	Dutch school children Aged 0 to 15 years	29.42	29.42
	American football	Individual activities	7.3	14.6
		Non-contact drills	31.6	63.2
		Contact drills	165.7	331.4
		Practice games	547.9	1 095.8
		Games	5 100.0	10 200.0
	Soccer	Youth male	14.00	29.17
		Youth female	32.00	66.67
	Endurance sports	Training and competition	71.96	71.96
	Body contact sports	Training and competition	82.45	82.45
	Non-contact sports	Training and competiton	65.30	65.30
	Explosive sports	Training and competition	65.26	65.26
	Scottish heavy	Training and competition	75.00	75.00
	Volleyball	Tournament – Time-loss injuries	23.00	23.0
		– All injuries	197.00	197.00
	International ice hockey	Matches – Time-loss injuries	791.6	791.6
		Matches – Lacerations	708.3	708.3
		Matches – Nuisance injuries	458.3	458.3
		Matches – All injuries	1 958.3	1 958.3

Data based on information from: Backx *et al.* (1989); Halpern *et al.* (1987); Lorentzon *et al.* (1988); McLennan and McLennan (1990); Schafle *et al.* (1990); Watson, (1993).

Level of competition

There is often a higher than average risk of injury when an individual takes up a new sport. This is due both to deficiencies of skill and to lack of adaptation of the body to the new stresses imposed upon it. Two types of sport provide a particular risk of early injury: (1) repetitive endurance sports such as running, rowing and swimming where specific muscles and joints are subjected to repeated trauma that produces over-use injuries; and (2) activities that place the individual in an 'unnatural' environment where a reasonable level of skill must be acquired in order to avoid mishap. Skiing and parachute jumping are examples of such activities where the level of injuries to novices is high (Bouter 1987; Steinberg 1989).

After initial adaptation to a new sport, the injury rate drops. It then rises as the standard increases and in all sports studied it is high in top-level participants (van Vulpen 1989; Watson 1993). This is illustrated in Table 6.5.

The *type* of injury sustained also changes with the level of competition. In sports as different as badminton and soccer, the number of over-use injuries rises and the incidence of acute injuries declines as the level of competition increases (Keller *et al.* 1987; Jorgensen and Winge 1990).

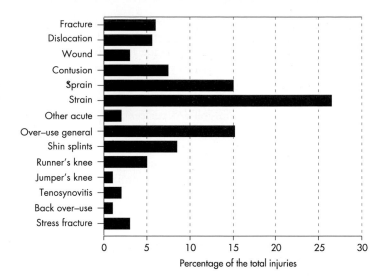

Figure 6.12. The most common injuries in a cross-section of endurance, body contact, non-contact and explosive sports. (Data adapted from Watson 1993.)

Site of injury The most common site of injury is the lower limb. There is obviously some variation between different sports but a great many activities involve weight being carried by the legs and feet and the stresses that are developed produce lower limb injuries. Where the lower limb is also subjected to violence from opponents, such as in soccer, the injury rate is even higher. The susceptibility of the lower limb to injury is illustrated by a study on the triathlon where the majority of injuries were found to occur in the running phase of the event (Collins *et al.* 1989).

Type of injury

Type of injury varies with the sport undertaken but also with the method of data collection. When only medically treated injuries are considered (which tended to be the case with older studies) sprains and contusions are the most commonly reported injuries (Figure 6.12), but many strains (pulled muscles) are not medically treated and their incidence is considerably underestimated in the scientific literature.

The same is true for over-use injuries, many of which restrict participation rather than prevent it completely. In children, 75 per cent of sports injuries are acute in onset (Backx 1991), but the proportion of over-use injuries increases with age and level of competition so that they become the major problem in many top-level sports.

Sport and the incidence of injury In Europe, the majority of sports injuries are sustained in soccer (28.9 per cent of the total in the UK compared with 7.5 per cent in keep fit, the next highest activity: Nicholl *et al.* 1992). This is partly attributable to the high participation rate. The *risk* of injury is less in soccer than it is in rugby and many other activities.

High-risk activities Parachuting appears to carry a high risk of serious injury. It is reported that during military training jumps, 0.22 hospital-treated injuries resulted per 100 jumps. There were also 4 deaths per 51 828 jumps (Lowdon and Wetherill 1989).

197

Death in sporting activities

There are relatively few published studies on the incidence of death in sport. Ragosta *et al.* (1984) analysed 81 non-traumatic deaths that occurred during or immediately after sport in the state of Rhode Island between 1 January 1975 and 1 May 1982. Most of the fatalities (88 per cent) were attributed to coronary heart disease and occurred in subjects over 29 years of age. In all but 7 per cent of these subjects there were previous signs of coronary heart disease or known risk factors. The majority of deaths occurred in golf (23 per cent), jogging (20 per cent) and swimming (11 per cent). This may appear surprising but it is due to the relatively high average age of the victims: 70 of the 81 deaths were in individuals over 40 years of age.

Only 6 of the 81 deaths occurred in individuals under 29. All of these were due to congenital cardiac or vascular abnormalities of which there were no previous signs.

Cantu (1992) has analysed high school and college sporting fatalities due both to

Table 6.6. Deaths in high school sport, USA, 1982–90 (data from Cantu 1992).

Sport	Deaths in sport due to accidental cause		Deaths in sport due to medical problems	
	n	Deaths per 100 000 participants	n	Deaths per 100 000 participants
Cross country	0		5	0.40
Football	43	0.40	46	0.44
Soccer	1	0.06	5	0.32
Basketball	0		22	0.49
Gynmastics	1	0.54	0	
Ice hockey	1	0.54	0	
Swimming	0		3	0.15
Wrestling	2	0.10	8	0.41
Baseball	2	0.06	4	0.12
Lacrosse	0		1	0.75
Track	6	0.16	11	0.26
Tennis	0		1	0.10
Total	56		106	

Table 6.7. Fatalities per 100 million occasions.

Activity	Estimated death rate
Climbing	>793
Air sports	>640
Motor sports	146
Water sports excluding swimming, diving, fishing	67.5
Horse riding	34.3
Rugby	15.7
Boxing/wrestling	5.2
Soccer	3.8
Cricket	3.1
Hockey	2.9
Track and field	1.0
Tennis	0.7

trauma and to underlying pathology (Table 6.6). Between 1931 and 1986 traumatic deaths in football outnumbered non-traumatic deaths by a factor of 2:1. Head and neck injuries were the single most common cause of fatalities. Since that time the number of traumatic deaths has declined due to changes in rules, equipment and conditioning methods, while the incidence of non-traumatic deaths has remained constant. Hypertrophic cardiomyopathy accounts for approximately half the non-traumatic fatalities in young sports people.

Fatal accident rates per 100 million occasions or days of participation have been estimated for the UK by Nicholl *et al.* (1992), and are summarised in Table 6.7.

Causes of sports injuries

A study of the causes of sports injuries is useful because it is the first step in the development of effective prevention programmes. At the most basic level, the cause of all injuries is extremely straightforward. Injuries occur when the stresses imposed upon a part of the body are greater than it is able to resist: mechanical failure is then the inevitable consequence. For example, when the outward force on an ankle exceeds a certain level the lateral ligaments rupture and a sprained ankle results. The reason why an individual gets into this position is usually much more complex. It could be that the ankle is weak as a result of previous injury, or the forces imposed upon the ankle may be excessive. This could be due to a variety of causes, including: an uneven playing surface; foul play by an opponent; the casualty being over weight or exceptionally tall — both of which increase the mechanical stress on the ankle.

Some of the above factors may themselves be the result of other causes. For example, the uneven surface may have been partly the result of the weather; the foul play may have been precipitated by poor refereeing which caused the match to get out of control. It is also possible that had the casualty been fresher he or she might have been able to take avoiding action in time. Thus in practice, most sports injuries

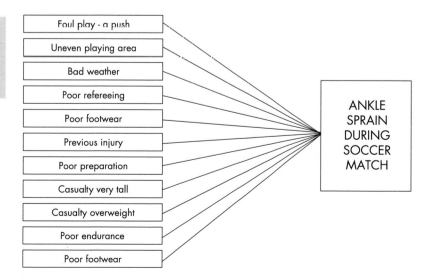

Figure 6.13. Summary of possible contributory factors to an ankle sprain sustained during a soccer match.

result from the interaction of a large number of different contributory factors (Figure 6.13).

An understanding of the causes of sports injuries, and the ways in which different factors interact, is essential for effective work on injury prevention. Unfortunately this is not an easy area in which to conduct research and investigators are frequently forced to rely upon the opinions of athletes and coaches as to the relative importance of different factors. This leads to an overestimate of the importance of the more obvious causes – like surfaces and foul play – and to an underestimate of the effects of the more complex biological ones.

Consequences of injury for the practising athlete

Although a few sports injuries are potentially very serious, the most important consequence of the majority is the extent to which they disrupt competition and training. Until recently, studies of sports injuries tended to be confined to the more dramatic varieties. Strains and over-use injuries were often ignored and an athlete was considered injured only if *completely* incapacitated. In practice, minor injuries which take the edge off performance and restrict training programmes are a more common problem. Competition is now so intense in all sports that any condition that restricts performance has very serious consequences for the athlete.

Factors influencing sports injuries

Intrinsic factors

Biological

Age and gender   The influence of these factors was considered on page 194.

Physique   A number of studies have demonstrated that athletes who are tall or overweight are more likely to suffer from injury (Watson 1986; Lijsens 1987; Taimela *et al.* 1990; Nicholl *et al.* 1992). This is an important finding as these two risk factors are extremely easy to identify. Individuals who fall into either of these categories should receive special attention in injury prevention programmes.

The relationship between somatotype and the risk of injury has been less well investigated. A study in our laboratory found that athletes rated 5.5 or above in mesomorphy were injured for an average of 68.5 days per year compared with 32.6 days for sportsmen with lower mesomorphy scores. This is probably due to the choice of sport of the former group of subjects and also to the manner in which they approached them. In a study on female gymnasts it was found that individuals high in mesomorphy were more likely to be injured than subjects with lower scores (Steele and White 1986).

Medical

Clinical defects   Many clinical defects make participation in certain activities unsafe, or require that special precautions be taken. The situation can occur in any age group, but it is more likely to occur in older individuals. Body contact sports are unsafe in middle and old age and very strenuous activities are often unwise. Medical advice should be obtained before a new activity is started, particularly following a prolonged period of inactivity.

A number of medical conditions make certain types of physical activity dangerous at any age. It is beyond the scope of this book to enter into a detailed discussion beyond stating that diseases of the nervous, respiratory, cardiovascular and musculo-skeletal systems often cause particularly serious problems. The absence of one of a pair of organs – eye, lung, kidney, ovary, testicle – is a contra-indication for participation in any activity that is likely to place the surviving organ at risk. Individuals with medical problems should not be discouraged from participation in sport, but should be directed towards alternative forms of physical activity that carry lower risks.

Asthma, diabetes mellitis and epilepsy are commonly encountered in young sportspeople. They should not prevent participation, but special precautions are necessary. There is an increased risk of injury in diabetics as a result of hypoglycaemia (van Vulpen 1989).

Short-term illness   Competition and training should be stopped during the acute phase of any illness, especially if body temperature is elevated.

Previous injury   Previous injury is one of the major factors that predisposes an individual to sports injury for a number of reasons. Firstly, unless special steps have been taken the factors that led to the first injury will not have been removed. A second injury will then occur from the same cause as the first. Secondly, the body is weaker after an injury unless special exercises have been taken to strengthen it. Thirdly, many athletes resume activity before they have recovered fully.

In a review of six major studies of soccer injuries, Keller *et al.* (1987) concluded that re-injury is extremely common and attributed this to incomplete rehabilitation. Ekstrand and Gillquist (1983a and b) found that 20 per cent of minor injuries to Swedish soccer players were followed within two months by a more serious injury to those same players. In the majority of cases this was a more serious version of the original injury. Requa *et al.* (1993) report that a history of injury doubled the chances of a subsequent injury on all sites except the knee, where the risk was increased three times.

Laxity of ligaments   This may predispose to sprains and dislocation, especially in body contact sports. For example, in one study it was found that 71 per cent of knee injuries to senior soccer players occurred in individuals with lax ligaments (Ekstrand and Gillquist 1983a and b).

Skill

Lack of skill in an activity can increase the risk of acute injury. It has been shown that inexperience increases the risk of injury in skiing and parachute jumping (Bouter 1987; Steinberg 1989). Poor technique is said to increase the risk of over-use injuries such as tendonitis and tennis elbow.

Long simple- and choice-reaction times to visual stimuli are thought to predispose to sports injury (Taimela *et al.* 1990).

Psychological factors

Psychological factors are likely to play an important part in the susceptibility to injury. However, the precise characteristics that predispose to injury are far from clear. It has been suggested that factors relating to anxiety and attention predispose to injury in endurance athletes. But Bond *et al.* (1988) found that the results could not be repeated on swimmers. Similarly, high scores on tests of 'Life Stress' have been associated with injuries in footballers and students but the results do not seem to apply to other sports such as volleyball (Williams *et al.* 1986). It may be that more sensitive psychological tests are required, or perhaps different considerations apply to different sports.

Attitudes   Lijsens (1986) and Bouter (1987) both found that lack of caution and low trait anxiety resulted in risk-taking behaviour that led to accidents and injuries. For example, skiers who said before a skiing holiday that they were not afraid of injury were the ones most likely to become injured.

Recklessness   Together with foul play, recklessness is the major cause of injury in school sport (Watson 1984a, 1986). It occurs for two reasons: 'showing off' and because children lack the knowledge and experience to evaluate the risks involved in particular situations. Correction of this type of behaviour through programmes of education offers considerable potential for a reduction in the number of sports injuries.

Fitness

Muscle development   Isometric muscle contractions help to stabilise joints. It has been shown that adequate levels of static strength reduce the likelihood of sports injury (Lijsens 1986; van Vulpen 1989; see also Figure 6.14).

Muscle balance   Imbalance in the strength of opposing muscle groups (Figure 6.15) predisposes to strain injury of the weaker group. The most common example is weakness of the hamstrings in relation to the quadriceps, which has been shown to increase the risk of hamstring strain in footballers and soccer players (Burkett 1970; Poulmedis 1989).

Flexibility   Lack of flexibility is a major cause of injuries such as muscle strains and tendonitis. The association has been demonstrated empirically in soccer players (Ekstrand and Gillquist 1983c), rowers and track and field athletes (Watson 1989), students (Lijsens 1986) and badminton players (Jorgensen and Winge 1990). The latter study also found that a daily stretching programme reduced the incidence of over-use injuries such as tendonitis. Watson (1989) demonstrated a reduction in both acute and over-use injuries when flexibility was improved. A number of studies suggest that injuries due to lack of flexibility are a particular problem in older sportspeople. Studies on the incidence of different types of injuries (page 197) shows that those that can be attributed to poor flexibility are among the most common. This suggests that improving flexibility is likely to be one of the more effective methods of injury prevention.

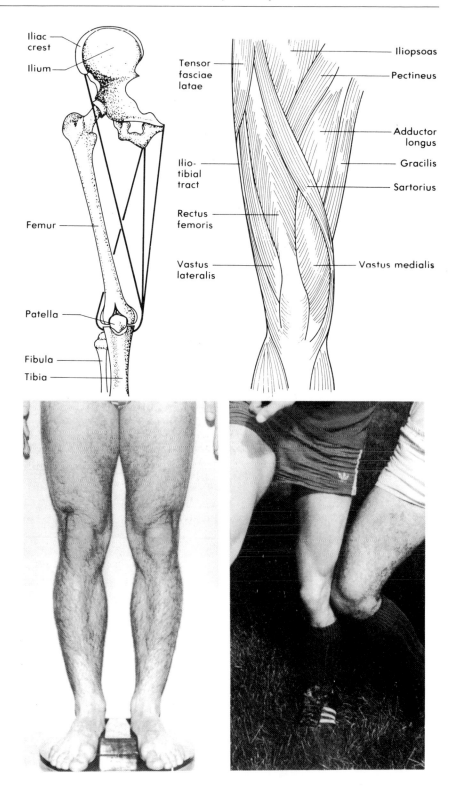

Figure 6.14. *Top*: much of the stability of the knee joint is derived from the strength of muscles which run from the pelvis to the bones of the leg. *Bottom*: well-developed muscles around the knee joint and the type of situation in which the knee joint is vulnerable to injury.

Iliac crest

Ilium

Tensor fasciae latae

Iliopsoas

Pectineus

Ilio-tibial tract

Adductor longus

Gracilis

Sartorius

Femur

Rectus femoris

Vastus lateralis

Vastus medialis

Patella

Fibula

Tibia

Figure 6.15. Superficial muscles of the abdomen and thorax.

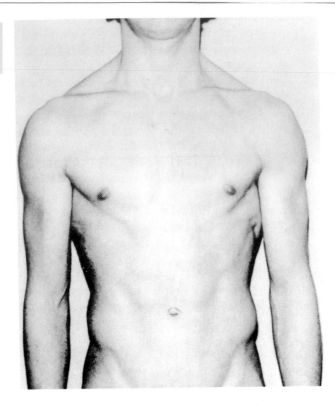

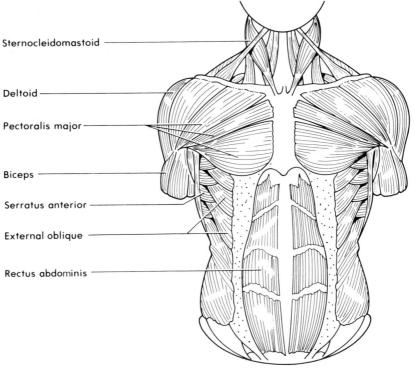

Sternocleidomastoid

Deltoid

Pectoralis major

Biceps

Serratus anterior

External oblique

Rectus abdominis

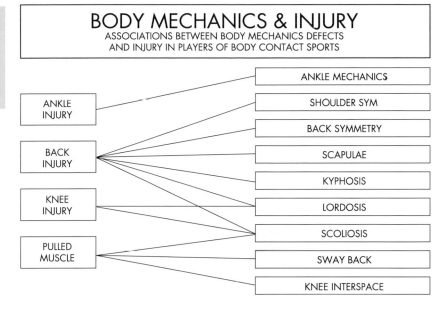

Figure 6.16.
Associations between
body mechanics defects
and sports injury in
players of body contact
sports. (Unpublished
data by the author.)

Endurance   It is probable that a poor level of endurance will increase the risk of injury by causing premature fatigue. This will prevent athletes from extricating themselves from potentially dangerous situations that they would otherwise be able to avoid.

Explosive power   In a 1986 study Lijsens found that subjects with high levels of explosive strength were more likely to suffer from acute injuries than individuals with lower scores. This was attributed to their developing greater power during sports activities, so being at greater risk of violent, acute injuries. The present author has obtained similar results.

Posture   The relationship between defects of body mechanics and the incidence of sports injuries has been studied by a number of groups. Some traditional views on the topic have been shown to be incorrect (Powell *et al.* 1986; Warren and Jones 1987), but recent research demonstrates a link between specific defects and particular kinds of sports injuries.

   The results of an investigation, carried out on footballers in our own laboratory, is summarized in Figure 6.16. This showed that the incidence of strains and over-use injuries was as high in players of body contact sports as it was in endurance athletes, and that a number of injuries were associated with the presence of body mechanics defects. Other research has demonstrated a greater incidence of sports injuries in athletes with the following conditions: a high 'Q' angle, unequal leg length, asymmetric distribution of weight onto the feet, poor spinal posture, and defects of foot mechanics (Klein 1983; Messier and Pitalla 1988; Steele and White 1986; Shambaugh *et al.* 1991). Recent research suggests that deviations of posture are a more important cause of sports injury than poor flexibility (Steele and White 1986; Shambaugh *et al.* 1991; Hennessy and Watson 1993).

Body fat   There is a popular misconception that fat acts as a protection against blows and other contact trauma. There is no evidence to support this theory and excessive body fat actually increases the likelihood and seriousness of injuries such as sprains and those caused by falling.

Diet   An adequate diet is necessary for successful participation in sport, but there is no evidence that dietary modification is capable of reducing the incidence of injuries.

Preparation

Training   Correct training is an important means of reducing the incidence of sports injuries. The topic is considered in Chapter 4. **Training errors** are a major cause of over-use injuries, and the most common include:

1 Over-training. Too much mileage, duration or intensity
2 Insufficient rest periods or 'easy days'
3 Too sharp an increase in duration or intensity
4 Errors of technique
5 Use of unsuitable exercises
6 Over-development of one area of the body or one aspect of fitness in relation to others.

Warm-up/cool-down   Warm-up prepares the body for exercise and is an important part of injury prevention. The warm-up undertaken by many athletes does not adequately prepare them for participation in sport. The topic is considered in detail in Chapter 3.

Hygiene   Poor hygiene may result in skin problems and other pathologies that have similar adverse effects to sports injuries. The most common conditions are: fungal infections like athlete's foot and jock itch, and plantar warts (verrucae) which are transmitted by a virus. Because of the use of communal changing and showering facilities, and the contact between players that takes place in some sports, the possibilities for the transmission of disease in sport are extensive and should be taken seriously. Blood–blood contact between two injured players, or a person attempting to administer first aid, opens the possibility of the transmission of hepatitis or HIV.

Extrinsic factors   *Personal equipment*

Footwear   Sports footwear is a topic that has received considerable attention from manufacturers and those responsible for marketing sports goods. Although modern sports shoes are much safer than the 'plimsolls' of former years, it is unfortunate that there have been few independent studies of the effectiveness of such equipment. The requirements of safety and enhanced performance must be balanced against each other as footwear which maximises energy return and unrestricted movement of the foot may increase the risk of injury (Smith and Bunch 1986). Footwear must also be designed to suit particular sporting activities and to have the correct amount of friction with the surface on which it is used. Research has shown that unsuitable footwear is one of the major causes of injury in sports as diverse as badminton and American football (Jorgensen and Winge 1990; Mueller and Blyth 1974). In the latter study it was found that changes in boots resulted in a 22 per cent reduction in sports injuries. The role of different types of boot in the prevention of ankle sprains has not been conclusively demonstrated. Barrett et al. (1993) found no evidence that high-topped boots or boots with an inflatable air chamber were more effective in preventing injuries than low-top shoes.

Kit   Sports kit needs to have the following characteristics:

1   It should make the athlete look and feel good so that the individual performs at his or her best.
2   It should allow necessary freedom of movement.
3   It should offer protection – for example, in body contact sports.
4   It should offer support.
5   It should regulate body temperature appropriately. For warm-up and for some cold weather activities good insulating properties are necessary in sports clothing. For endurance activities, particularly in hot weather, kit that facilitates heat loss is essential.

Different clothes are required for different activities and often for different stages of one particular sport.

Protective equipment   Proper protective equipment is a vital aspect of safety in many sports and can make a significant reduction in the incidence of injury. A list of common protective items is given in Table 6.8.

However, protective equipment must be properly designed, manufactured and maintained or the incidence of injury may actually increase (Figure 6.17). For example, it has been shown that incorrect adjustment of ski bindings is a major cause

Table 6.8. Examples of protective items used in selected sports.

Item	Example of sport
Helmets	Motorised sports, cycling, equestrian sports, canoeing, climbing, skiing, ice hockey, hurling, cricket, American football
Eye protectors	Motorised sports, winter sports, swimming, squash
Gum shields	Football, boxing
Face guards	Fencing, American football, ice hockey
Shoulder pads	American football
Groin protectors	Cricket
Knee pads	Volleyball
Shin pads	Soccer
Thigh pads	Cricket

Figure 6.17. Mechanical testing of a protective helmet. This kind of evaluation is essential for all types of protective equipment. (Photo reprinted with permission of Blackwell Scientific Publications from *Sports Injuries: Basic Principles of Prevention and Care, Vol IV of the Encyclopaedia of Sports Medicine.* An IOC Medical Commission Publication in collaboration with the International Federation of Sports Medicine, edited by P.A.F.H. Renstrom.)

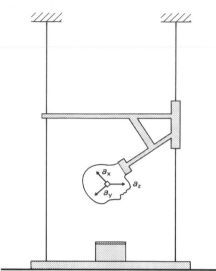

of injury (Johnson *et al.* 1980). Some manufacturers market equipment that has not been scientifically designed or evaluated, or sell it for purposes for which it is not suited. A number of successful legal actions have been brought against such companies.

Knee and ankle supports   Knee bandages have no effect in preventing injuries and even elaborate mechanical braces seem to be of doubtful value. Of the seven published studies, three found a decrease in the injury rate, three an increase, and one no change as a result of the use of knee braces (Pinkowski and Paulos 1993). Taping and the use of lace-up stabilisers appear to be more effective in the prevention of ankle sprains (Garrick and Requa 1973; Rovere *et al.* 1988).

Personal equipment   Personal equipment, such as racquets that are poorly designed, damaged, or of the wrong size or weight, can cause a variety of acute and over-use injuries (see p. 118 – tennis elbow).

Playing environment

Surfaces   Slippery surfaces offer low friction and increase the chances of injury due to falling. Surfaces with moderate amounts of friction have the reverse effect and are safer. Paradoxically, many modern indoor and outdoor surfaces that have extremely high levels of friction produce an increased risk of injury. They do this because they anchor the athlete's footwear so firmly. This allows greater force to be developed and improves performance, but at the cost of an increase in over-use injuries, strains and sprains. Players eventually adapt to new types of surface but the risk of injury is increased if they alternate between different surface types (Ekstrand and Nigg 1989). Surfaces and shoes need to be matched. In a study on American football, Mueller and Blythe (1974) found a 31 per cent reduction in knee and ankle injuries as a result of improved playing surfaces and a reduction of 46 per cent when both playing surface and boots were changed. Two studies of soccer both attribute 25 per cent of injuries to playing surfaces (Sullivan *et al.* 1980; Ekstrand and Gillquist 1983a).

Hard surfaces increase the likelihood of jarring injuries to the feet, legs and back – shin splints is universally attributed to running on hard surfaces like roads. They also increase the likely seriousness of a fall. Less-hard surfaces are kinder to the body but if too soft they absorb a significant amount of energy which reduces power output and increase fatigue.

Uneven surfaces are an important cause of injury. They cause trips, falls, ankle and knee sprains; and also lead to dangerous deviations of the ball in such games as hockey and cricket.

Temperature Extremes of temperature may affect the playing environment, in addition to causing direct injury to the athlete. High temperatures adversely affect some playing surfaces while frost makes grass and other outdoor surfaces dangerous for many sports.

Weather High winds on their own may be dangerous in a number of adventure sports. Wind has a considerable chill factor which, in cold weather, increases the risk of hypothermia. The hazard is greater in wet conditions because of the cooling effects of evaporation and because water reduces the insulating properties of most clothing.

Physical environment The physical environment has an important influence on the safety of sport. Some examples of factors that may cause injuries are listed in Table 6.9.

	Factor	Example
Table 6.9. Factors that may increase the risk of injury.	Poor fixed equipment	Unsafe or unstable wall bars, take off boards, diving boards etc Un-padded goal posts Metal objects rusted or with dangerous projections
	Obstructions	Equipment/chairs stored in playing area
	Atmosphere	Condensation on playing surface or approaches
	Illumination	Level too low, uneven, or glare a problem
	Poor acoustics	Causes confusion
	Approaches	Slippery, uneven or obstructed
	Glass	Clear glass doors are dangerous
	Spectators	Must be separated from playing area

People and organisation

Rules   Rules have an important influence on the incidence of sports injuries and should be formulated with safety considerations uppermost. For example, rule changes in American football resulted in a dramatic decrease both in cervical spine injuries and those that resulted in quadriplegia (Torg *et al.* 1990).

Opponents: Sensible and appropriate   Foul play is said to be responsible for one-third of injuries in soccer (Ekstrand and Gillquist 1983a; Keller *et al.* 1987) and is the most important cause of injury in school sport (Watson 1986). Serious injury is more likely if there is a mis-match of age, size, physical maturity and experience between opponents.

Injury prevention

Injury prevention involves eliminating, or reducing, the effects of factors that have been shown to cause sports injuries in the discussion on the preceding pages. These have been considered in some detail in order that the coach and athlete may focus on the aspects of prevention of special relevance to their own situation. A summary of the factors that need to be considered is given in Figure 6.18. Factors of a biological nature and those concerned with fitness are considered in detail in Chapters 2, 3 and 4.

Sports injuries are now so common that training programmes, and other aspects of preparation for sport, need to be planned with injury prevention as a primary objective. The problem is essentially one of education and behaviour modification. The same principles apply as in other types of health education.

Education of athletes and coaches

Continental sporting organisations – particularly those in Holland – have had considerable experience in organising injury prevention programmes. The steps involved are summarised in Figure 6.19.

The initial, education, phase is vital and must be an ongoing process if behavioural changes are to be achieved and maintained. A number of different approaches should be used:

- Posters, leaflets, booklets
- Attention from the local and national media
- Lectures, talks, etc.
- Seminars, workshops, etc.
- Recording and analysis of injuries in sports clubs
- Screening clinics for individual athletes

Experience in Holland indicates that prevention is most effective when a combination of methods is used. Media coverage introduces the problem to the community. Screening clinics make it a reality for the individual athlete. Leaflets and booklets help to maintain interest and behaviour modification.

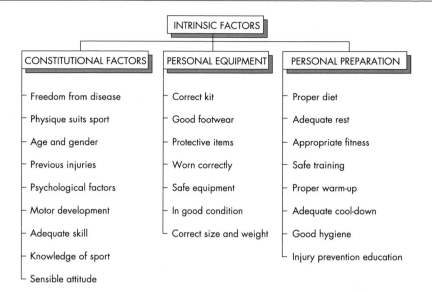

INTRINSIC FACTORS

CONSTITUTIONAL FACTORS
- Freedom from disease
- Physique suits sport
- Age and gender
- Previous injuries
- Psychological factors
- Motor development
- Adequate skill
- Knowledge of sport
- Sensible attitude

PERSONAL EQUIPMENT
- Correct kit
- Good footwear
- Protective items
- Worn correctly
- Safe equipment
- In good condition
- Correct size and weight

PERSONAL PREPARATION
- Proper diet
- Adequate rest
- Appropriate fitness
- Safe training
- Proper warm-up
- Adequate cool-down
- Good hygiene
- Injury prevention education

EXTRINSIC FACTORS

PLAYING ENVIRONMENT
- Playing surfaces
- Good illumination
- Good visability
- Good acoustics
- Safe fixed equipment
- No broken objects
- No obstructions
- No condensation
- Controlled spectators
- Temperature and humidity
- Environment and weather

PEOPLE AND ORGANISATION
- Sensible rules
- Good refereeing
- Appropriate opponents
- Sensible opponents
- Good coaching
- Realistic expectations
- Adequate support

Pre-participation screening examinations

Pre-participation medical examinations are common in certain parts of the world, and in some European countries they are compulsory. Where the effectiveness of such procedures has been studied it has been shown that medical examinations carried out by non-specialists are of no value in reducing the incidence of sports injuries (Meeuwisse and Fowler 1988; Inklaar 1989).

211

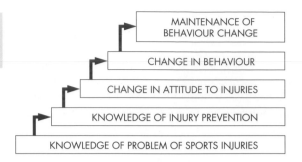

Figure 6.19. Steps in a successful injury prevention programme.

MAINTENANCE OF BEHAVIOUR CHANGE

CHANGE IN BEHAVIOUR

CHANGE IN ATTITUDE TO INJURIES

KNOWLEDGE OF INJURY PREVENTION

KNOWLEDGE OF PROBLEM OF SPORTS INJURIES

There are probably two reasons for this. Firstly, although medical practitioners are highly trained in the recognition and diagnosis of disease, the prevention of sports injuries is not a significant part of the curriculum of any of the leading medical schools. Secondly, the infrastructure, of which the general practitioner is a part, is geared towards the investigation and treatment of disease – not the prevention of injuries. The majority of sports injuries are caused by faults of technique, preparation and equipment, or by deficiencies of flexibility, body mechanics and muscle balance. A more effective way of preventing injuries is to identify and reduce the risk factors associated with a particular sport. Examples of what can be achieved are summarised in Table 6.10.

Table 6.10. Effects of some injury prevention measures.

Sport	Prevention measure	Percentage reduction in sports injuries	Reference
American Football	New type of boot	22.3	Mueller and Blyth (1974)
	New surface	30.5	
	New surface and new boot	46	
	Helmet standard, influence on fatalities 1975–89	90	
Skiing	Information and improved equipment	25–71	Johnson *et al.* (1980)
Cyclists	Helmets, Binding-type pedals, equipment inspection and medical coverage	50	
Ice hockey	Helmets, influence on head injuries 1986–89	66	
	Facial protection and eye injuries 1974–79	81	
Irish élite athletes	Coach education	40	Watson (1990)
	Physiological screening	60	

Summary 1 Injuries are a serious hazard in sport and training. The risk increases with age, the level of competition and the frequency of participation.

2   Strains and over-use injuries constitute a much more serious problem than is generally realised. Injuries which restrict performance and training are extremely common.

3   There is little point in training regularly in order to reach a high level of fitness unless precautions are also taken to reduce the risk of sustaining an injury.

4   The most common injuries in sport are: strains, sprains and various kinds of over-use injury. The incidence of these conditions is influenced by intrinsic factors that can be modified through training.

5   The incidence of sports injuries can be reduced but only by means of a properly designed and executed intervention programme. This is likely to involve:

- Education about the problem of sports injuries
- Education about methods of preventing injuries
- Individual injury prevention screening
- Adoption of injury prevention measures
- Reinforcement
- Behaviour modification
- Maintenance of modified behaviour.

6   Extrinsic factors such as equipment and the playing environment have an important influence on the incidence of sports injuries. Athletes and coaches should do all they can to ensure a high standard. They should decline to compete in conditions that are clearly unacceptable.

7   The most important intrinsic factors in injury prevention are:

- Choice of a sport that suits the subject's age, physique and physical conditions
- Freedom from physical defects
- A suitable training programme
- Adequate flexibility of relevant muscle groups
- Freedom from defects of body mechanics
- Sufficient muscle development to support and protect joints
- Balance between the strength of different muscle groups
- A properly constructed warm-up
- A below-average level of body fat
- Adequate aerobic endurance
- Full recovery from any previous injury.

8   Flexibility is an important factor in relation to injury prevention, but many athletes have poor flexibility because they do not realise its importance and do not know how to train effectively. Stretching only during warm-up is not adequate for injury prevention.

9   Body mechanics defects are a major predisposing factor to sports injuries. Participation in sport can lead to the development of such defects.

10 Much of the strength of joints is derived from the muscles that surround them. Static muscle strength can help give protection against sprains and other joint injuries.

11 A balance between the strength of different muscle groups is necessary otherwise the stronger ones may develop so much force that they injure the weaker ones.

12   An adequate warm-up prepares the body for exercise and reduces the risk of injury. The warm-up carried out by many sportspeople is not adequate and offers no protection.

13   Incomplete recovery from previous injury is one of the major causes of further sports injury.

14   Protective items – such as helmets, gum shields, shin pads and goggles – play an important part in injury prevention, but only if they are properly designed, manufactured and worn. Substandard items cause more problems than they prevent.

REFERENCES

Adams, K., O'Shea, J.P., O'Shea, K.L. and Climstein, M.: The effects of six weeks of squat, plyometric and squat plyometric training on power production. *Journal of Applied Sports Science Research* **6**: 36–41, 1992.

Adams, W.C., Bernauer, E.M., Dill, D.B. and Bonar, J.B.: Effects of equivalent sea-level and altitude training on $\dot{V}_{O_2max}$ and running performance. *Journal of Applied Physiology* **39**: 262–6, 1975.

Ahlborg, G., Hagenfeldt, L and Wahren, J.: Substrate utilisation by the inactive leg during one-leg or arm exercise. *Journal of Applied Physiology* **39**: 718–23, 1975.

Albert, M.: Descriptive three year data study of outdoor and indoor soccer injuries. *Athletic Training* **18**: 218–20, 1983.

Alen, M., Hakkinen, K. and Komi, P.V.: Changes in neuromuscular performance and muscle fibre characteristics of elite power athletes self administering androgenic and anabolic steroids. *Acta Physiologica Scandinavica* **122**: 525–44, 1984.

Alter, M.J.: *Science of Stretching*. Champaign, Illinois, Human Kinetics, 1988.

Anderson, T. and Cattanach, D.: Effects of three different rest periods on expression of developed strength. *Journal of Strength and Conditioning Research* **7**: 185 (abstract), 1993.

Anderson, T. and Kearney, J.T.: Effects of three resistance training programs on muscular strength and absolute and relative endurance. *Research Quarterly for Exercise and Sport* **53**: 1–7, 1982.

Asmussen, E. and Christensen, H.E.: *Compendium i Legemsovelsernes Specielle Teori*. Kobenhavn, Kobenhavens Universites Fond til Tilverjbringelse af Laremindler, 1967.

Astrand, P.O. and Rhyming, I.: A nomogram for calculation of aerobic capacity (physical fitness) from pulse rate during sub-maximal work. *Journal of Applied Physiology* **1**: 218–21, 1954.

Astrand, P.O. and Rodahl, K.: *Text Book of Work Physiology*. New York, McGraw-Hill, 1986.

Backous, D.D., Friedl, K.E., Smith, N.J., Parr, T.J. and Carpine, W.D.: Soccer injuries and their relation to physical maturity. *American Journal of Diseases in Childhood* **142**: 839–42, 1988.

Backx, F.J.G., Erich, W.B.M., Kemper, A.B.A. and Verbeek, A.L.M.: Sports injuries in school-aged children. *American Journal of Sports Medicine* **17**: 234–40, 1989.

Backx, F.J.G.: Sports injuries in youth. MD Thesis University of Utrecht. Published by Institute of Sports Health Care, Oosterbeek, Netherlands, 1991.

Baldwin, K.M., Klinkefuss, G.H., Terjung, R.L., Mole, P.A. and Holloszy, J.O.: Respiratory capacity of red, white and intermediate muscle: adaptive response to exercise. *American Journal of Physiology* **225**: 962–6, 1972.

Bangsbo, J. and Mizuno, M.: Morphological and metabolic alterations in soccer players with detraining and retraining and their relation to performance. In: *Science and Football*, pp. 114–24, Ed. Reilly, T., Lees, A., Davids, K. and Murphy, W.J. London, E & FN Spon, 1988.

Barnard, R.J., Edgerton, V.R. and Peter, J.B.: Effects of exercise on skeletal muscle. I: biochemical and histochemical properties. *Journal of Applied Physiology* **28**: 762–6, 1970.

Barnard, R.J. and Peter, J.B.: Effects of exercise on skeletal muscle. III: Cytochrome changes. *American Journal of Physiology* **31**: 904–8, 1971.

Barrett, J.R., Tanji, J.L., Drake, C., Fuller, D., Kawaski, R.I. and Fenton R.M.: High- versus low-top shoes for the prevention of ankle sprains in basketball players. *American Journal of Sports Medicine* **21**: 582–5, 1993.

Barry, A., Cantwell, T., Doherty. F., Folan, J.C., Ingolsby, M., Kevany, J.P., O'Brien, J.D., O'Connor, H., O'Shea, B., Ryan, B.A. and Vaughan, J.: A nutritional study of Irish athletes.

British Journal of Sports Medicine 15: 99–109, 1981.

Belcastro, A.N. and Bonen, A.: Lactate removal rates during controlled and uncontrolled recovery exercise. *Journal of Applied Physiology* 39: 932–6, 1975.

Berg, K., Olsen, R., McKinney, M., Hofschire, P., Latin, R. and Bell, W.: Effect of reduced training volume on cardiac function, $\dot{V}_{O_2max}$, and running performance. *Journal of Sports Medicine and Physical Fitness* 29: 245-52, 1989.

Berger, R.A.: Comparison of the effect of various weight training loads on strength development. *Research Quarterly* 36: 141–6, 1965.

Berger, R.A.: Effect of varied weight training programs on strength. *Research Quarterly* 33: 168–81, 1962.

Bergh, H., Thorstensson, A., Sjodin, B., Hulten, B., Piehl, K. and Karlsson, J.: Maximum oxygen uptake and muscle fibre types in trained and untrained humans. *Medicine and Science in Sports* 10: 151–4, 1978.

Bielen, E.C., Fagard, R.H. and Amery, A.K.: Inheritance of acute cardiac changes during bicycle exercise: an echocardiographic study in twins. *Medicine and Science in Sports and Exercise* 23: 1254–9, 1991.

Billeter, R. and Hoppeler, H.: Muscular basis for strength. In: *Strength and Power in Sport*, Ed. Komi, P.V. Oxford, Blackwell, 1992.

Binkhorst, R.A., Hoofd, L. and Vissers, A.C.A.: Temperature and force–velocity relationship of human muscles. *Journal of Applied Physiology* 42: 471–5, 1977.

Blattner, S.E. and Noble, L.: Relative effects of isokinetic and plyometric training on vertical jumping performance. *Research Quarterly* 50: 583–8, 1979.

Bobbert, M.F., Huijing, P.A. and Van Ingen Schenau, G.J.: Drop jumping II: The influence of dropping height on the biomechanics of drop jumping. *Medicine and Science in Sports and Exercise* 19: 339–46, 1987.

Bond, J.W., Miller, B.P. and Christfield, P.M.: Psychological prediction of injury in elite swimmers. *International Journal of Sports Medicine* 9: 345–8, 1988.

Bonjer, F.N.: Measurement of working capacity by assessment of the aerobic capacity in a single session. *Federation Proceedings* 25: 1363–5, 1966.

Bosco, C.: Evaluation and control of basic and specific muscle behaviour, Part II. *Track Technique* 124: 3947–52, 1993

Bosco, C.: Stretch-shortening cycle in skeletal muscle function. In: *Studies in Sport, Physical Education and Health*, Ed. Komi, P.V. Finland, University of Jyvaskyla, 1982.

Bosco, C., Luhtanen, P., Komi, P.V.: Kinetics of the take-off in long jump. In: *Biomechanics* VB. Komi P. (ed): University Park Press, Baltimore, MD. 174–180, 1976.

Bosco, C., Komi, C.V.: Mechanical characteristics and fibre composition of human leg extensor muscles. *European Journal of Applied Physiology* 41: 275–84, 1979.

Bosco, C., Luhtanen, P., Komi, P.V.: A simple method for the measurement of mechanical power in jumping. *European Journal of Applied Physiology* 50: 273–82, 1983.

Bosco, C., Montanari, G., Ribacchi *et al.*: Relationship between the efficiency of muscular work jumping and the effects of running. *European Journal of Applied Physiology* 56: 138–43, 1987.

Bouchard, C.: Heredity and the path to overweight and obesity. *Medicine and Science in Sports and Exercise* 23: 285–91, 1991.

Bouchard, C., Godbout, P., Mondor, J.C. and Leblanc, C.: Specificity of maximum aerobic power. *European Journal of Applied Physiology* 40: 85–93, 1979.

Bouchard, C., Taylor, A.W., Simoneau, J.-A. and Dulac, S.: Testing anaerobic power and capacity. In: *Physiological Testing of the High-Performance Athlete*, Ed. MacDougal, J.D., Wenger, H.A. and Green, H.J. Champaign, Illinois, Human Kinetics, 1991.

Bouter, L.M.: Accident risk in downhill skiing. In: *Sports Injuries and their Prevention*. Proceedings of Council of Europe 2nd meeting, Papendal, Netherlands, 1987.

Brady, T., Cahill, B. and Bodnar, L.: Weight training related injuries in the high school athlete. *American Journal of Sports Medicine* 10: 1–5, 1982.

Brien, A.J. and Simpson, T.L.: Effects of red blood infusion on 1500 m race time. In: *Abstracts – New Horizons of Human Movement* 13: 149. SOSCOC, Seoul, 1988.

Brooks, G.A.: The lactate shuttle during exercise and recovery. *Medicine and Science in Sports and*

Exercise **18**: 360–8, 1986.

Brouns, F., Saris, W.H.M. and Rehrer, N.J.: Abdominal complaints and gastrointestinal function during long-lasting exercise. *International Journal of Sports Medicine* **8**: 175–89, 1987.

Brown, M.E., Mayhew, J.L. and Boleach, M.A.: Effect of plyometric training on vertical jump performance in high school basketball players. *Journal of Sports Medicine and Physical Fitness* **26**: 1–4, 1986.

Burke, R.E. and Edgerton, V.R.: Motor unit properties and selective involvement in movement. *Exercise and Sports Science Reviews* vol III, Ed. Wilmore, J.H. and Kreogh, J.F. New York, Academic Press, 1975.

Burkett, N.L.: Causative factors in hamstring strains. *Medicine in Science and Sports* **7**: 195–7, 1970.

Cantu, R.C.: Congenital cardiovascular disease – the major cause of athletic deaths in high school and college. *Medicine and Science in Sports and Exercise* **24**: 279–80, 1992.

Chatard, J.C., Lavoie, J.M. and Lacour, J.R.: Analysis of determinants of swimming economy in front crawl. *European Journal of Applied Physiology* **61**: 88–92, 1990.

Chow, R.K., Harrison, J.E., Brown, C.F. and Hajek, V.: Physical fitness effects on bone mass in postmenopausal women. *Archives of Physical Medicine and Rehabilitation* **67**: 231–4, 1986.

Christensen, E.H. and Hansen, O.: Arbeitsfahigkeit und Ehrnahrung. *Scandinavian Archives of Physiology* **81**: 160–75, 1939.

Chu, D.A.: *Jumping Into Plyometrics*. Champaign, Illinois, Human Kinetics, 1992.

Clarkson, P.M.: Vitamins and trace minerals. In: *Ergogenics – Enhancement of Performance in Exercise and Sport*, pp. 123–82, Ed. Lamb, D.R. and Williams, M.H. Dubuque, Iowa, Brown & Benchmark, 1991.

Clarkson, P.M., Nosaka, K. and Braun, B.: Muscle function after exercise induced muscle damage, and rapid adaptation. *Medicine and Science in Sports and Exercise* **24**: 512–20, 1992.

Clarys, J.P., Martin, A.F. and Drinkwater, D.T.: Gross tissues masses in adult humans: data from 25 dissections. *Human Biology* **56**: 459–73, 1984.

Clayton, M.L., Miles, J.S. and Abdulla, M.: Experimental investigation of ligamentous healing. *Clinical Orthopaedics* **61**: 146–53, 1968.

Coast, J.R. and Krause, K.M.: Relationship of oxygen consumption and cardiac output to work of breathing. *Medicine and Science in Sports and Exercise* **25**: 335–40, 1993.

Collins, K., Wagner, M., Peterson, K. and Storey, M.: Overuse injuries in triathletes: a study of the 1986 Seafair Triathlon. *American Journal of Sports Medicine* **17**: 675–80, 1989.

Corbin, C.B. and Noble, L.: Flexibility: a major component of fitness. *The Journal of Physical Education and Recreation* **51**: 23 4 and 57–60, 1980.

Costill, D.L.: *Inside Running: Basics of Sports Physiology*. Indianapolis, USA, Benchmark Press Inc., 1986.

Costill, D.L. and Miller, J.M.: Nutrition for endurance sport: carbohydrate and fluid balance. *International Journal of Sports Medicine* **1**: 2–14, 1988.

Costill, D.L. and Saltin, B.: Factors influencing gastric emptying during rest and exercise. *Journal of Applied Physiology* **37**: 679–83, 1987.

Costill, D.L., Dalskey, G.P. and Fink, W.J.: Effects of caffeine ingestion on metabolism and endurance performance. *Medicine and Science in Sports* **10**: 155–8, 1978.

Costill, D.L., Coyle, E.F., Fink, W.F., Lesmes, G.R. and Witzmann, F.A.: Adaptations in skeletal muscle following strength training. *Journal of Applied Physiology* **46**: 96–9, 1979a.

Costill, D.L., Daniels, J., Evans, W., Fink, W., Krahenbuhl, G. and Saltin B.: Skeletal muscle enzymes and fibre composition in male and female track athletes. *Journal of Applied Physiology* **40**: 149–54, 1976a.

Cotes, J.E. and Woolmer, R.F.: A comparison between 27 laboratories of the analysis of an expired air sample. *Journal of Physiology* **163**: 37P, 1962.

Coyle, E.F., Costill, D.L. and Lesmes, G.R.: Leg extensor power and muscle fibre composition. *Medicine and Science in Sports* **11**: 12–15, 1979.

Coyle, E.F., Hammert, M.K. and Coggan, A.R.: Effects of detraining on cardiovascular responses to exercise: role of blood volume. *Journal of Applied Physiology* **60**: 95–9, 1986.

Coyle, E.F., Sidossos, L.S., Horowitz, J.F. and Beltz, F.D.: Cycling efficiency is related to the percentage of Type I muscle fibres. *Medicine and Science in Sports and Exercise* 24: 782–8, 1992.

Cullinane, E.M., Sady, S.P., Vadeboncoeur, L., Burke, M. and Thompson P.D.: Cardiac size and $\dot{V}_{O_2max}$ do not decrease after short-term exercise cesssation. *Medicine and Science in Sports and Exercise* 18: 420–4, 1986.

Cumming, G.R. and Danziger, R.: Bicycle ergometer studies in children. *Pediatrics* 32: 202–8, 1963.

Cunningham, D.A., McCrimmon, D. and Vlach, L.F.: Cardiovascular response to interval and continuous training in women. *European Journal of Applied Physiology* 41: 187–97, 1979.

Daniels, J., Oldbridge, N., Nagle, F. and White, B.: Differences and changes in VO2max among young runners 10 to 18 years of age. *Medicine and Science in Sports* 10: 200–3, 1978.

Daniels, J.T., Scardina, N.J. and Foley, P.: VO2max during five modes of exercise. In: *Proceedings of the World Congress of Sports Medicine*, pp. 904–15, Ed. Backl, N., Prokop, L. and Sucket, R. Vienna, Urban and Schwartszenberg, 1984.

Davies, R.E.: The dynamics of the energy rich phosphates. In: *Limiting Factors of Human Performance*, Ed. Keul, J. Stuttgard, Theime, 1971.

Davies, S.F., Iber, C., Keene, S.A., McArthur, C.D. and Path, M.J.: Effect of respiratory alkalosis during exercise on blood lactate. *Journal of Applied Physiology* 61: 948–52, 1986.

DeHaven, K.E. and Lintner, D.M.: Athletic injuries: comparison by age, sport and gender. *American Journal of Sports Medicine* 14: 218–24, 1986.

DeLorme, T.L., Ferris, B.G. and Gallagher, J.R.: Effect of progressive exercise on muscular contraction time. *Archives of Physical Medicine* 33: 86–97, 1952.

Dempsey, J.A.: Is the lung built for exercise? *Medicine and Science in Sports and Exercise* 18: 143–55, 1986.

Depocas, F., Minaire, Y. and Chatonnet, J.: Rates of formation and oxidation of lactic acid in dogs at rest and during moderate exercise. *Canadian Journal of Physiology and Pharmacology* 47: 603–10, 1969.

Dionne, F.T., Turcotte, L., Thibault, M., Boulay, M.R., Skinner, J.S. and Bouchard, C.: Mitochondrial DNA sequence polymorphism, $\dot{V}_{O_2}$ and response to endurance training. *Medicine and Science in Sports and Exercise* 23: 177–85, 1991.

Dodd, S.L., Brooks, E., Powers, S.K. and Tully, R.: The effects of caffeine on graded exercise performance in caffeine naive versus habituated subjects. *European Journal of Applied Physiology* 62: 424–9, 1991.

Douge, B.: Football: the common threads between the games. In: *Science and Football*, pp. 3–19, Ed. Reilly, T., Lees, A., Davids, K. and Murphy, W.J. London, E & FN Spon, 1988.

Drinkwater, B.L. and Horvath. S.M.: Heat tolerance and aging. *Medicine and Science in Sports* 11: 49–55, 1979.

Eddy, D.O., Sparks, L.L. and Adeliz, D.A.: The effects of continuous and interval training in women and men. *European Journal of Applied Physiology* 37: 83–92, 1977.

Ekblom, B., Astrand, P.O., Saltin, B., Stenberg, J. and Wallstrom, B.: Effects of training on circulatory response to exercise. *Journal of Applied Physiology* 24: 518–28, 1968.

Ekstrand, J. and Gillquist, J.: Soccer injuries and their mechanisms: a prospective study. *Medicine and Science in Sports and Exercise* 15: 267–70, 1983a.

Ekstrand, J. and Gillquist, J.: The avoidability of soccer injuries. *International Journal of Sports Medicine* 4: 124–8, 1983b.

Ekstrand, J. and Gillquist, J.: The frequency of muscle tightness and injuries in soccer players. *American Journal of Sports Medicine* 10: 75–8, 1983c.

Ekstrand, J. and Nigg, B.M.: Surface related injuries in soccer. *Sports Medicine (New Zealand)* 8: 56–62, 1989.

Eldred, E., Hutton, R.S. and Smith, J.L.: Nature of the persisting changes in the afferent discharge from muscle following its contraction. *Progressive Brain Research* 44: 157–71, 1976.

Erikson, M.A., Schwarzkopf, R.J. and McKenzie, R.D.: Effects of caffeine, Fructose and glucose ingestion on muscle glycogen utilization during exercise. *Medicine and Science in Sports and Exercise* 19: 579–83, 1987.

Eriksson, B., Gollnick, P. and Saltin, B.: Muscle metabolism and enzyme activities after training in boys 11–13 years. *Acta Physiologica Scandinavica* 87: 485–97, 1973.

Falch, D.K. and Strømme, S.B.: Pulmonary blood flow and interventricular circulation time in physically trained and untrained subjects. *European Journal of Applied Physiology* 40: 211–18, 1979.

Felig, P.: Amino acid metabolism in exercise. In: *The Marathon: Physiological, Medical, Epidemiological, and Psychological Studies*, pp. 56–63, Ed. Milve, P. New York, The New York Academy of Sciences, 1977.

Fleck, S.J. and Kraemer, W.J.: *Designing Resistance Training Programs*. Champaign, Illinois, Human Kinetics, 1987.

Foster, C., Costill, D.L. and Fink, W.J.: Effects of pre-exercise feeding on endurance performance. *Medicine and Science in Sports* 11: 1–5, 1979.

Fox, E.L., Bowers, R.W. and Foss, M.L.: *The Physiological Basis of Physical Education and Athletics*. Philadelphia, Saunders, 1988.

Friden, J. and Lieber, R.L.: Structural and mechanical basis of exercise induced muscle injury. *Medicine and Science in Sports and Exercise* 24: 521–30, 1992.

Gaesser, G.A. and Poole, D.C.: Lactate and ventilatory thresholds: disparity in time course of adaptations to training. *Journal of Applied Physiology* 61: 999–1004, 1986.

Galen, W. van: Injuries in the Netherlands. In: *Sports Injuries and their Prevention*. Proceedings of Council of Europe 3rd meetings, pp. 7–20, Papendal, Netherlands, 1988.

Gallagher, S.S., Finison, K., Guyer, B. and Goodenough, S.: The incidence of injuries among 87,000 Massachusetts children and adolescents. *American Journal of Public Health* 74: 1340–7, 1984.

Garrick, J. and Requa, R.: Role of external support in the prevention of ankle sprains. *Medicine and Science in Sports and Exercise* 5: 200–3, 1973.

Gisolfi, C.V.: Work heat tolerance derived from interval training. *Journal of Applied Physiology* 35: 349–54, 1973.

Gisolfi, C.V. and Dutchman, S.M.: Guidelines for optimum replacement beverages for different athletic events. *Medicine and Science in Sports and Exercise* 24: 679–87, 1992.

Gisolfi, C.V., Summers, R.W., Schedl, H., Bleiler, T.L. and Oppliger, R.A.: Human intestinal water absorption: direct vs indirect measurements. *American Journal of Physiology* 258: G216–22, 1990.

Glassford, R.G., Baycroft, G.H.Y., Sedgwick, A.W. and MacNab, R.B.J.: Comparison of maximum oxygen uptake values determined by predicted and actual methods. *Journal of Applied Physiology* 20: 509–13, 1965.

Glenhill, N.: Blood doping and related issues: a brief review. *Medicine and Science in Sports and Exercise* 14: 45–8, 1982.

Goldfinch, J., McNaughton, L. and Davis, P.: Induced metabolic alkalosis and its effect on 400 m race time. *European Journal of Applied Physiology* 57: 45–8, 1988.

Gollnick, P.D., Armstrong, R.B., Saltin, B., Saubert, C., Sembrowich W. and Shephard, R.: Effects of training on enzyme activity and fibre composition of human skeletal muscle. *Journal of Applied Physiology* 34: 107–11, 1973.

Gollnick, P.D., Armstrong, R.B., Saubert IV, C.W., Piehl, K. and Saltin, B.: Enzyme activity and fibre composition in skeletal muscle of untrained and trained men. *Journal of Applied Physiology* 33: 312–19, 1972.

Gorostiaga, E.M., Walter, C.B., Foster, C. and Hickson, R.C.: Uniqueness of interval and continuous training at the same maintained exercise intensity. *European Journal of Applied Physiology* 63: 101–7, 1991.

Guth, L.: 'Trophic' influences of nerve on muscle. *Physiology Review* 48: 645–87, 1968.

Gutin, B., Stewart, K., Lewis, S. and Kruper, J.: Oxygen consumption in the first stages of strenuous work as a function of prior exercise. *Journal of Sports Medicine* 16: 60–5, 1976.

Guyton, A.C.: *Cardiac Output and its Regulation*. Philadelphia, Saunders, 1963.

Guyton, A.C.: Regulation of cardiac output. *Anaesthesiology* 29: 314, 1968.

Guyton, A.C.: *Textbook of Medical Physiology*, 8th edition. Philadelphia, Saunders, 1991.

Haennel, R., Koon-Kang, T., Quinney, A. and Kappagoda, T.: Effects of hydraulic circuit training on cardiovascular function. *Medicine and Science in Sports and Exercise* 21: 605–12, 1989.

Hagberg, J.M. and Coyle, E.F.: Physiological determinants of endurance performance as studied in competitive racewalkers. *Medicine and Science in Sports and Exercise* 15: 287–93, 1983.

Hagberg, J.M., Hickson, R.C., Ehsani, A.A. and Holloszy, J.O.: Faster adjustment to and recovery from submaximal exercise in the trained state. *Journal of Applied Physiology* 48: 218–24, 1980.

Hagermann, F.C., McKirnan, M.D. and Pompei, J.A.: Maximum oxygen consumption of conditioned and unconditioned oarsmen. *Journal of Sports Medicine* 15: 43–8, 1975.

Haglund. Y. and Eriksson, E.: Does amateur boxing lead to chronic brain damage? *American Journal of Sports Medicine* 21: 97–109, 1993.

Hakkinen, K.: Factors influencing trainability of muscular strength during short term and prolonged training. *National Strength and Conditioning Association Journal* 2: 32–7, 1985.

Hakkinen, K.: Neuromuscular and hormonal adaptations during strength and power training – a review. *Journal of Sports Medicine and Physical Fitness* 29: 9–26, 1989.

Hakkinen, K., Alen, M. and Komi, P.V.: Changes in isometric force and relaxation-time, electromyographic and muscle fibre characteristics of human skeletal muscle during strength training and detraining. *Acta Physiologica Scandinavica* 125: 573–85, 1985a.

Hakkinen, K., Kauhanen, H. and Komi, P.V.: Aerobic, anaerobic, assistant exercise and weightlifting performance capacities in elite weightlifters. *Journal of Sports Medicine* 27: 240–6, 1987.

Hakkinen, K., Komi, P.V. and Alen, M.: Effect of explosive type strength training on isometric force and relaxation-time, electromyographic and muscle fibre characteristics of leg extensor muscles. *Acta Physiologica Scandinavica* 125: 587–600, 1985b.

Hakkinen, K., Komi, P.V. and Kauhanen, H.: EMG, muscle fibre and force production characteristics of leg extensor muscles of elite weight lifters during isometric, concentric and various stretch-shorten cycle exercises. *International Journal of Sports Medicine* 7: 144–51, 1986.

Halpern, B., Thomson, N., Curl, W.W., Andrews, J.R., Hunter, S.C. and Boring J.R.: High school football injuries: identifying the risk factors. *American Journal of Sports Medicine* 15: 316–20, 1987.

Haymers, E.M., McCormick, J.R. and Buskirk, E.R.: Heat tolerance of exercising lean and obese pre-pubertal boys. *Journal of Applied Physiology* 39: 457–61, 1975.

Hejna, W.F., Rosenberg, A., Buturusis, D.J. and Kireger, A.: The prevention of sports injuries in high school students through strength training. *National Strength and Conditioning Association Journal* 4: 28–31, 1982.

Henane, R., Flandrois, R. and Charbonnier, J.P.: Increase in sweating sensitivity by endurance conditioning in man. *Journal of Applied Physiology* 43: 822–8, 1977.

Hennessy, L.: A comparison of three different methods of training and their influence on selected strength and speed performances. Unpublished dissertation. Thomond College of Education, Limerick, 1981.

Hennessy, L.: Plyometrics – important technical observations. *Athletics Coach* 24: 18–21, 1990.

Hennessy, L. and Watson, A.W.S.: Relationship of flexibility and posture to hamstring injury. *British Journal of Sports Medicine* 27: 243–6, 1993.

Hennessy, L.C. and Watson, A.W.S.: The interference effects of simultaneously training for strength and endurance. *Journal of Strength and Conditioning Research* 8: 12–9, 1994.

Hetzler, R.K., Knowlton, R.G., Kaminsky, L.A. and Kamimori, G.H.: Effect of warm-up on plasma free fatty acid response to heavy exercise. *Research Quarterly* 57: 223–8, 1986.

Hickson, R.C.: Interference of strength development by simultaneously training for strength and endurance. *European Journal of Applied Physiology* 45: 255–63, 1980.

Hickson, R.C. and Rosenkoetter, M.A.: Reduced training frequencies and maintenance of increased aerobic power. *Medicine and Science in Sports and Exercise* 13: 13–6, 1981.

Hickson, R.C., Dvorak, B.A., Gorostiaga, E.M., Kurowski, T.T. and Foster, C.: Potential for strength and endurance training to amplify endurance performance. *Journal of Applied Physiology* 65: 2285–90, 1988.

Hickson, R.C., Foster, C., Pollock, M.L., Gallassi, T.M. and Rich, S.: Reduced training intensities and loss of aerobic power, endurance and cardiac growth. *Journal of Applied Physiology* 58: 492–99, 1985.

Hickson, R.C., Kanakis Jr, C., Davis, J.R., Moore, A.M. and Rich, S.: Reduced training duration effects on aerobic power, endurance, and cardiac growth. *Journal of Applied*

Physiology 53: 225–9, 1982.

Hickson, R.C., Hagberg, J.M., Conlee, R.K., Jones, D.A., Ehsani, A.A. and Winder, W.W.: Skeletal muscle enzyme alterations after sprint and endurance training. *European Journal of Applied Physiology* 40: 868–72, 1979.

Holloszy, J.O.: Biochemical changes in muscle: effects of exercise on mitochondrial oxygen uptake and respiratory enzyme activity. *Journal of Biological Chemistry* 242: 2278–82, 1967.

Hooper, S.L., MacKinnon, L.T., Gordon, R.D. and Bachmann, A.W.: Hormonal response of elite swimmers to overtraining. *Medicine and Science in Sports and Exercise* 25: 741-7, 1993.

Hortobagyi, T., Katch, F.I. and Lachance, P.F.: Effects of simultaneous training for strength and endurance on upper and lower body strength and running performance. *Journal of Sports Medicine and Physical Fitness* 31: 20–30, 1991.

Houston, M.E. and Thomson, J.A.: The response of endurance adapted adults to intense anaerobic training. *European Journal of Applied Physiology* 36: 207–13, 1977.

Hoy, K., Lindblad, B.E., Terkelsen, T.J., Helleland, H.E. and Terkelsen, C.J.: European soccer injuries. *American Journal of Sports Medicine* 20: 318–22, 1992.

Iashvili, A.V.: Active and passive flexibility in athletes specialising in different sports. *Soviet Sports Review* 18: 30–2, 1983.

Ibara, G., Fisher, A.G. and Conlee, R.K.: Effects of anaerobic training on selected aerobic factors in well-trained endurance runners. *Medicine and Science in Sports and Exercise* 13: (abstract) 109, 1981.

Ikai, M. and Steinhaus, A.: Some factors modifying the expression of human strength. *Journal of Applied Physiology* 16: 157–63, 1961.

Ingjer, F.: Capillary supply and mitochondrial content of different skeletal muscle fibre types in untrained and endurance trained men: a histochemical and ultrastructure study. *European Journal of Applied Physiology* 40: 197–209, 1979.

Ingjer, F. and Strømme, S.B.: The effects of active, passive or no warm-up on physiological response to heavy exercise. *European Journal of Applied Physiology* 40: 273–82, 1979.

Inklaar, H.: An experimental soccer injury prevention programme. In: *Sports Injuries and their Prevention*. Proceedings of Council of Europe 3rd Meeting, Papendal, Netherlands, 1989.

Inklaar, H.: Continuous morbidity registration, sentinel stations. *Survey of Sports Injuries 1979–83*. Oosterbeek, Netherlands, NISGZ, 1986.

Issekutz, B., Shaw, W.A. and Issekutz, A.C.: Lactate metabolism in resting and exercising dogs. *Journal of Applied Physiology* 40: 312–19, 1976.

Ivy, J.L., Katz, A.L., Cutler, C.L., Sherman, W.M. and Coyle, E.F.: Muscle glycogen synthesis after exercise. effect of time of carbohydrate ingestion. *Journal of Applied Physiology* 64: 1480 5, 1988.

Ivy, J.L., Costill, D.L., Fink, W.L. and Lower, R.W.: Influence of caffeine and carbohydrate feeding on endurance performance. *Medicine and Science in Sports and Exercise* 11: 6–11, 1979.

Jackson, A.S. and Pollock, M.L.: Generalised equations for predicting body density of man. *British Journal of Nutrition* 40: 497–504, 1978.

Jacobs, I., Westlin, N., Karlsson, J., Rasmusson, M. and Houghton, B.: Muscle glycogen and diet in elite soccer players. *European Journal of Applied Physiology* 48: 297–302, 1982.

Johnson, B.L., Adanczyk, J.W., Tennoe, K.O. and Strømme, S.B.: A comparison of concentric and eccentric muscle training. *Medicine and Science in Sports* 8: 35–8, 1976.

Johnson, R.J., Ettlinger, C.F., Campbell, R.J. and Pope, M.H.: Trends in skiing injuries. analysis of 6-year study (1972–1978). *American Journal of Sports Medicine* 8: 106–13, 1980.

Jones, D.A., Priest, J.D., Hayes, W.C., Tichnor, C.C. and Nagel, D.A.: Humeral hypertrophy in response to exercise. *Journal of Bone and Joint Surgery* 59a: 204–8, 1977.

Jorfeldt, L., Juhlin-Dannfelt, A. and Karlsson, J.: Lactate release in relation to tissue lactate in human skeletal muscle during exercise. *Journal of Applied Physiology* 44: 350–2, 1978.

Jorgensen, U. and Winge, S.: Injuries in badminton. *Sports Medicine* 10: 59–64, 1990.

Kamien, M.: The incidence of tennis elbow and other injuries in tennis players. *Australian Journal of Science and Medicine in Sport* 21: 18–22, 1989.

Kanehisa, H. and Miyashita, M.: Specificity of velocity in strength training. *European Journal of Applied Physiology* 52: 104–6, 1983.

Karlsson, J. and Saltin, B.: Diet, muscle glycogen and endurance performance. *Journal of Applied Physiology* **31**: 203–6, 1971.

Karlsson, J., Nordesjo, L., Jorfeldt, L. and Saltin, B.: Muscle lactate, ATP and CP levels during exercise after physical training. *Journal of Applied Physiology* **33**: 199–203, 1972.

Kavanagh, T., Shephard, R. and Pandit, V.: Marathon running after myocardial infarction. *Journal of the American Medical Association* **229**: 1602–5, 1974.

Keizer, H.A., Kuipers, H., Van Kranenburg, G. and Geurten, P.: Influence of liquid and solid meals on muscle glycogen resynthesis, plasma hormone response, and maximal physical working capacity. *International Journal of Sports Medicine* **8**: 99–104, 1987.

Keller, C.S., Noyles, F.R. and Buncher, C.R.: The medical aspects of soccer epidemiology. *American Journal of Sports Medicine* **15**: S105–12, 1987.

Keul, J., Doll, E. and Keppler, D.: *Energy Metabolism in Human Muscle.* Basel, Karger, 1972.

Keys, A. and Brozek, J.: Body fat in adult man. *Physiological Review* **33**: 245–325, 1953.

Klausen, K.: Strength and weight training. In: *Physiology of Sports*, Ed. Reilly, T., Secher, N., Snell, P. and Williams, C. London, E & FN Spon, 1990.

Klein, K. K.: Developmental asymmetries and knee injuries. *Physician and Sportsmedicine* **11**: 67–72, 1983.

Knapik, J. J., Mawdsley, R.H. and Ramos, M.U.: Angular specificity and test mode specificity of isometric and isokinetic strength training. *Journal of Orthopaedic Sports Physical Therapy* **5**: 58–65, 1983a.

Knapik, J.J., Jones, B.H., Toner, M., Daniels, W.L. and Evans, W.J.: Influence of caffeine on serum substrate changes during running in trained and untrained individuals. *Biochemistry of Exercise* **13**: 514–19, 1983b.

Knutten, H.G.: Aerobic capacity of adolescents. *Journal of Applied Physiology* **22**: 655–8, 1967.

Komi, P.V.: Physiological and biomechanical correlates of muscle function: effects of muscle structure and strength-shortening cycle on force and speed. In: *Exercise and Sports Science Reviews* **12**: 81–122. Toronto, DC Heath, 1984.

Komi, P.V. and Buskirk, E.R.: Effects of concentric and eccentric muscle conditioning on tension and electrical activity of human muscle. *Ergonomics* **15**: 417–34, 1972.

Komi, P.V., Vittasalo, R., Rauramaa, R. and Vihko, V.: Effects of isometric strength training on mechanical, electrical and metabolic aspects of muscle function. *European Journal of Applied Physiology* **40**: 45–55, 1978.

Komi, W., Rusko, H., Vos, J. and Vihko, J. Anaerobic performance capacity in athletes. *Acta Physiologica Scandinavica* **100**: 107–14, 1977.

Krahenbuhl, G.S. and Williams, T.J.: Running economy: changes with age during childhood and adolescence. *Medicine and Science in Sports and Exercise* **24**: 462–6, 1992.

Kulund, D.: *The Injured Athlete.* Philadelphia, Lippincott, 1988.

LeBlanc, J., Jonin, N., Cote, J., Samson, P. and Labrie, A.: Enhanced metabolic response to caffeine in exercise-trained human subjects. *Journal of Applied Physiology* **59**: 832–7, 1985.

Leighton, J.R., Holmes, D., Benson, J., Wooten, B. and Schmerer, R.: A study of the effectiveness of ten different methods of progressive resistance exercise on the development of strength, flexibility, girth and body weight. *Journal of the Association of Physical and Mental Rehabilitation* **21**: 78–81, 1967.

Lesmes, G.R., Costill, D.H., Coyle, E. and Fink, W.J.: Muscle strength and power changes during maximal isokinetic training. *Medicine and Science in Sports* **10**: 266–9, 1978.

Lijsens, R.J.J.: A study of the intrinsic risk factors of sports injuries in young adults. In: *Sports Injuries and their Prevention*. Proceedings of Council of Europe 1st meeting. Papendal, Netherlands, 1986.

Lijsens, R.J.J.: Epidemiological surveillance of sports injuries through a network of sentinel generating general practitioners in Belgium. In: *Sports Injuries and their Prevention*. Proceedings of Council of Europe 2nd meeting. Papendal, Netherlands, 1987.

Logan, G.A. and Egstrom, G.H.: The effects of slow and fast stretching on the sacro-femoral angle. *Journal of the Association for Physical and Mental Rehabilitation* **15**: 86–9, 1961.

Lorentzon, R., Wedren, H., Pietila, T. and Gustavsson, B.: Injuries in international ice hockey. *American Journal of Sports Medicine* **16**: 389–91, 1988.

Loucks, A.B.: Osteoporosis prevention begins in childhood. In: *Competitive Sports for Children and Youth: An Overview of Research and Issues*, pp. 213–23, Ed. Brown, E.W. and Bravta, C.F. Champaign, Illinois, Human Kinetics, 1988.

Lowdon, I.M. and Wetherill, M.H.: Parachuting injuries during training descents. *Injury* 20: 257–8, 1989.

MacDougal, J.D., Elder, G.B.C., Sale, D.G., Moraz, J.R. and Sutton, J.R.: Effects of strength training and immobilisation on human muscle fibres. *European Journal of Applied Physiology* 43: 25–34, 1980.

Magel, J.R., Foglia, G.F., McCardle, W.D., Gutin, B., Pechar, G.S. and Katch, F.I.: Specificity of swim training on maximum oxygen uptake. *Journal of Applied Physiology* 38: 151–5, 1975.

Maher, J.T., Beller, G., Foster, J.M. and Hartley, L.H.: Radiographic changes in cardiac dimensions during exhaustive exercise in man. *Journal of Sports Medicine* 18: 263–69, 1978.

Malarecki, I.: Investigation into the physiological effect of so-called 'warming-up'. *Acta Physiol Pol* 5: 543–6, 1954.

Malina, R.M. and Bouchard, C.: *Sport and Human Genetics*. Champaign, Illinois, Human Kinetics, 1986.

Malina, R.M. and Bouchard, C.: *Growth, Maturation and Physical Activity*. Champaign, Illinois, Human Kinetics, 1991.

Manning, R.J., Graves, J.E., Carpenter, D.M., Leggett, S.H. and Pollock, M.L.: Constant vs variable resistance knee extension training. *Medicine and Science in Sports and Exercise* 22: 397–401, 1990.

Margaria, R., Cerretelli, P. and Mangili, F.: Kinetics and mechanism of oxygen debt contraction in man. *Journal of Applied Physiology* 19: 623–8, 1964.

Margaria, R., Edwards, H.T. and Dill, D.B.: The possible mechanism of contracting and paying the oxygen debt and the role of lactic acid in muscular contraction. *American Journal of Physiology* 106: 687–715, 1933.

Maron, M.B., Wagner, J.A. and Horavath, S.M.: Thermoregulatory responses during competitive marathon running. *Journal of Applied Physiology* 42: 909–14, 1977.

Martin, A.D., Howie, J.L., Baily, D.A. and Houston, C.S.: Osteoporosis and bone dynamics: a radiological prospective. In: *Kinathropometry III*. Ed. Reilly, T., Watson, J. and Borms, J. London, E & FN Spon, 1986.

Martin, P.E., Heise, G.D. and Morgan, D.W.: Interrelationships between mechanical power, energy transfer, and walking and running economy. *Medicine and Science in Sports and Exercise* 25. 508–15, 1993.

Martin, B.R., Robinson, S., Wiegman, D.L. and Anlick, L.H.: Effects of warm-up or metabolic response to strenuous exercise, *Medicine and Science in Sports* 7: 146–9, 1975.

Matveyev, L.P.: Modern procedures for the construction of macrocycles. *Modern Athlete and Coach* 30: 32–4, 1992.

Maughan, R.J.: Marathon Running. In: *Physiology of Sports*, Ed. Reilly, T., Secher, N., Snell, P. and Williams, C. London, E & FN Spon, 1990.

Maughan, R.J. and Leiper, J.B.: Aerobic capacity and fractional utilisation of aerobic capacity in elite and non-elite male and female marathon runners. *European Journal of Applied Physiology* 52: 80–7, 1983.

Mazess, R.B., Peppler, W.W., Chesney, R.W., Lange, T.A., Lingren, W. and Smith, E. Jr: Total body and regional bone mineral by dual-photo absorbtiometry in metabolic bone disease. *Calcified Tissue International* 36: 8–13, 1984.

McArdle, W.D., Magel, J.R., Dekio, D.J., Toner, M. and Chase, J.M.: Specificity of run training on VO_2max and heart rate during running and swimming. *Medicine and Science in Sports* 10: 16–20, 1978.

McCulloch, R.G., Baily, D.A., Houston, C.S. and Dodd. B.L.: Effects of physical activity, dietary calcium intake and selected lifestyle factors on bone density in young women. *Canadian Medical Association Journal* 142: 221–32, 1990.

McLennan, J.G. and McLennan, J.E.: Injury patterns in Scottish heavy athletes. *American Journal of Sports Medicine* 18: 529–32, 1990.

McMaster, W.C. and Walter, M.: Injuries in soccer. *American Journal of Sports Medicine* 6: 354–7, 1978.

References

McMorris, R. and Elkins, E.: A study of production and evaluation of muscular hypertrophy. *Archives of Physical Medicine and Rehabilitation* **35**: 420–6, 1954.

Meeuwisse, W.H. and Fowler, P.J.: Frequency and predictability of sports injuries in intercollegiate athletes. *Canadian Journal of Sports Science* **18**: 35–42, 1988.

Messier, S.P. and Pittala, K.A.: Etiological factors associated with selected running injuries. *Medicine and Science in Sports and Exercise* **20**: 501–5, 1988.

Meulen, J.C., Van: Present state of knowledge on processes of healing in collagen structures. *International Journal of Sports Medicine* **3**: suppl. 1, 4–8, 1982.

Mikesell, K.A. and Dudley, G.A.: Influence of intense endurance training on aerobic power of competitive distance runners. *Medicine and Science in Sports and Exercise* **16**: 371–5, 1984.

Milner-Brown, H.S., Stein, R.B. and Yemm, R.: The orderly recruitment of human motor units during voluntary isometric contractions. *Journal of Physiology* **230**: 359–70, 1973.

Minaire, T.: Origine et destiné du lactate plasmatique. *Journal of Physiology (Paris)* **66**: 229–57, 1973.

Moffatt, R.J., Stamford, B.A. and Neill, R.D.: Placement of tri-weekly training sessions: importance regarding enhancement of aerobic capacity, *Research Quarterly* **48**: 583–91, 1977.

Mokha, R., Kaur, G. and Sidhu, L.S.: Effect of training on the reaction time of Indian Female hockey players. *Journal of Sports Medicine and Physical Fitness* **32**: 428–31, 1992.

Moore, M. and Hutton, R.S.: Electromyographic investigation of muscle stretching techniques. *Medicine and Science in Sports and Exercise* **12**: 322–9, 1980.

Moravec, P., Ruzicka, J., Susanka, P., Dostal, E., Kodejs, M. and Nosek, M.: The 1987 International Athletic Foundation/IAFF scientific project report: Time analysis of the 100 metres events at the world championships in Athletics. *New Studies in Athletics* **3**: 61–96, 1988.

Morgan, D.W. and Craib, M.: Physiological effects of running economy. *Medicine and Science in Sports and Exercise* **24**: 456–61, 1992.

Morgan, R.E. and Adamson, G.T.: *Circuit Training*. London, Bell & Sons, 1962.

Muller, E.A.: Influence of training and inactivity on muscle strength. *Archives of Physical Medicine and Rehabilitation* **51**: 449–62, 1970.

Mueller, F.O. and Blythe, C.S.: North Carolina high school football injury study: equipment and prevention. *Journal of Sports Medicine* **2**: 1–10, 1974.

Muller, E.A. and Hettinger, T.: Die Bedeutung der Trainingsgeschwindigkeit atrophierter von Muskelin. *Arbeitsphysiologie* **15**: 223–30, 1954.

Nadel, E.R. (Ed.): *Problems with Temperature Regulation during Exercise*. New York, Academic Press, 1977.

Nadel, E.R.: Control of sweating rate while exercising in the heat. *Medicine and Science in Sports* **11**: 31–5, 1979.

Nicholl, J.P., Coleman, P. and Williams, B.T.: *Injuries in Sport and Exercise*. London, Sports Council, 1992.

Nishiitsutsuji-Uwo, J.M., Ross, B.M. and Krebs, H.A.: Metabolic activities of the isolated perfused rat kidney. *Biochemistry Journal* **103**: 852–62, 1967.

Olsen, R., Berg, K., Latin, R. and Blanke, D.: Comparison of two intense interval training programs on maximum oxygen uptake and running performance. *Journal of Sports Medicine and Physical Fitness* **28**: 158–64, 1988.

Parkhouse, W.S. and McKensie, D.C.: Possible contribution of skeletal muscle buffers to enhanced anaerobic performance: a brief review. *Medicine and Science in Sports and Exercise* **16**: 328-38, 1984.

Pendersen, P. and Jorgensen, K.: Maximum oxygen uptake in young women with training, inactivity and retraining. *Medicine and Science in Sports* **10**: 233–7, 1978.

Perrine, J.J. and Edgerton, V.R.: Muscle force–velocity and power–velocity relationships under isokinetic loading. *Medicine and Science in Sports* **10**: 159–66, 1978.

Peter, J.B., Sawaki, A., Barnard, R.J., Edgerton, R.J. and Gillespie, C.A.: Lactate dehydrogenase isoenzymes: distribution in fast-twitch red, fast-twitch white and slow-twitch intermediate fibres of guinea pig skeletal muscle. *Archives of Biochemistry and Biophysiology* **144**: 304–7, 1971.

Pette, D., Smith, M.E., Staudte, W.H. and Vribova, G.: Effects of long term electrical stimulation on some contractile and metabolic characteristics of fast twitch rabbit muscles. *Pfleugers Archives* **338**: 257–72, 1973.

Pfundt, K.: *Bedeutung und Charakteristics von Heim und Freizeitunfallen.* Cologne, HUK Association, Publication No. 26, 1985.

Pinkowski, J.P. and Paulos, L.E.: Prophylactic knee and ankle orthoses. In: *Sports Injuries,* Ed. Renstrom, P.A.F.H. Oxford, Blackwell, 1993.

Pipes, T.V.: Variable resistance versus constant resistance strength training in adult males. *European Journal of Applied Physiology* **39**: 27–35, 1978.

Pipes, T.V. and Wilmore, J.: Isokinetic vs. isotonic training in adult men. *Medicine and Science in Sports* **7**: 262–74, 1975.

Pollock, M.L., Gettman, L.A., Milesis, C.A., Bah, M.D., Durstine, L. and Johnson, R.M.: Effects of frequency and duration of training on attrition and incidence of injury. *Medicine and Science in Sports* **9**: 31–9, 1977.

Pollock, N.A., Eisman, J.A., Yeats, M.G., Sambrook, F.N. and Eberl, S.: Physical fitness is a major determinant of femoral neck and lumbar spine bone mineral density. *Journal of Clinical Investigation* **78**: 618–21, 1986.

Poortmans, J.R. and Jeanloz, R.W.: Quantitative immunological determination of 12 plasma proteins excreted in human urine collected before and after exercise. *Journal of Clinical Investigation* **47**: 386–93, 1978.

Potteiger, J.A., Judge, L. and Cerny, J.A.: Lean body mass and hormonal changes using a periodised training program in weight event athletes. *Journal of Strength and Conditioning Research* **7**: 182 (abstract), 1993.

Poulmedis, P.: Muscular imbalance and strains in soccer. In: *Sports Injuries and their Prevention.* Proceedings of Council of Europe 3rd meeting, pp. 53–8. Papendal, Netherlands, 1989.

Powell, K.E., Kohl, H.W., Caspersen, C.J. and Blair, S.N.: An epidemiological perspective on the causes of running injuries. *Physician and Sportsmedicine* **14**: 100–14, 1986.

Prendergast, D.R., Prampero, P.E. di, Craig, A.B., Wilson, D.R. and Rennie, D.W.: Quantitative analysis of the front crawl in men and women. *Journal of Applied Physiology* **43**: 475–9, 1977.

Ragosta, M., Crabtree, J., Sterner, W.Q. and Thomson, P.D.: Death during recreational exercise in the state of Rhode Island. *Medicine and Science in Sports and Exercise* **16**: 339–42, 1984.

Ramsey, J.M. and Pipoly, S.W., Jr: Response of erythrocyte 2-, 3-diphosphoglycerate to strenuous exercise. *European Journal of Applied Physiology* **40**: 227–33, 1979.

Rasch, P.J. and Morehouse, E.L.: Effects of static and dynamic exercises on muscular strength and hypertrophy. *Journal of Applied Physiology* **11**: 29–34, 1957.

Reilly, T.: Football. In: *Physiology of Sports,* pp. 371–427, Ed. Reilly, T., Secher, N., Snell, P. and Williams, C. London, E & FN Spon, 1990.

Requa, R.K., DeAvilla, L.N. and Garrick, J.G.: Injuries in recreational activities. *American Journal of Sports Medicine* **21**: 461–7, 1993.

Robergs, R.A., Pascoe, D.D., Costill, D.L., Fink, W.J., Chwalbinskamoneta, J., Davis, J.A. and Hickner, R.: Effects of warm-up on muscle glycogenolysis during intense exercise. *Medicine and Science in Sports and Exercise* **23**: 37–43, 1991.

Roberts, A.D. and Morton, A.R.: Total and alactic oxygen debts after supra-maximal work. *European Journal of Applied Physiology* **38**: 281–9, 1978.

Robinson, S., Dill, D.B., Robinson, R.D., Tzankoff, S.P. and Wagner, J.A.: Physiological aging of champion runners. *Journal of Applied Physiology* **41**: 46–51, 1976.

Ross, J.R., Casson, I.R., Siegel, O. and Cole, M.: Boxing injuries: neurologic, radiologic and neuropsychologic evaluation. *Clinics in Sports Medicine* **6**: 41–51, 1987.

Rovere, G., Clarke, T., Yates, C. and Burley, K.: Retrospective comparison of taping and ankle stabilizers in preventing ankle injuries. *American Journal of Sports Medicine* **16**: 228–33, 1988.

Rowell, L.B.: Human cardiovascular adjustments to exercise and thermal stress. *Physiological Review* **54**: 75–157, 1974.

Rowland, T.W.: Aerobic responses to physical training in children. In: *Endurance in Sport,* Ed. Shephard, R.J. and Astrand, P.O. Oxford, Blackwell, 1992.

Sady, S.P., Worman, M. and Blank, D.: Flexibility training: ballistics, static or proprioceptive neuromuscular facilitation. *Archives of Physical Medicine and Rehabilitation* **63**: 261–3, 1982.

Sale, D.G.: Neural adaptation to strength training. In: *Strength and Power in Sport*, pp. 249–65, Ed. Komi, P.V. Oxford, Blackwell, 1992a.

Sale, D.G.: Testing strength and power. In: *Physiological Testing of the High-Performance Athlete*, Ed. MacDougal, J.D., Wenger, H.A. and Green, H.J. Champaign, Illinois, Human Kinetics, 1992b.

Sale, D.J., MacDougal, J.D., Jacobs, I. and Garner, S.: Interaction between concurrent strength and endurance training. *Journal of Applied Physiology* **68**: 260–70, 1990.

Salmons, S. and Vrbova, G.: The influence of activity on some contractile characteristics of mammalian fast and slow twitch muscles. *Journal of Physiology* **201**: 535–49, 1969.

Saltin, B.: Physiological effects of physical conditioning. *Medicine and Science in Sports* **1**: 50–6, 1969.

Saltin, B. and Stenburg, J.: Circulatory response to prolonged severe exercise. *Journal of Applied Physiology* **19**: 833–8, 1964.

Sapega, A.A., Quedenfield, T.C., Moyer, R.A. and Butler, R.A.: Biophysical factors in range-of-motion exercise. *The Physician and Sportsmedicine* **9**: 57–65, 1981.

Schafle, M.D., Requa, R.K., Patton, W.L. and Garrick, J.G.: Injuries in the 1987 National amateur volleyball tournament. *American Journal of Sports Medicine* **18**: 624–31, 1990.

Schmidtbleicher, D.: Training for power events. In: *Strength and Power in Sport*, pp. 381–95, Ed. Komi, P.V. Oxford, Blackwell, 1992.

Schultz, R.W.: Effect of direct practice and repetitive sprinting and weight training on selected motor performance tasks. *Research Quarterly* **38**: 108–18, 1967.

Scoles, G.: Depth jumping: does it really work? *Athletic Journal* **58**: 48–75, 1978.

Scripture, E.Q., Smith, T.L. and Brown, E.M.: On the education of muscular control and power. *Studies of Yale Psychological Laboratory* **2**: 114–19, 1894.

Secher, N.H.: The physiology of rowing. *Journal of Sports Sciences* **1**: 23–53, 1983.

Shambaugh, J.P., Klein, A. and Herbert, J.H.: Structural measures as predictors of injury in basketball players. *Medicine and Science in Sports and Exercise* **23**: 522–7, 1991.

Sharp, R.L. and Costill, D.L.: Influence of body hair removal on physiological responses during breaststroke swimming. *Medicine and Science in Sports and Exercise* **21**: 576–80, 1989.

Sharp, R.L., Troup, J.P. and Costill, D.L.: Relationship between power and sprint freestyle swimming. *Medicine and Science in Sports and Exercise* **14**: 53–6, 1982.

Shaver, L.G.: Cross transfer effects of conditioning and de-conditioning on muscular strength. *Ergonomics* **18**: 9–16, 1975.

Sheldon, W.H., with Dupertuis, C.W. and McDermott, E.: *Atlas of Men*. New York, Harper, 1954.

Sheldon, W.H., with Stevens, S.S. and Tucker, W.B.: *The Varieties of Human Physique*. New York, Harper, 1940.

Shephard, R.J.: *Endurance Fitness*. Toronto, University of Toronto Press, 1969.

Shephard, R.J.: Intensity, duration, and frequency of exercise as determinants of the response to a training regimen. *International Zeitschrift für angewandte Physiologie* **26**: 272–8, 1968.

Sherman, W.M., Armstrong, L.E., Murray, T.M., Hagermann, F.C., Costill, D.L., Staron, R.C. and Ivy, J.L.: Effect of a 42.2 km footrace and subsequent rest or exercise on muscular strength and work capacity. *Journal of Applied Physiology* **57**: 1668–73, 1984.

Shields, C.L., Zomar Beckwith, V. and Kurland. H.L.: Comparison of leg strength training equipment. *The Physician and Sportsmedicine* **13**: 49–56, 1985.

Silvester, L.J., Stiggins, C., McGown, C. and Byrce, G.: The effects of variable resistance and free weight training programs on strength and vertical jump. *National Strength and Conditioning Association Journal* **5**: 30–3, 1984.

Siri, W.E.: Body composition from fluid spaces and density: analysis of different methods. In: *Techniques for Measuring Body Composition*, Ed. Brozek, J. and Henschel, A. Washington, National Academy of Science and National Research Council, 1961.

Sjodin, B. and Svedenhag, J.: Applied physiology of marathon running. *Sports Medicine* **2**: 83–99, 1985.

Skinner, H.B., Wyatt, M.P., Stone, M.L., Hodgdon, J.A. and Barrack, R.L.: Exercise related knee joint laxity. *Medicine and Science in Sports and Exercise* **14**: 30–4, 1986.

Smith, D.P. and Stransky, F.W.: The effects of training and detraining on the body composition and cardiovascular response of young women to exercise. *Journal of Sports Medicine* **16**: 112–20, 1976.

Smith, L.S. and Bunch, R.: Athletic footwear. *Clinical Pediatrics and Medical Surgery* **3**: 637–47, 1986.

Smith, R. and Reischl, S.: Treatment of ankle sprains in young athletes. *American Journal of Sports Medicine* **14**: 465–71, 1986.

Snell, P.: Middle distance running. In: *Physiology of Sports*, pp. 101–20, Ed. Reilly, T., Secher, N., Snell, P. and Williams, C. London, E & RN Spon, 1990.

Stamford, A.B., Moffatt, R.J., Weltman, A., Maldonado, C. and Curtis, M.: Blood lactate disappearance after supra-maximal one-leg exercise. *Journal of Applied Physiology* **45**: 244–8, 1978.

Staron, R.S., Malicky, E.S., Leonardi, M.J., Falkel, J.E., Hagermann, F.C. and Dudley, G.A.: Muscle hypertrophy and fast fiber type conversions in heavy resistance trained women. *European Journal of Applied Physiology* **60**: 70–9, 1989.

Staudte, W.H., Exner, G. and Pette, D.: Effects of short-term high-intensity (sprint) training on some contractile and metabolic characteristics of fast and slow twitch muscle of the rat. *Pfluegers Archives* **344**: 159–68, 1973.

Steben, R.E. and Steben, A.H.: The validity of the stretch-shortening cycle in selected jumping events. *Journal of Sports Medicine* **21**; 28–37, 1981.

Steele, V. A. and White, J.A.: Injury prediction in female gymnasts. *British Journal of Sports Medicine* **20**: 31–3, 1986.

Steinberg, P.J.: Injuries to sports parachutists. In: *Sports Injuries and their Prevention*. Proceedings of Council of Europe 3rd meeting, pp. 29–42. Papendal, Netherlands, 1989.

Stone, M.H.: Connective tissue and bone response to strength training. In: *Strength and Power in Sport*, Ed. Komi, P.V. Oxford, Blackwell, 1992.

Stone, M.H., O'Bryant, H. and Garhammer, J.: A hypothetical model for strength training. *Journal of Sports Medicine* **21**: 342–51, 1981.

Sullivan, J.A., Gross, R.H. and Grana, W.A.: Evaluation of injuries in youth soccer. *American Journal of Sports Medicine* **8**: 325–7, 1980.

Supinski, G.S., Levin, S. and Kelsen, S.G.: Caffeine effects on respiratory muscle endurance and sense of effort during loaded breathing. *Journal of Applied Physiology* **60**: 2040–7, 1986.

Suzuki, S. and Hutton, R.S.: Postcontractile motomeuron discharge produced by muscle afferent activation. *Medicine and Science in Sports* **8**: 258–64, 1976.

Taimela, S., Kujala, U.M. and Osterman, K.: Intrinsic risk factors and athletic injuries. *Sports Medicine (New Zealand)* **9**: 205–15, 1990.

Tanner, J.M.: *The Physique of the Olympic Athlete*. London, Allen & Unwin, 1964a.

Tanner, J.M.: Analysis and classification of physique. In: *Human Biology: An Introduction to Human Evolution, Variation and Growth*, Ed. Harrison, G.A., Weiner, J.S., Tanner, J.M. and Barnicott, N.A. Oxford, Clarendon Press, 1964b.

Terry, D.J. and Nethery, V.M.: Vertical jump changes during and following a combined plyometric and weight training program. *Journal of Strength and Conditioning Research* **7**: 181 (abstract), 1993.

Tesch, P.A., Thorsson, A. and Kaiser, P.: Muscle capillary supply and fiber type characteristics in weight and power lifters. *Journal of Applied Physiology* **56**: 35–8, 1984.

Thorstensson, A., Grimby, G. and Karlsson, J.: Force–velocity relationship and fibre composition in human knee extensor muscle. *Journal of Applied Physiology* **40**: 12–16, 1976a.

Thorstensson, A., Hulten, B., Von Dobeln, W. and Karlsson, J.: Effect of strength training activities and fibre characteristics in human skeletal muscle. *Acta Physiologica Scandinavica* **96**: 392–8, 1976b.

Thorstensson, A., Larsson, L., Tesch, P. and Karlsson, J.: Muscle strength and fibre composition in athletes and sedentary men. *Medicine and Science in Sports* **9**: 26–30, 1977.

Thorstensson, A., Sjodin, B. and Karlsson, J.: Enzyme activities and muscle strength after sprint training in man. *Acta Physiologica Scandinavica* **94**: 313–18, 1975.

Torg, J.S., Vegso, J.J., O'Neill, M.J. and Sennett, B.: Analysis of football induced cervical spine trauma. *American Journal of Sports Medicine* 18: 50–7, 1990.

Tropp, H., Ekstrand, J. and Gillquist, J.: Stabilometry in functional instability of the ankle and its value in predicting injury. *Medicine and Science in Sports and Exercise* 16: 64–6, 1984.

Tursz, A. and Crost, M.: Sports-related injuries in children. *American Journal of Sports Medicine* 14: 294–9, 1986.

Vihko, V., Soimajarvi, J., Karvinen, E., Rahkila, P. and Havu, M.: Lipid metabolism during exercise. I: Physiological characteristics of normal healthy subjects in relation to their physical fitness. *European Journal of Applied Physiology* 39: 209–18, 1978.

Vulpen, A.T., van: *Sports Injuries and their Prevention*. Scientific report. Netherlands, Oosterbeek, NISGZ, 1989.

Vuori, I.: Education and the prevention of sports injuries in Finland. In: *Sports Injuries and their Prevention*. Proceedings of Council of Europe 3rd meeting, pp. 135–44. Papendal, Netherlands, 1988.

Warmolts, J.R. and Engel, W.K.: Correlation of motor unit behaviour with histochemical myofibre type in humans by open-biopsy electromyography. In: New developments in Elecromyography and Clinical Neurophysiology vol 1. Basel, Karger, 1973.

Warren, B.L. and Jones, C.J.: Predicting plantar fasciitis in runners. *Medicine and Science in Sports and Exercise* 19: 71–3, 1987.

Warren, C.G., Lehmann, J.F. and Koblanski, J.N.: Elongation of rat tail tendon: effects of load and temperature. *Archives of Physical Medicine and Rehabilitation* 52: 465–74, 1971.

Warren, C.G., Lehmann, J.F. and Koblanski, J.N.: Heat and stretch procedures: an evaluation using rat tail tendon. *Archives of Physical Medicine and Rehabilitation* 57: 122–6, 1976.

Watson, A.W.S.: Weight changes during prolonged exercise, *British Journal Sports Medicine* 7: 338–9, 1973.

Watson, A.W.S.: A three year study of the effects of exercise on active young men. *European Journal of Applied Physiology* 40: 107–15, 1979.

Watson, A.W.S.: Factors predisposing to sports injury in schoolboy rugby players. *Journal of Sports Medicine* 21: 417–22, 1982.

Watson, A.W.S.: Posture and participation in sport. *Journal of Sports Medicine and Physical Fitness* 23: 231–9, 1983.

Watson, A.W.S.: Sports injuries in one academic year in 6799 Irish school children. *American Journal of Sports Medicine* 12: 65–71, 1984a.

Watson, A.W.S.: Distribution of subcutaneous fat in sportsmen: relationship to anaerobic power output. *Journal of Sports Medicine and Physical Fitness* 24: 195–204, 1984b.

Watson, A.W.S.: The physique of sportsmen: a study using factor analysis. *Medicine and Science in Sports and Exercise* 16: 279–93, 1984c.

Watson, A.W.S.: *Sports Injuries in Irish Second-Level Schools during the School Year 1984–1985*. Dublin, Department of Education, 1986.

Watson, A.W.S.: Discriminant analysis of the physiques of schoolboy rugby players, hurlers and non-team members. *Journal of Sports Sciences* 6: 131–40, 1988a.

Watson, A.W.S.: Quantification of the influence of body fat content on selected physical performance variables in adolescent boys. *Irish Journal of Medical Science* 157: 383–4, 1988b.

Watson, A.W.S.: Sports injuries: relationship to deficiencies of flexibility and body mechanics and the effectiveness of different intervention strategies. In: *Sports Injuries and their Prevention*. Proceedings of Council of Europe 3rd meeting. Papendal, Netherlands, 1989.

Watson, A.W.S.: *Fitness of Children in Irish Primary Schools*. Report No. 4, Sports Research Committee. Dublin, Department of Education, 1990.

Watson, A.W.S.: Incidence and nature of sports injuries in Ireland: analysis of four types of sport. *American Journal of Sports Medicine* 21: 137–43, 1993.

Watson, A.W.S. and O'Donovan, D.J.: The reliability of measurements of physical working capacity. *Irish Journal of Medical Science* 145: 308, 1976.

Watson, A.W.S. and O'Donovan, D.J.: Factors relating to the strength of male adolescents. *Journal of Applied Physiology* 43: 834–8, 1977a.

Watson, A.W.S. and O'Donovan, D.J.: The effects of five weeks of controlled interval training on youths of diverse pre-training condition. *Journal of Sports Medicine and Physical Fitness* 17:

139–46, 1977b.

Watson, R.C.: Bone growth and physical activity in young males. *International Conference on Bone Mineralisation.* US Department of Health, Education and Welfare. Publication NIH 75-683: pp. 380–5, 1974.

Weiner, J.S. and Lourie, S.A.: *Human Biology: A Guide to Field Methods.* IBP Handbook, Oxford, Blackwell, 1969.

Wilkerson, J.E. and Evonuk, E.: Changes in cardiac and skeletal muscle ATP-ase activities after exercise. *Journal of Applied Physiology* 30: 328–30, 1971.

Wilkes, D., Glenhill, N. and Smyth, R.: Effects of acute induced metabolic acidosis on 800 m race time. *Medicine and Science in Sports and Exercise* 15: 277–80, 1983.

Wilkie, D.R.: *Muscle.* London, Arnold, 1968.

William, W.W.: Effect of intravenous caffeine on liver glycogenolysis during prolonged exercise. *Medicine and Science in Sports and Exercise* 18: 192–6, 1986.

Williams, J.G.P.: *A Colour Atlas of Injury in Sport.* London, Wolfe Medical Publications, 1980.

Williams, J.M., Tonymon, P. and Wadsworth, W.A.: Relationship of life stress to injury in intercollegiate volleyball. *Journal of Human Stress* 12: 38–43, 1986.

Williams, M.H. and Ward, A.J.: Hemotological changes elicited by prolonged intermittent exercise. *Research Quarterly* 48: 606–16, 1977.

Williams, M.H., Wesseldine, T.S. and Schuster, R.: The effects of induced erythrocythemia upon 5-mile treadmill time. *Medicine and Science in Sports and Exercise* 13: 167–75, 1981.

Wilson, G.J., Elliott, B.C. and Wood, G.A.: Stretch-shorten cycle performance enhancement through flexibility training. *Medicine and Science in Sports and Exercise* 24: 116–23, 1992.

Wolfe, L.A., Cunningham, D.A., Rechnitzer, P. and Nichol, P.M.: Effects of endurance training on left ventricular dimensions in healthy men. *Journal of Applied Physiology* 47: 207–12, 1979.

Wyndham, C.H.: Effects of acclimatisation on the sweat-rate/temperature relationship. *Journal of Applied Physiology* 22: 27–92, 1967.

Wyndham, C.H.: The physiology of exercise under heat stress. *Journal of Applied Physiology* 35: 193–220, 1973.

Yamakawa, J. and Ishiko, T.: Standardisation of physical fitness tests for rowers. In: *Proceeding of the International Congress on Sports Sciences.* Tokyo, Japanese University of Sports Sciences, 1966.

Zaricznyj, B., Shattuck, L.J. and Mast, T.A.: Sports related injuries in school aged children. *American Journal of Sports Medicine* 8: 318–24, 1980.

Zuntz, N., Loewy, A., Muller, F. and Caspari, W.: *Hohenklima und Bergwanderungen in ihrer Wirkung auf den Menschen.* Berlin, Deutsches Verlogshaus Bong & Co., 1906.

Zuti, W.R. and Golding, L.A.: Comparing diet and exercise as weight reduction tools. *The Physician and Sportsmedicine* 4: 49–56, 1976.

INDEX